CO-AUM-649

OXFORD MEDIEVAL TEXTS

*General Editors*

V. H. GALBRAITH   R. A. B. MYNORS
C. N. L. BROOKE

# PETER ABELARD'S
# *ETHICS*

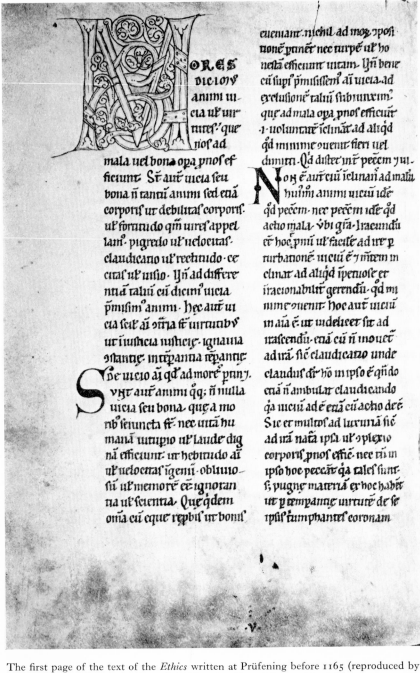

The first page of the text of the *Ethics* written at Prüfening before 1165 (reproduced by kind permission of the Bavarian State Library, Munich)

# PETER ABELARD'S
# *ETHICS*

AN EDITION WITH INTRODUCTION
ENGLISH TRANSLATION AND NOTES

BY

## D. E. LUSCOMBE

*Fellow of Churchill College*
*Cambridge*

OXFORD
AT THE CLARENDON PRESS
1971

*Oxford University Press, Ely House, London W. 1*

GLASGOW  NEW YORK  TORONTO  MELBOURNE  WELLINGTON
CAPE TOWN  SALISBURY  IBADAN  NAIROBI  DAR ES SALAAM  LUSAKA  ADDIS ABABA
BOMBAY  CALCUTTA  MADRAS  KARACHI  LAHORE  DACCA
KUALA LUMPUR  SINGAPORE  HONG KONG  TOKYO

PRINTED IN GREAT BRITAIN
AT THE UNIVERSITY PRESS, OXFORD
BY VIVIAN RIDLER
PRINTER TO THE UNIVERSITY

FOR MEGAN

# PREFACE

M Y interest in the problems posed by the conditions in which we know Abelard's writings was aroused before I learnt that Fr. E. M. Buytaert, O.F.M., was proceeding from his own studies of Abelard's writings to a large-scale edition of his theological works, though not of the *Ethics*, which is appearing in the *Continuatio mediaevalis* of the series *Corpus Christianorum*. His will be the great achievement of tackling the formidable problems involved in discovering methods for confining within the stable limits of a modern printed edition the fluid and mobile texts of, for example, Abelard's *Theologia* and *Sic et non*. I began work upon the present edition in 1965 because the problems surrounding the text of the *Ethics* were still unclear to me and also because Professor L. M. de Rijk, the editor of Abelard's *Dialectica* (Assen, 1956), was then abandoning his own preparations for an edition. I appreciate his kindly encouragement and in particular his acceptance in the journal *Vivarium* (vol. iii, 1965) of my preliminary survey of manuscripts.

A critical text is not the only need, and I have felt that a historical commentary upon the work would be of help to readers who, although they may know the main outlines of Abelard's thought, are unfamiliar with the fresh studies of twelfth-century morality which have been made by a succession of very fine scholars such as P. Anciaux, R. Blomme, and O. Lottin. My introductory historical survey of twelfth-century ethical thought rests upon a framework provided by a number of specialist studies by these and other scholars and it has grown out of a paper which I felt privileged to give to the Anglo-American Conference of Historians in London in 1966. I owe much to Professor C. R. Cheney, who convinced me of the desirability of completing this edition with a translation into English. Professor M. D. Knowles has provided much support, both general and special, and I am grateful also to Professor W. Ullmann for comments upon Abelard's discussion of the episcopacy and to Mrs. M. Cheney, Dr. R. W. Hunt, and Dr. R. W. Southern for further help. Dr. B. Scott most kindly read through the Latin text, offering both valuable comments and general agreement. The

British Academy generously made a Research Award which enabled me to travel to Germany to carry out the essential task of checking my transcriptions and of studying the manuscripts in their own habitats.

Two further acknowledgements are also most important. The Fellows of Churchill College have been generous in granting me both money and time to prepare this book. As the College is now just ten years old, it is perhaps permissible here to celebrate the generous, friendly, and enlightened way in which it fosters the *artes*. I am also deeply grateful to the general editors of the Oxford Medieval Texts for accepting this book into their admirable series, and in particular to Professor C. N. L. Brooke for the charm of his criticism and the wealth of his advice.

D. E. L.

Since this edition went into proof, two of the five volumes of E. M. Buytaert's editions of Abelard have become available (*Corpus Christianorum. Continuatio mediaevalis*, xi and xii) as well as an edition by R. Thomas of *Petrus Abaelardus, Dialogus inter Philosophum, Iudaeum et Christianum* (Stuttgart–Bad Cannstatt, 1970).

D. E. L.

# CONTENTS

# CONTENTS

# SHORT BIBLIOGRAPHY AND
# LIST OF ABBREVIATIONS

I. Editions of Abelard's works are discussed below, pp. xxxviii–xli.

II. Some general introductions to twelfth-century thought and culture are:

C. Brooke, *The twelfth century renaissance* (London, 1969).
J. de Ghellinck, *L'essor de la littérature latine au XII<sup>e</sup> siècle* (Brussels–Paris, 1946).
J. de Ghellinck, *Le mouvement théologique du XII<sup>e</sup> siècle* (2nd edn., Bruges, 1948).
G. Paré, A. Brunet, P. Tremblay, *La renaissance du douzième siècle. Les écoles et l'enseignement* (Paris–Ottawa, 1933).
R. W. Southern, *The making of the Middle Ages* (London, 1953).

III. Four modern studies of Abelard are:

E. Gilson, *Héloïse and Abélard* (Eng. trans., London, 1953).
J. Jolivet, *Arts du langage et théologie chez Abélard* (Paris, 1969).
D. E. Luscombe, *The school of Peter Abelard* (Cambridge, 1969).
R. E. Weingart, *The Logic of Divine Love* (Oxford, 1970).

IV. Many studies of twelfth-century ethics, particularly those by P. Delhaye, are cited in the notes accompanying the introduction below.

V. The following titles are abbreviated in this book:

| | |
|---|---|
| Anciaux, *La théologie du sacrement de pénitence* | P. Anciaux, *La théologie du sacrement de pénitence au XII<sup>e</sup> siècle* (Louvain–Gembloux, 1949). |
| BGPTMA | Beiträge zur Geschichte der Philosophie und der Theologie des Mittelalters (Münster, 1891– ). |
| Blomme, *La doctrine du péché* | R. Blomme, *La doctrine du péché dans les écoles théologiques de la première moitié du XII<sup>e</sup> siècle* (Louvain, 1958). |
| CCL | *Corpus Christianorum. Series latina* (Turnholti). |
| Clm. | Codex latinus monacensis (Bavarian State Library, Munich). |
| CSEL | *Corpus scriptorum ecclesiasticorum latinorum.* Editum consilio et impensis Academiae Litterarum Caesareae Vindobonensis (Vienna, 1866– ). |

| | |
|---|---|
| Cousin, *Opera P.*<br>  *Abaelardi* | V. Cousin, *Opera Petri Abaelardi* (2 vols.,<br>Paris, 1849, 1859). |
| Lottin, *Psychologie et*<br>  *morale* | O. Lottin, *Psychologie et morale aux XII$^e$*<br>*et XIII$^e$ siècles* (6 vols., Louvain–Gembloux,<br>1942–60). |
| *PL* | J. P. Migne, *Patrologia latina* (Paris, 1844–64). |
| Schmitt, *Anselmi opera* | F. S. Schmitt, *S. Anselmi Cantuariensis*<br>*archiepiscopi Opera omnia* (6 vols., Edinburgh,<br>1938–61). |

VI. The following *sigla* are used to refer to the MSS. of the *Ethics*:

    A Munich, Bavarian State Library, lat. (= Clm.) 14160, 12th century; see p. xli.

    B Munich, Bavarian State Library, lat. (= Clm.) 28363, 12th century; see p. xliv.

    C Oxford, Balliol College 296, 14th century; see p. l.

    D Mainz, Stadtbibliothek lat. 76, 15th century; see p. xlviii.

    E Munich, Bavarian State Library, lat. (= Clm.) 18597, 15th century; see p. xlv.

# PETER ABELARD AND
# TWELFTH-CENTURY ETHICS

## I. ABELARD

OF the many periods when France has been foremost in the cultivation of thought and letters in western Europe, the twelfth century remains peculiarly attractive as a time of creative renewal. The best organized centres for the study of classical, Biblical, and Patristic writing were the monasteries and abbeys of canons such as Clairvaux under St. Bernard, Cluny under Peter the Venerable, Mont-Saint-Michel under Robert of Torigny, Saint-Denis under Suger or Saint-Victor under Hugh. The cathedrals of France succeeded in making their schools highly attractive to clerics from many parts of Europe, who sought an education in philosophy at Chartres under Bernard or at Paris under William of Champeaux or Thierry of Chartres or Gilbert of Poitiers, or who sought to be taught theology at Laon under Anselm and Ralph or at Rheims under Alberic and Lotulph. Great churches that were then built or rebuilt remain to testify in some of their details to this educational ferment; the ancient philosophers were sculpted at Chartres, and Saint-Denis was re-planned according to the Platonic symbolism of the Pseudo-Denis. The masters and scholars survive now through their writings, though these are frequently scanty and their origin is often obscure. Within this scene Peter Abelard (1079–1142) is in many ways the great exception. The outline of his career is extraordinarily well known, largely because he wrote his autobiography, known as the *History of My Troubles*. In a world of wandering and sometimes protesting students, he became a wandering and a frequently protesting master. Not even on the Mont Sainte Geneviève, where Abelard taught John of Salisbury, did he remain for more than a few years continuously. Most reputable masters and most monks led settled lives; Abelard's was turbulent in the extreme. He appeared to scoff and to insult. He was twice condemned for heresy, in 1121 at the synod of Soissons and again in 1140 at the council of Sens. He fathered a child and, although he was a master, he married and then dismissed

his wife. He was castrated as the result of a personal enmity. He was punished by being ordered to enter a monastery, from which he fled. He was an abbot until attempts were made upon his life. Yet he became in his last days an exemplary and pious Cluniac.

His scholarly and intellectual achievement was also in many ways exceptional. As a logician he was probably the one who did most to force out of fashion the idealism that was then prevalent; his lifetime coincided with the decline of Platonic exemplarism—a decline that may be compared with the collapse in Britain in the early twentieth century of the idealism of a Hegel or a Bradley. As a theologian Abelard was perhaps the best of those who in his day showed the way to come to grips with the vastness and the seeming incoherence of Patristic and of post-Patristic teaching; in his *Sic et non* Abelard both revealed the magnitude of the apparent discordances among the authorities and formulated rules for their resolution. Above all, perhaps, Abelard critically probed some of the most firmly established religious convictions of his time. The comparison with Socrates sprang readily to the minds of his friends, for he explored with considerable oral brilliance various possibilities of thought and he reviewed other men's ideas without himself leaving any well-constructed framework or system of doctrine.[1] Following St. Anselm, abbot of Bec and archbishop of Canterbury (d. 1109), he revised the current picture or interpretation of the Redemption and placed a very heavy emphasis not upon God's Son paying a ransom to the devil for the release of captive mankind, but upon the Wisdom of God which by sane teaching and supreme love inspires men in their turn to love him. Optimistically and through logic Abelard also attempted to show that all was for the best in the best of all possible worlds. Moreover, he attempted to devise a new language for expressing the persons of the Trinity and the relations between the persons in terms of the properties or attributes of God and thus to draw closer to classical pagan descriptions of God. A brief summary of Abelard's opinions cannot convey how miscellaneous and fluid they sometimes were nor how eagerly and yet tentatively they were presented. However, Abelard's desire to overhaul and to reformulate current ethical assumptions also occupied a prominent place

[1] How Abelard made the arts of the trivium contribute to theology is thoroughly explained by J. Jolivet, *Arts du langage et théologie chez Abélard*, Études de philosophie médiévale, lvii (Paris, 1969).

*He is still a man, even with his hook stack.*

among his ambitions and this may appropriately be more closely
examined.

## II. TWELFTH-CENTURY ETHICS

Abelard's ethical thinking reflects the concerns of the thinkers of
his own and of previous times. Like them he wanted to know what
it is in men which produces good behaviour or evil and how to
distinguish between conduct worthy of praise or blame by God.
Like them also, although his outlook was dominated by the teachings of the Old and New Testaments, much of his moral vocabulary came from the ancient pagan moralists, especially from
Cicero. Moreover, like very many of his contemporaries he was
enthralled by a desire to study comparatively Christian morality
and the moral philosophies of the ancient Graeco-Roman world.
Accordingly, by way of introduction to this new edition of Abelard's
*Ethics*, it is worth delineating the leading features of ethical thought
in the twelfth century and suggesting Abelard's relationship to this
thought. The twelfth century, as much as the twentieth century,
was tormented by grave and common practical moral problems,
such as the presence of violence and corruption within society and
the problems which arise from legal punishment. As Bartholémy
Hauréau long ago observed,[1] Abelard possessed a social doctrine
and he was an impassioned critic of some of the evils of his society.
Moreover, and to a degree which was possibly more intense and
more explicit than it is in popular education today, the twelfth
century was preoccupied with the question of the moral formation
of the person and with a person's need to know his moral self and
to have a carefully formulated moral language with which to study
his own character and conduct. Abelard's own distinguished contribution to the re-structuring of the concepts used in moral
thought is principally contained in his *Ethics*.

Ethical thought was promoted in the twelfth century by theologians, who were usually monks or canons or schoolmen (*schola-
stici*), and by the teachers and students of the liberal arts.[2] Peter
Abelard was both a theologian and a logician. He was also both a

---

[1] 'Le poème adressé par Abélard à son fils Astrolabe', *Notices et extraits de la
Bibliothèque nationale*, xxxiv. 2 (1895), 155.

[2] For a brief introduction to educational organization in the twelfth century
see P. Delhaye, 'L'organisation scolaire au XIIᵉ siècle', *Traditio*, v (1947),
211–68.

monk who spent many years in various cloisters and a schoolman
who taught openly in several scholastic centres such as Laon,
Paris, Melun, the Mont Sainte Geneviève, and even in the
countryside on an experimental basis at Quincey. Monks and
schoolmen—monasticism and scholasticism—did not wholly share
identical ethical interests and outlooks. Within the monastic
cloister in the twelfth century the problems of the moral life were
studied intensively with a special emphasis upon the needs of the
spiritual life. Monastic writers expressed their utter abhorrence
of sin, their depreciation of earthly values, the impossibility of
unaided moral initiative, the duty of obedience to and of identification with God's will, the joys of spiritual friendship, the satisfactions brought by grace and the superiority of the contemplative
over the active life.[1] For St. Anselm, man was not endowed with the
unfettered power of choosing between good and evil but only with
the power of not acting contrary to the will of God, the power of
freely obeying without which man is not free.[2] For St. Bernard,
abbot of Clairvaux (d. 1153), the witness to our moral obligations
is within us; it is conscience or the remorse which inhabits the
sinful soul and allows of no tranquillity. God is always present in
the good conscience and all our actions are selected or omitted in the
presence of the divine judge.[3] Bernard's thought was meditative
and affective in character and drew heavily upon Biblical and
Patristic sources. Some monastic moralists were liable to denounce
any appeal to pagan morality. A clear example is the criticism which
Rupert, abbot of Deutz (d. 1129/30), directed against the four
principal virtues listed by Macrobius, on the ground that pagan
writers did not know their heavenly or spiritual worth.[4] However,
the assumption that there existed a community of feeling and of
interests between Christian and pagan moral ideals was a venerable

[1] A survey has been provided by F. Vandenbroucke, *Pour l'histoire de la
théologie morale: la morale monastique du XIᵉ au XVIᵉ siècle*, Analecta mediaevalia Namurcensia, xx (Louvain, 1960). The best general initiation to monastic
authors from Benedict to Bernard of Clairvaux is that of J. Leclercq, *L'amour
des lettres et le désir de Dieu* (Paris, 1957).

[2] Cf. R. W. Southern, *Saint Anselm and his Biographer* (Cambridge, 1963),
pp. 102–7, here p. 104.

[3] Cf. P. Delhaye, *Le problème de la conscience morale chez S. Bernard étudié
dans ses œuvres et dans ses sources*, Analecta mediaevalia Namurcensia, ix (Namur,
1957).

[4] *De gloria et honore filii hominis*, iv (*PL* 168. 1401D–1403A), v (1422D). Cf.
H. Silvestre, 'Note sur la survie de Macrobe au moyen âge', *Classica et Mediaevalia*, xxiv (1963), 170–80, here pp. 175–7.

one. To this community of feeling the writings of St. Ambrose of Milan in the fourth century, of St. Martin of Braga in the sixth, of St. Isidore in the seventh, and of Hadoard in the ninth stood witness. There were many monastic moralists in the twelfth century who were ready to make appeal to a variety of non-Patristic and non-Scriptural sources. For all, the profoundest Biblical expression of the theme of spiritual love was provided in the Song of Songs, but when Ailred, the Cistercian abbot of Rievaulx in Yorkshire, in the last years of his life, probably in 1163, wrote his treatise on *Spiritual Friendship* he modelled it upon Cicero's *On Friendship*.[1] Bernard's friend, William of Saint-Thierry, absorbed large amounts of the *Letters* of Seneca.[2] Yet another Cistercian, Thomas of Perseigne, introduced into his commentary on the Song of Songs about one hundred and sixty classical quotations, and Helinand of Froidmont, the troubadour turned Cistercian, constantly cited the pagans as moral authorities.

The theologians in the non-monastic or open schools also said much about sin, virtue, and grace. At the beginning of the twelfth century the theological school of Anselm of Laon (d. 1117) and of William of Champeaux (d. 1121) viewed man as a creature of ignorance, sensually disordered, stained by sin, and in need of grace. The problems of human responsibility were enmeshed in the problems surrounding the Fall of man and the fact of concupiscence. There was, however, a general feeling for the importance of conscience as providing a subjective norm of morality and for intention as a source of morality, itself influencing the degree of merit or blame accorded to man by God.[3] The traditions of the school of Laon lay heavily on the theological thought of the twelfth century. Above all in the school of Saint-Victor in Paris, which was founded by William of Champeaux, which boasted of such famous

---

[1] Ailred's treatise is printed in *PL* 195. 659–702. An English translation has been made by C. H. Talbot, *Christian Friendship by Saint Ailred of Rievaulx* (London, no date, perhaps 1942). The *Christian Friendship* of Peter of Blois, archdeacon of Bath (d. after 1204), was influenced by Ailred's initiative; ed. M. M. Davy, *Un traité de l'amour du XIIᵉ siècle. Pierre de Blois* (Paris, 1932). On both works see P. Delhaye, 'Deux adaptations du *De amicitia* de Cicéron au XIIᵉ siècle', *Recherches de théologie ancienne et médiévale*, xv (1948), 304–31. On Ailred see further A. Squire, *Aelred of Rievaulx* (London, 1969), chap. 5.

[2] Cf. J.-M. Déchanet, '*Seneca Noster*. Des lettres à Lucilius à la lettre aux Frères de Mont Dieu' in *Mélanges J. de Ghellinck*, Museum Lessianum, Section historique, xiii–xiv (Gembloux, 1951), ii. 753–66.

[3] Cf. Blomme, *La doctrine du péché*, pp. 3–99, especially pp. 46–9, 58–61, 85–7.

masters as Hugh and Richard of Saint-Victor, and which formed the mind of the great Sentencer, Peter Lombard, the conservative, orthodox, Augustinian tradition followed by Anselm of Laon remained alive.

Ethics had found no place among the seven liberal arts as they were described in the programmes of Boethius, Cassiodore, and Isidore. In the twelfth century attempts were made to find a place for it in systems of teaching. Some writers, such as Honorius of Autun, Stephen of Tournai, and Godfrey of Saint-Victor, freely appended ethics to the end of the list of the seven arts.[1] Hugh of Saint-Victor sandwiched it, as a part of practical philosophy, between logic (grammar, dialectic, and rhetoric) and theoretical philosophy (theology, physics, and mathematics).[2] William of Conches advised that after a student had studied eloquence (grammar, dialectic, and rhetoric) and before he approached theoretical philosophy (the study of corporeal beings in mathematics and physics and of incorporeal beings in theology) he should be instructed in practical philosophy, in ethics, economics, and politics.[3]

In practice, however, the incorporation of moral education into the school curriculum was more easily achieved. This was because wherever the liberal arts were best taught—in the chapter schools of the cathedral towns and also in the schools of the regular canons—the ancient Roman tradition of pedagogy continued. This literary tradition aimed to produce men of letters and culture and moral worth by the means of reading and commenting and imitating the ancient pagan writers. Quintilian had suggested in his *De institutione oratorica* that the teacher of oratory should concern himself with the moral development of the young; eloquence and wisdom should go together. Bernard of Chartres—'the most

[1] Cf. P. Delhaye, '"Grammatica" et "Ethica" au XIIe siècle', *Recherches de théologie ancienne et médiévale*, xxv (1958), 59–110, here pp. 61–7.
[2] *Didascalicon*, vi. 14 (*PL* 176. 809–10). Cf. P. Delhaye, 'L'enseignement de la philosophie morale au XIIe siècle', *Medieval Studies*, xi (1949), 77–99, here p. 77.
[3] 'Des commentaires inédits de Guillaume de Conches et de Nicolas Triveth sur la Consolation de Boèce', ed. C. Jourdain in *Notices et extraits des manuscrits de la Bibliothèque impériale*, xx. 2 (1862), 74. Cf. P. Delhaye, 'L'enseignement de la philosophie morale', p. 77, and id., 'La place de l'éthique parmi les disciplines scientifiques au XIIe siècle' in *Mélanges E. D. Arthur Janssen*, Bibliotheca Ephemeridum Theologicarum Lovaniensium, series i, vol. 2 (Louvain, 1948), pp. 29–44, here p. 37.

abundant fountain of letters in Gaul'—had behind him the figure and example of Quintilian. In his classes he thoroughly expounded Latin texts from a grammatical point of view and he did so with the aim of edifying faith and morals.[1] As his admirer John of Salisbury confidently believed,[2] no man can devote himself both to letters and to vice and in Virgil and Lucan are revealed the bases of morality. Similarly in the literary studies of the twelfth century, Juvenal, Horace, and Statius, the Roman satirists and poets, were seen as teachers of ethics who inspire their readers to flee from vice and to imitate heroes. Ovid and Virgil were moralized. Cicero's rhetorical treatise *On Invention* was held to be a moral classic; in the second book Cicero distinguished honesty from utility and discoursed of virtue.[3] Seneca, the reputed correspondent of St. Paul and according to Abelard 'the greatest builder of morality among all the philosophers',[4] was likewise treated as an authority in ethics.[5] Teachers of grammar and of rhetoric, no less than the commentators of Scripture, practised the art of *moralisatio*.[6]

Earlier, in the ninth century, Heiric of Auxerre and Sedulius Scottus had compiled *florilegia* or collections of classical tags and proverbs chosen expressly for their ethical content.[7] In the twelfth century this fashion revived and was intensified.[8] For example, the so-called Brussels *florilegium*,[9] after outlining Cicero's scheme

---

[1] John of Salisbury, *Metalogicon* i. 24, ed. C. C. J. Webb (Oxford, 1929), pp. 53–7.                    [2] *Metalogicon* i. 22, ed. Webb, pp. 51–2.

[3] See, for example, the extracts from the commentary of Thierry of Chartres upon the *De inuentione* published by P. Delhaye, 'L'enseignement de la philosophie morale', Appendix C, pp. 97–9. On this see further F. Masai in *Scriptorium*, v (1951), 117–20, 308–9.

[4] *Epist.* viii (*PL*. 178. 297B).

[5] On Seneca in the twelfth century see L. D. Reynolds, *The Medieval Tradition of Seneca's Letters* (Oxford, 1965), pp. 112–24, and K.-D. Nothdurft, *Studien zum Einfluss Senecas auf die Philosophie und Theologie des zwölften Jahrhunderts* (Leyde–Cologne, 1963).

[6] Cf. G. Paré, A. Brunet, P. Tremblay, *La renaissance du XIIᵉ siècle. Les écoles et l'enseignement*, Publications de l'Institut d'études médiévales d'Ottawa, iii (Paris–Ottawa, 1933), 120–1.

[7] On these see the introduction by C. H. Talbot to the second part of the edition of the *Florilegium morale Oxoniense*, Analecta Mediaevalia Namurcensia, vi (Louvain, 1956), 12–13, and, in addition to the references there given, see the edition of R. Quadri, *I collectanea di Eirico di Auxerre*, Spicilegium Friburgense, xi (Freiburg, 1966).

[8] Two leading examples are the *Florilegium Gallicum*, ed. A. Gagner (Lund, 1936), and the *Florilegium morale Oxoniense* (*MS. Bodl. 633*), ed. P. Delhaye and C. H. Talbot, Analecta Mediaevalia Namurcensia, v–vi (Louvain, 1955–6).

[9] The Brussels *florilegium* is contained in cod. Bruxellensis 10106–13 and is

of the virtues, presents a collection of philosophers' sayings or sentences which support and illustrate ethical notions. The anonymous author of this modest *florilegium* has skimmed the moral cream from the classics to compile a dictionary of ethical teaching. In its celebrity the most important adaptation of Cicero's *De officiis* was the *Moralium dogma philosophorum*.[1] The author, whoever he was—and he may have been William of Conches, the teacher of John of Salisbury and of the future King Henry II of England[2]—retained the plan of Cicero's inquiry into honesty and utility and the relationships between the two;[3] he set out to 'teach summarily the ethics of Tully and to imitate Tully and Seneca' and to bring together 'nearly all the more elegant sayings of the moral doctors'[4]—Sallust, Horace, Terence, and Lucan among them. The result was a *catena* of definitions and quotations, a textbook, a series of lists organized around rather vague questions. By far the longest part of the *Moralium dogma philosophorum* concerns the subject of honesty and treats, like Cicero, of the four cardinal virtues of prudence, justice, fortitude, and temperance. Like other twelfth-century moralists—for example, the author of the *Ysagoge in theologiam*[5] and after him Alan of Lille[6]—the author of the *Moralium dogma philosophorum* was particularly interested

inedited; see, however, P. Delhaye, 'Un petit florilège moral conservé dans un manuscrit bruxellois' in *Medioevo e Rinascimento. Studi in onore di Bruno Nardi*, i (Florence, 1955), 199–215.

[1] Ed. J. Holmberg, *Das Moralium dogma philosophorum, lateinisch, altfranzösisch und mittelniederfränkisch* (Uppsala, 1929).

[2] Such, at least, is the opinion of P. Delhaye, *Gauthier de Chatillon est-il l'auteur du Moralium Dogma?*, Analecta Mediaevalia Namurcensia, iii (Namur–Lille, 1953).

[3] Cf. P. Delhaye, 'Une adaptation du *De officiis* au XIIe siècle. Le *Moralium Dogma Philosophorum*', *Recherches de théologie ancienne et médiévale*, xvi (1949), 227–58, and xvii (1950), 5–28; N. E. Nelson, 'Cicero's *De officiis* in Christian Thought: 300–1300' in *Essays and Studies in English and Comparative Literature*, University of Michigan Publications, Language and Literature, x (Ann Arbor, 1933), 59–160, here pp. 90–9.

[4] Cf. the anonymous prologue *Quia mores* which was added to the *Moralium dogma*, ed. J. Holmberg, pp. 77, 73.

[5] Ed. A. M. Landgraf, *Écrits théologiques de l'école d'Abélard*, Spicilegium Sacrum Lovaniense, xiv (Louvain, 1934), 61–289, here pp. 73–8 Cf. my article 'The Authorship of the *Ysagoge in theologiam*', *Archives d'histoire doctrinale et littéraire du moyen âge*, xxxv (1968), 7–16.

[6] The treatment of virtues and vices by Alan, in the *Moralium dogma*, and in the *Ysagoge* is often similar, and the three authors are interdependent; cf. P. Delhaye, 'Une adaptation du *De officiis*', and id., *Gauthier de Chatillon est-il l'auteur du Moralium Dogma?*

in classifying and in subdividing the virtues, and he found further assistance in Cicero's *De inuentione*, ii. 52–6, and in Macrobius' *Commentary* on the *Dream of Scipio* (i. 8). Little attempt was made to baptize this pagan morality, probably because the author's main intention was to reproduce the teaching of Cicero and others for the benefit of students who perhaps were unable to obtain these sources for themselves.

Classical ethics thus found a place in twelfth-century programmes of education; its attraction was mainly felt in *belles-lettres*, and any lingering doubts about the advisability of educating Christian boys with pagan books could be countered by emphasizing the moral and literary values of this method. However, this teaching of Latin language and literature suggested the way to a philosophical study of the rational ethics of Greece and Rome in comparison with the revealed morality found in Scripture and in Christian teaching. Graeco-Roman paganism no longer constituted the same kind of threat to Christianity as it had done in Jerome's or in Augustine's day; in the twelfth century the influence of the classical world was felt uniquely through the literary and other physical memorials that survived, not through cults or through personal encounters. When the *Moralium dogma philosophorum* raised again Cicero's questions on the relationship between honesty and utility, the questions had no edge or sharpness and were, for this author, only pegs from which to dangle classical quotations. This writer transforms Cicero's emphasis on the respectability and on the rightness in itself of being honest into an emphasis on the obligation and duty to be virtuous and obedient. It is true that he refers not to God but to the gods, but this would not be taken seriously amiss in a collection of classical texts. In an age that was so exuberant and prolific in both its philosophizing and its classicizing activities, the minds which aspired to consider seriously and on a philosophical level the fundamental ethical problems transmitted in the classics were few.

One interesting confrontation with pagan ethical teaching was provided by the poet and theologian Alan of Lille (d. 1203). In his *Treatise on Virtues and Vices and the Gifts of the Holy Spirit*, which he wrote perhaps in the 1170s,[1] he asked how the natural

---

[1] On the text and the date of this work and on its place in Alan's *corpus* and its subsequent influence see M. T. d'Alverny, *Alain de Lille. Textes inédits avec une introduction sur sa vie et ses œuvres*, Études de philosophie médiévale, lii

virtues described by philosophers such as Cicero and Macrobius relate to the higher Pauline or catholic virtues of faith, hope, and charity.[1] Can the political virtues, that is, the virtues which are not oriented towards God and which suit men living in society, become catholic virtues? Alan himself often wrote in the name of reason and of nature. As a theologian he was sympathetic to Aristotle, to dialectical methods, to the traditions established by Abelard and by Gilbert of Poitiers. He knew that the virtues of the philosophers were on the level of nature, of reason, and of man, whereas the leading Christian virtue of charity is of divine inspiration. For Cicero, religion was merely part of the virtue of justice, that part which concerned the rendering of what is due to God as distinct from one's neighbour;[2] but for Alan, who saw the sense in which Cicero was right, religion was also in a more important sense higher than justice. The cult of God comprised the theological virtues of faith, hope, and charity.[3] So Alan argued that the natural or political virtues, which are, as Abelard and his school had chosen to say,[4] habits of the well-ordered mind, rise to the level of being virtues *simpliciter* when they are directed towards God and conform to the laws of the Church and when they are animated or informed by the divine charity which is the mother or form of all virtues. Political or natural virtues are not essentially different from catholic or given virtues; their difference arises from the uses to which they are put. Catholic virtues do not efface natural virtues but transform them. *Data fiunt dona.*[5] Alan therefore attempts to control and to come to grips with pagan teachings on virtue by attaching them to Christian theological belief.

An interesting discussion of ancient theses of the supreme good and of the end of the moral life is contained in the *Policraticus* which John of Salisbury completed in 1159 and which he dedicated to Thomas Becket. The *Policraticus* is about courtiers' trifles and philosophers' examples, about the problems of being a man of affairs, the problems, that is, which had preoccupied the

(Paris, 1965), 61–4, and Lottin, *Psychologie et morale*, vi. 27–43. The best ed. is by Lottin, ibid., pp. 45–92.

[1] On Alan's discussion cf. Lottin, *Psychologie et morale*, iii. 109–21; vi. 40–2, and P. Delhaye, 'La vertu et les vertus dans les œuvres d'Alain de Lille', *Cahiers de civilisation médiévale*, vi (1963), 13–25.

[2] *De inuentione*, ii. 57.

[3] *Tractatus de uirtutibus*, ed. Lottin, *Psychologie et morale*, vi. 53–4.

[4] Cf. Lottin, *Psychologie et morale*, iii. 103–4.

[5] *Tractatus de uirtutibus*, ed. Lottin, *Psychologie et morale*, vi. 57–60.

Roman moralists. It is well known that John of Salisbury was so influenced by Cicero's *De officiis* iii. 6, as well as by examples in Scriptural and ecclesiastical history, that he revived the doctrine of tyrannicide;[1] the *De officiis* also gave John the thesis that political life must be based on a complete harmony between the principles of usefulness and honesty.[2] In the seventh and eighth books of the *Policraticus*, under the stimulus of Boethius' *Consolation of Philosophy*, John discusses Epicureanism and the search for happiness through the four rivers of the terrestrial pleasures of riches, ambition, sensual delights, and pride. John recognized that the happy life sought by Epicurus himself consisted of an absence of sadness and trouble and that it was nobler and sounder than that sought by his disciples. John's courtly contemporaries also fail to realize the supreme good and in practice follow the mistaken way of Epicurus' disciples. In his diatribe against the corrupt view of pleasure, against the confusion of what is honest with what is useful, against the love of riches and power and the longing for popularity and for social prestige, John excels in his deployment of classical illustration, of contemporary anecdote, and of human detail, as well as in his manipulation of Patristic and of classical literature. The human point of view, the argument of moderation, prevails with him as he counsels that men should maintain a moral attitude to the money, the power, and the pleasures of this world, which not all can be expected to renounce. But men will not be able to maintain this truly philosophical attitude without the gifts of grace. John searches for a compromise between renunciation of the world and reform of society and of courtly life. He uses Cicero to help him to balance the Bible.[3]

It is significant that Alan and John had in common strong dialectical and philosophical interests. In a cultural context where

---

[1] *Policraticus siue De nugis curialium et uestigiis philosophorum*, iii. 15 and viii. 18, ed. Webb (Oxford, 1909), i. 232 and ii. 364. Cf. also ibid. v. 6 and viii. 20–1 (Webb, i. 298–307; ii. 372–96) and on John's discussion cf. H. Liebeschütz, *Medieval Humanism in the Life and Writings of John of Salisbury* (London, 1950), pp. 50–5. For further discussion of John's political views see Liebeschütz, 'Chartres und Bologna, Naturbegriff und Staatsidee bei Johannes von Salisbury', *Archiv für Kulturgeschichte*, l (1968), 3–32.

[2] Cf. Liebeschütz, *Medieval Humanism*, pp. 79–80.

[3] Cf. Liebeschütz, *Medieval Humanism*, pp. 28–33, 78–84, and P. Delhaye, 'Le bien suprême d'après le Policraticus de Jean de Salisbury', *Recherches de théologie ancienne et médiévale*, xx (1953), 203–21. For a further critique of Epicureanism see John's *Entheticus de dogmate philosophorum*, ed. C. Petersen (Hamburg, 1843), pp. 20–2.

pagan ethics were mainly studied in the trivium in the course of reading literature and where most theologians restricted the scope of the dialectical arts, sustained ethical analysis was unlikely to arise unless a theologian with a dialectician's zeal were to confront this body of pagan thought. One such man, with Alan and John one of Huizinga's three pre-Gothic spirits,[1] a dialectician, a connoisseur of the classics, and in addition a theologian, was Peter Abelard.

### III. ABELARD AND PAGAN MORALITY

How then does Abelard stand in relation to his contemporary and near-contemporary background? Abelard had as high an esteem as any in his day for pagan philosophy and for pagan ethics. The great appeal which he formulated in his *Theologia* that Christians should study pagan doctrine on God and on the Trinity—an appeal for which Abelard provided the guarantee of Patristic authority—was supported by reference to the good examples which pagan philosophers set in the conduct of their own lives.[2] Abelard tells how the Fathers went to the schools of the philosophers to learn how to describe virtue. The debate which Abelard presents in his autobiography, the *Historia calamitatum*, and in which Abelard and Héloïse discuss whether they should marry, contains many references to the opinions of pagan philosophers. Héloïse is allowed to argue in favour of the philosophers' ideal of love without marriage.[3] In the verses of advice which Abelard composed for his son Astralabe, he paraded, Polonius-wise, a capricious collection of moral maxims, spicy rules of practical morality inspired probably by the *Distichs* of Cato as well as by his own moral theories. The maxims are largely of the kind that appealed to

---

[1] Cf. J. Huizinga, 'Ein praegothischer Geist: Johannes von Salisbury', in *Parerga* (Basel, 1945), p. 35.

[2] *Theologia 'Summi boni'*, I. v–vi, ed. H. Ostlender, *Peter Abaelards Theologia 'Summi boni'*, BGPTMA, xxxv. 2–3 (Münster, 1939), pp. 11–27; *Theologia christiana*, ii (*PL* 178. 1165 et seq.); *Theologia 'Scholarium'*, I. xv–xxv; II. i–ii (*PL* 178. 1004–46).

[3] Ed. J. Monfrin, *Abélard. Historia Calamitatum*, Bibliothèque des textes philosophiques (2nd edn., Paris, 1962), *ll.* 425–558. Cf. Abelard, *Theologia christiana*, ii (*PL*. 178. 1195 et seq.). Also P. Delhaye, 'Le dossier antimatrimonial de l'Adversus Jovinianum et son influence sur quelques écrits latins du XIIᵉ siècle', *Medieval Studies*, xiii (1951), 65–86.

florilegists: publish as late as possible, learn before you teach, distrust women.[1]

Abelard brought pagan moral themes into theology. For example, at the beginning of the second book of his *Scito te ipsum* he underlined what Boethius had found in Aristotle's *Categories* concerning virtue as a habit. According to Aristotle, habit is more than a simple disposition of character; it is a quality acquired by effort and perseverance and anchored in one's being, producing a mark in the soul which is difficult to efface. Virtue is like this.[2] In his *Dialogue between a Philosopher, a Jew, and a Christian* Abelard makes the Philosopher define and classify the cardinal virtues of prudence, justice, fortitude, and temperance.[3] In this appreciation of virtue as a habit of mind, as a natural quality acquired by human effort, Abelard and his school stood out from contemporary theologians. On the subject of virtue the school of Laon had been, in the word of Dom Lottin,[4] dumb. Hugh of Saint-Victor in his *De sacramentis* concentrated upon a theological approach to virtue and upon relating virtue to grace.[5] Among theologians it was Abelard who first in his time attempted a serious philosophical discussion of natural virtue and who first really put the human virtues upon the theological map.

This particular venture was not incidental to Abelard's other concerns, for he had something of importance to say about the relationship of pagan to Christian morality. He said it in his imaginary *Dialogue between a Philosopher, a Jew, and a Christian*.[6]

---

[1] The best edn. is by B. Hauréau, 'Le poème adressé par Abélard à son fils Astrolabe', *Notices et extraits des manuscrits de la Bibliothèque nationale*, xxxiv. 2 (1895), 153–87.

[2] See below, pp. 128–9 and the references there cited.

[3] *Dialogus* (*PL* 178. 1652A–1658A). Abelard also, by means of Macrobius' *Commentary* on the *Dream of Scipio* (i. 8. 5, 8) reproduced Plotinus' fourfold division of the virtues into political, purifying, purified, and exemplary virtues; cf. *Theologia christiana*, ii (*PL*. 178. 1185C), and *Dialogus* (1649C).

[4] Cf. Lottin, *Psychologie et morale*, iii. 99 et seq.

[5] *De sacramentis christianae fidei*, I. vi. 17; II. xiii (*PL* 176. 273–5, 525–50).

[6] The *Dialogus* is only nowadays beginning to receive the attention which it has long lacked. A lengthy commentary upon it is R. Thomas, *Der philosophisch-theologische Erkenntnisweg P. Abaelards im Dialogus inter philosophum, Judaeum et Christianum*, Untersuchungen zur allgemeine Religionsgeschichte, N.F. vi (Bonn, 1966). H. Liebeschütz has argued that Abelard's conception of Judaism was inspired by the Church Fathers rather than by current Jewish exegesis, 'The significance of Judaism in Peter Abaelard's Dialogus', *Journal of Jewish Studies*, xii (1961), 1–18; in this article Liebeschütz also suggested that the dialogue form was inspired by Cicero's *De natura deorum*. R. Roques has noticed that

As one starts to read it, the *Dialogue* appears to be a debate between not very personalized figures who appear before Abelard in a dream and ask him to judge, on the basis of their arguments, which religion is the most reasonable.[1] The three interlocutors have in common the worship of one God, but each has a different faith and life; the Philosopher is content with the natural law, the Christian and the Jew have the Scriptures. At first the debate seems to be staged in order to produce the conclusion that only a very few Christians, chief among them being Abelard, are reasonable and capable of satisfying the demands of both faith and philosophy. The Philosopher goes so far as to explain that the three disputants, having failed to reach agreement among themselves, have chosen Abelard as a judge because he knows the strength of philosophical reasons and 'the muniments of both laws' and is the only man whom they could find who did not belong to one of the three sects.[2] The Philosopher, moreover, is allowed to pay handsome tributes to Abelard.[3] The *Dialogue* thus appears to be Abelard's *apologia pro vita sua*, a philosophical counterpart to his autobiographical and historical *apologia*, the so-called *Historia*

the Philosopher is a composite figure, not merely of the pagan gentile such as Paul or Augustine encountered, but also a circumcised Ismaelite. He was a pre-Islamic pagan (*Dialogus*, PL 178. 1644A) content with the natural law (1611A) and having no Scriptures; but the Jew speaks of Ismael as a father of the Philosopher and the Philosopher himself appeals to the first Patriarchs as 'our Prophets' (1619C, 1634C). See Roques, *Structures théologiques. De la gnose à Richard de Saint-Victor*, Bibliothèque de l'École des Hautes Études, Section des sciences religieuses, lxxii (Paris, 1962), 260–4, or, earlier, in *Die Metaphysik im Mittelalter*, ed. P. Wilpert, Miscellanea Mediaevalia, ii (Berlin, 1963), 196–9. J. Jolivet, 'Abélard et le philosophe', *Revue de l'histoire des religions*, clxiv (1963), 181–9, also believes that Abelard's Philosopher is partly a Muslim who pursues purely natural philosophy and may be inspired by a faint knowledge of Ibn-Bājja (Avempace; d. A.D. 1138), who was considered by some to be a philosopher emancipated from religious faith. A closer study of the arguments used by the Jew, the Philosopher, and the Christian is needed to throw further light on these observations.

[1] In his poem to Astralabe, Abelard noted the absence of what we now call the comparative study of religions, ed. B. Hauréau in *Notices et extraits des manuscrits de la Bibliothèque nationale*, xxxiv. 2 (Paris, 1895), 167:

> Tot fidei sectis diuisus mundus habetur
> Vt quae sit uitae semita uix pateat.
> Quod tot habet fidei contraria dogmata mundus
> Quisque facit generis traditione sui.
> Denique nullus in his rationem consulere audet,
> Dum quacumque sibi uiuere pace studet.

[2] *Dialogus* (PL 178. 1613B).
[3] Ibid. (1613CD).

*calamitatum.* However, the *Dialogue*, incomplete and therefore difficult to assess as it is, is more than such a *pièce justificative*. It is not, as used to be thought, one of Abelard's very last works written as a final fling at Saint-Marcel after the defeat and condemnation of 1140. On the contrary, it was written before Abelard wrote his Commentary on the *Hexaemeron* and after he had composed his *Theologia christiana*, perhaps in the mid or late 1130s.[1] It falls into two main parts, not just in the sense in which it is conveyed in the Oxford manuscript, Balliol College 296, where the Philosopher has what is called a first *collatio* with the Jew and then a second *collatio* with the Christian, but in the sense that the first theme, displayed by the Philosopher and the Jew, is the relationship between Scriptural faith and reason, with special reference to the sufficiency or otherwise of the life according to reason and nature, while later the leading theme is the confrontation of pagan with Christian morality. Here the Philosopher and the Christian face each other with their rival ethics and here Abelard takes it upon himself to challenge and to examine the pagan morality that was then exciting so much fashionable attention. Whereas most twelfth-century writers who were attracted by the pagan moralists remained more or less on a level of literary appreciation, the level of cultivated fashion, of practical moral instruction within the grammatical-rhetorical tradition, and whereas most theologians in their theology left all this well alone, a few, more dialectically minded inquirers, such as Alan of Lille and John of Salisbury, but above all Abelard, submitted ancient theses to a probing inquiry. In the *Dialogue* Abelard gives them the most thorough examination that they ever received in the twelfth century.

The discussion between the Philosopher and the Christian has two main objects, the nature of supreme good and supreme evil and the means or discipline required to attain the supreme good or supreme evil. As regards the second object, the Christian asks the Philosopher to define and to distinguish the virtues and vices. The Philosopher does this at length, taking his major definitions largely from Cicero's *De inuentione* ii. 53–4, and some of his divisions from Macrobius' *Commentary* on the *Dream of Scipio*, i. 8. 7, but also introducing parts of Abelard's own theories of the moral indifference of human actions and his use of Aristotle's

[1] Cf. E. M. Buytaert, 'Abelard's Collationes', *Antonianum*, xliv (1969), 18–39.

distinction between habit and disposition.¹ However, in the discussion of the nature of supreme good and supreme evil, the Philosopher, who is the natural leader of the debate, loses hold of his initiative in favour of his Christian protagonist. He presents ancient theses on the supreme good; he shows, as John of Salisbury was later to do as well, that the Epicurean doctrine of pleasure properly refers, not to the base pleasures of the flesh, but to an inner tranquillity of the soul achieved through virtue.² Thus the Philosopher is able to harmonize Epicureanism, as it is found in Seneca ('the greatest edifier of morals'), with the Socratic-Platonic view that happiness, which is attained by excelling in virtue, is the supreme good.³ Moreover, since tranquillity of soul is best assured where there are no afflictions and no suffering,⁴ he claims that the happiness sought by Epicurus does not consist of earthly advantages and is none other than the kingdom of heaven preached by Christ; the names of the reward are different, but the thing is the same.⁵

Now, however, the Christian moves into the attack and directs the Philosopher's attention to Stoicism. He suggests that perhaps ancient philosophy is not in such harmony with Christianity as the Philosopher has made it appear. Christ preached contempt of the world and encouraged the desire for happiness in the next life. Pagan doctors believed that virtue should be pursued for its own sake rather than for the sake of a greater hope and Cicero distinguished the search for what is honest and pleasing in itself from the pursuit of advantage.⁶ Moreover, the single supreme good for man cannot consist in happiness *tout court*, since men, being unequal in virtue, are unequally rewarded.⁷ The Philosopher replies that Stoicism has the merit of avoiding two pitfalls. First, Cicero, whom, the Philosopher says, the Christian has fairly represented, did not advocate the pursuit of merely temporal reward but neither did he exclude all reward. Secondly, he did not erect virtue itself into the supreme good.⁸ It is true that Stoicism teaches that all good men are equally virtuous and that all sins are equal,⁹ but Augustine said that all the virtues have a single name,

¹ *Dialogus* (PL 178. 1651c–7d).     ² Ibid. (1642AB).
³ Ibid. (1644cd).     ⁴ Ibid. (1643A–d).
⁵ Ibid. (1645d–1646A).     ⁶ Ibid. (1645A–c).
⁷ Ibid. (1646A–d).     ⁸ Ibid. (1645c–6A).
⁹ Ibid. (1647A–8b). Cf. Cicero, *De officiis* ii. 9–10, §§ 34–5 and *Paradoxon* iii. Cf. also Abelard, *Ethica*, below, pp. 74, 75.

which is charity, and just as the virtuous man is a man of all the virtues, so too the man of charity has all the virtues, because all virtue is charity. The Christian again resists the Philosopher, because although it is true that only charity can win merit with God, not all good men are equally fired by charity; no man can be better than the good man, but one good man may be better than another good man.[1]

So the core of the debate is reached. The Philosopher and the Christian compare their definitions of the supreme good and the supreme evil. They agree that the supreme good is God. Where they differ is in defining the supreme good for man and the supreme evil for man. The Philosopher believes that man's supreme good is the perpetual rest or joy which is earned by merits and which is granted in the future life in the vision or knowledge of God, and that man's supreme evil is perpetual punishment or misery also earned by merits.[2] The Christian caps this by defining man's supreme good and supreme evil, not in terms of the reward or the penalties gained—punishments are themselves good, not evil—but in terms of the highest inner state that a man can achieve and in terms of what actually earns for man his eternal reward, namely his supreme love for God or the fault which actually makes him evil.[3]

The discussion between the Christian and the Philosopher is not yet complete. The Christian next elaborates the Christian faith relative to the experience of happiness in the vision of God and to the experience of hell,[4] and he then discusses the nature of good and evil in general, with special reference to the equivocalness of the word 'good'.[5] Here the work breaks off unfinished, but long before this point the Philosopher has been relegated to the role of merely asking questions, and he confesses the inadequacy of his predecessors in providing definitions of good and evil.[6] It is clear that in the *Dialogue* Abelard is far from merely wishing to uphold to his contemporaries the excellences of pagan philosophy. In so far as this is his aim, it is secondary to his main concern. Certainly Abelard presents a Philosopher who, by reason, accepts the immortality of the soul, the existence of rewards and punishments in an after life, and the identity of the highest good with God.

---

[1] *Dialogus (PL* 178. 1648B–50B).  
[2] Ibid. (1658AB).  
[3] Ibid. (1658C–61C).  
[4] Ibid. (1661C–75B).  
[5] Ibid. (1675B–82A).  
[6] Ibid. (1675C).

Abelard's Philosopher recalls the eighth book of *The City of God* where Augustine shows that pagan philosophy is in many ways close to Christianity. But the Philosopher of the *Dialogue* begins by assuming that Christians are mad;[1] and his assumption manifestly fails to be vindicated as the conversation proceeds. The Philosopher fails to bring enlightenment to the Christian; the Christian gains command of the argument and defines from a position of advantage the relationship between Christian morality and that of classical paganism. This relationship needed to be defined in Abelard's day.

## IV. ABELARD'S *ETHICS*

Abelard was engaged in finishing his *Ethics* within, at the most, a few years of issuing his *Dialogue*. In his *Commentary* upon the Epistle to the Romans he reserved certain questions for discussion in the *Ethics*,[2] and in the *Ethics* he refers readers to the third book of his *Theologia 'Scholarium'*. This *Theologia* was written in stages; the third book first appeared in its third recension, within the years 1133 and 1138/9.[3] At the very end of the first book of the *Ethics* Abelard criticized the hostility towards obvious truth of those who were at the time prominent in religious life.[4] A few quotations in chapters xii and xiii of the *Disputatio* written against Abelard by Abbot William of Saint-Thierry early in 1139 may well indicate that the *Ethics* was then circulating among Abelard's disciples.

Abelard entitled his book of ethics *Scito te ipsum, Know Thyself*, and elsewhere he referred to this work as his *Ethics*.[5] The term

---

[1] *Dialogus* (*PL* 178. 1613B).

[2] *Expositio in Epistolam ad Romanos*, ii. 4; v. 13, 14 (*PL* 178. 842A, 951A, 959D).

[3] See below, p. 96, where Abelard refers to a part of his *Theologia 'Scholarium'*, iii, which has only been edited by V. Cousin in *Opera Petri Abaelardi*, ii (Paris, 1859), 148–9, from the Oxford MS., Balliol College 296, which itself represents the fifth recension of the work. But the third book of the *Scholarium* first appeared in the third recension; see H. Ostlender, 'Die Theologia Scholarium des Peter Abaelard', in *Aus der Geisteswelt des Mittelalters*, BGPTMA, Supplementband, iii. 1 (1935), p. 270. On the date of the third recension see E. M. Buytaert, 'An Earlier Redaction of the "Theologia Christiana" of Abelard', *Antonianum*, xxxvii (1962), 495, who also dates the fourth and fifth recensions to 1139 or early 1140. According to an earlier estimate the *Commentary* on Romans, the *Scholarium*, and the *Ethics* were all assigned to the years between *c.* 1128 and 1138; J. Cottiaux, 'La conception de la théologie chez Abélard', *Revue d'histoire ecclésiastique*, xxviii (1932), 262, 268.

[4] See below, pp. 126, 127.    [5] See below, p. 130 n. 2.

*ethica* often signified in the twelfth century the rational ethics of the *ethici*, the pagan moralists. Socrates, for example, was thought of as the inventor of ethics and as the author of an *Ethica* and of twenty-four books on positive justice.[1] 'Know thyself', the Delphic oracle, was the principle of Socratic interiority.[2] Yet Abelard's *Scito te ipsum* is not a treatise on rational morality considered in the light of pagan doctrine. In two books, the second of which survives only in a fragment, Abelard proposed to study evil and goodness, contempt of God and obedience to God. In the first book, which is complete, Abelard considers actual, as distinct from original, sin and also the remedies for sin—penance, confession, absolution, and satisfaction. The sources cited are almost exclusively Scriptural and Patristic; pagan authorities and ideas are much less evident. Yet the title of this book is justified. Isidore of Seville had used the word *ethica* to indicate the four principal virtues of which prudence consisted in the profession of the true faith and in the knowledge of the Scriptures according to their historical, figurative, and spiritual senses.[3] Abelard's *Ethica* is a theological monograph upon the moral aspects of the Christian religion. It is the counterpart of his *Theologia*, which is a theological monograph upon God and the Trinity. As for the title *Scito te ipsum*, it serves aptly and allusively to hint at Abelard's concern for

---

[1] Cf. Hugh of Saint-Victor, *Didascalicon*, iii. 2; vi. 14 (*PL* 176, 766B, 810B) for a contemporary example; also Isidore, *Etymologiae*, II. xxiv. 5, and Augustine, *De ciuitate dei*, viii. 3. In the *Dialogue* Abelard's Philosopher uses the term ethics to signify rational ethics: *scientia morum quam ethicam dicimus* (*PL* 178 1614B) and his Christian interlocutor does likewise: *quam quidem uos ethicam, id est moralem, nos diuinitatem nominare consueuimus* (1636C); Christ, moreover, *ueram ethicam consummauit* (1636C).

[2] For an outline of sources and allusions to this epigram see J. Taylor's translation of *The Didascalicon of Hugh of St. Victor* (Columbia University Press, 1961), p. 177 n. 4; R. Javelet, *Image et ressemblance au douzième siècle, de saint Anselme à Alain de Lille* (Paris, 1967), I. 368–71, II. 278–81, and B. Bischoff, *Mittelalterliche Studien* (Stuttgart, 1967), II. 235, 245, 274–5. Cf. also Juvenal, *Satura* xi. 27.

[3] *Differentiarum liber*, ii, *cap.* 39, nn. 154–5 (*PL* 83. 94–5). The ambiguity of the usage of the term *ethica* may be seen in the prologue *Quia mores* to the *Moralium dogma philosophorum* where *moralis philosophia* is stated to consist in 'ethics and in all theology', ed. J. Holmberg, *Das Moralium dogma philosophorum* (Uppsala, 1929), p. 77. Hugh of Saint-Victor, having named Socrates, Plato, and Cicero in his *Didascalicon*, iii. 2 (*PL* 176. 766BC) as authors in ethics, counsels those who wish to know how virtues are acquired and vices avoided to read Scripture (v. 7 (794CD)). Cf. P. Delhaye, *Gauthier de Chatillon est-il l'auteur du Moralium Dogma?* Analecta Mediaevalia Namurcensia, iii (Lille–Namur, 1953), 23–6.

the inner point of view in moral discussion, the attitudes of a man rather than the nature of his deeds.

The centre of interest in Abelard's *Ethics* is the theory of intention and the definition of sin. Abelard argued, with an abiding appeal and force, that God thinks not of what is done but in what mind it is done; merit and praise accrue to a human agent not for his actions but for his intentions. Deeds, being common to the damned and to the elect, are all in themselves indifferent and are called good or evil only on account of the intention of their agent.[1] To call Abelard's outlook moral subjectivism would be to offer an imprecise description for, as S. M. Deutsch observed,[2] although Abelard argued that no human action is morally good or bad in itself, none the less he upheld the existence of objective criteria of right and wrong. Our intentions determine the morality of our actions but our intentions should be informed with the standards of divine law. Abelard certainly argued that if one does wrong thinking it is right, one is not guilty; he did not argue that if one does wrong thinking it is right, it is therefore right or worthy of merit.

It has sometimes been thought that Abelard's emphasis upon the disposition and the intention of the sinner and the penitent was prompted by reaction to the crudities of an existing penitential system under which penances were imposed on sinners according to tariffs which were still set out in current manuals of penance and which were, in the judgement of some, imposed with insufficient regard for the dispositions of the individual penitent or sinner.[3] The development in the twelfth century of the practice of private confession—a development to which Abelard himself in his *Ethics* gave considerable support—brought into sharper relief the importance of taking into account the psychology of the individual sinner or penitent, but it did not at once render obsolete the old penitential collections with their lists of sins,[4] nor were the best of these penitentials, even in the Carolingian age, less

[1] Excellent studies have been made of the main aspects of Abelard's ethical theories, and for fuller discussions the reader should refer to Lottin, *Psychologie et morale*, to Blomme, *La doctrine du péché*, 2ᵉ partie, pp. 101–294, and to Anciaux, *La théologie du sacrement de pénitence*, pp. 66–7, 286–92.

[2] *Peter Abaelard, ein kritischer Theologe des zwölften Jahrhunderts* (Leipzig, 1883), p. 348.

[3] For this view see Blomme, *La doctrine du péché*, p. 202 n. 1; also p. 109.

[4] As an example see P. Michaud-Quantin, 'Un manuel de confession archaïque dans le manuscrit Avranches 136', *Sacris Erudiri*, xvii (1966), 5–54.

concerned with the dispositions of the soul than with tariffs for
evil deeds.[1] Abelard refers to the *instituta sanctorum patrum* and
*instituta canonum*, but he sees these *instituta* as bulwarks which
protect the faithful from arbitrary penances which are, none the
less, frequently imposed by ignorant prelates.[2] He does not see
them as impersonal rules which crudely mistake the proper meaning of sin and of penance. He denounces bishops who arbitrarily
commute canonical penances.[3] Moreover, he defends the bishop
who imposes a penalty upon a poor mother who in love and with
no contempt of God accidentally suffocates her baby.[4] The *Scito
te ipsum* does not suggest that Abelard wished to support the
desire of some in the twelfth century to soften ecclesiastical punishments.[5] With the increasing refinement of thought in the eleventh
and twelfth centuries, the theologian-canonists sought to formu-
late more discerning views on the dispositions required for the
commission and the absolution of sins, and Abelard as a dialectical
theologian may well have profited from the example of a Burchard
or an Ivo when deciding to establish a notion of sin which is always
and everywhere verifiable and which emphatically recognizes the
role of intention.[6] But he was no reformer of the penitential system.

The thesis that sin is consent to evil and contempt of God is
presented by Abelard in his *Scito te ipsum* with all the appearance
of originality. In this demonstration he rarely cites any authority
other than Scripture. He had possibly been helped on his way to
defining sin by the theologians of the school of Laon who, plough-
ing their Augustinian furrow, had brought into a modest promi-
nence the 'interior' aspects of sin such as conscience, intention,
and will.[7] More important is the relationship, which the French

[1] See on this the pertinent remarks of J. Leclercq, *A History of Christian Spirituality*, ii (London, 1968), 82.
[2] Below, pp. 104, 105, 108, 109.
[3] Below, pp. 108, 109.
[4] Below, pp. 38, 39.
[5] On the existence of a desire to soften existing severities of penitential practice see especially P. Michaud-Quantin, 'A propos des premières Summae Confessorum. Théologie et droit canonique', *Recherches de théologie ancienne et médiévale*, xxvi (1959), 264-306, and P. Delhaye, 'Deux textes de Senatus de Worcester sur la pénitence', *Recherches de théologie ancienne et médiévale*, xix (1952), 203-24.
[6] For a short introduction to the large subject of canonical writings on penance in the eleventh and twelfth centuries see Anciaux, *La théologie du sacrement de pénitence*, pp. 8-14, 121-31.
[7] See above, p. xvii.

scholar J. Rohmer has underlined,[1] between Abelard's thesis and the voluntarist psychology of St. Augustine, who had emphasized will as the principle by which we act. For Augustine sin consists in the will to retain or to pursue that which justice forbids and from which one is free to abstain.[2] The lusts of the flesh are neither good nor bad in themselves and they become sinful only when our will consents to their incitement.[3] The Law prescribes only charity and forbids only cupidity.[4] These Augustinian themes had become commonplaces of medieval writing; they recur, for example, in the works of Anselm of Bec[5] and of Bernard of Clairvaux.[6] What Abelard did was to extend Augustine's argument. First, he agreed that to acquire merit a good intention is needed in the human agent and to incur guilt requires a bad intention; hence original sin in us is not our fault, because we did not intend the Fall of which we bear the penalty. Secondly, in his *Scito te ipsum* Abelard ceases to speak of sin as an act of will.[7] Will is too equivocal a word; it may mean concupiscence and our desires, but in this sense an evil will does not constitute sin unless consent is given to it. Properly speaking, therefore, consent to an evil will constitutes sin, not the will for evil. Abelard's intention in this as in much else seems to have been to reorganize the language of traditional discussion. He rephrased Augustine's precisions in order to fashion a more rigid and unambiguous vocabulary. Augustine gave Abelard the idea of the importance of consent in the enactment of sin. Abelard thereupon selected the factor of consent to evil as the univocal definition of sin, because it was the unvarying and indispensable constituent of sin which must not be confused with the temptation or appetite or even the will which may precede it or with the action which may ensue upon it. Augustine also gave to Abelard a heightened awareness that the commands of Christ

---

[1] J. Rohmer, *La finalité morale chez les théologiens de saint Augustin à Duns Scot*, Études de philosophie médiévale, xxvii (Paris, 1939), pp. 31–49.

[2] *De duabus animis*, xi. 15 (*PL* 42. 105).

[3] Cf. Augustine, *De continentia*, c. 2 (*PL* 40. 350); *Expositio propositionum ex Epistola ad Romanos*, xiii–xviii (*PL* 35. 2066); *Sermo VI de verbis Apostoli*, c. 1 (*PL* 38. 841), and *Enarratio in Psalm. CXVIII, Sermo III* (*PL* 37. 1507–8, or *CCL* xl. 1671–2).

[4] See below, pp. 26, 27.

[5] Cf. *Liber de conceptu uirginali et originali peccato*, c. 4, ed. F. S. Schmitt, *Anselmi opera*, ii. 143–5.

[6] Cf. *De gratia et libero arbitrio*, cc. 11, 12 (*PL* 182. 1021AB, 1024A).

[7] On the evolution of Abelard's thinking on this point see below, p. 8 n.

concerned two things only, love and cupidity; upon this basis Abelard established his argument that works, unlike intention and consent, do nothing in themselves to earn merit or damnation and are morally neutral. In pursuing a coherent description of the morality of conduct Abelard carried the principles of intention and of consent beyond Augustine's own limits. Augustine believed that man did share in Adam's fault and guilt and that man's actions determine his merit; Peter Lombard and the school of Saint-Victor in Paris rejoined Augustine in affirming this and in contesting Abelard.[1]

By directing attention upon the need to know oneself in respect of the quality and the rightness of one's intentions, Abelard laid a striking emphasis upon man's faculty of choice and upon the importance of considering his ability to have knowledge of divine law. He placed more emphasis, in formulating his concept of sin, upon the knowing and deciding mind than upon will. Anselm of Bec had shown the power of the sanctified will to be free from the possibility of erroneous choice; Abelard underlined the faultlessness of the mind that consents to a wrong which it does not truly know. For Abelard, the consent that constitutes sin is consent to what is known to be evil. Abelard stressed the ways in which ignorance is an excuse from sin. In earlier theological discussion of the problem of ignorance, a stock example was Eve deceived by the serpent. Her ignorance did not excuse her from sin,[2] and ignorance generally was treated as a constituent feature of original sin.[3] It is a measure of the provocativeness of Abelard that he chose the case of those who crucified Christ in order to argue that in so far as the crucifiers did not believe that Christ was the Son of God and in so far as they thought they were doing right, they did not offer contempt to God nor did they consent to evil. The monastic reaction to this thesis was sharp. Anselm of Bec had already applied the idea that ignorance lessened the gravity of a sin to the case of Christ's crucifiers,[4] but, as Bernard of Clairvaux observed, Christ

[1] On the reaction to Abelard's teaching see below, pp. 24 n, 46 n. See also my *School of Peter Abelard*, pp. 193–4, 209–10, 211, 241, 276–8, 294–6.

[2] Cf. Isidore, *Sententiae*, ii. 17, nn. 3–6 (*PL* 83. 620). Also Gregory the Great, *Moralia*, xxv. 11–12, nn. 28–9 (*PL* 76. 339–40), referring to St. Paul's misbehaviour before his conversion. For the twelfth century cf. *Summa Sententiarum*, III. vi (*PL* 176. 98AB); III. xi (107 A–D) and Peter Lombard, *Sententiarum liber* II. xxii. 4–5 (2nd edn., Ad Claras Aquas, 1916), pp. 412–15.

[3] Cf. Lottin, *Psychologie et morale*, iii. 12–18.

[4] *Cur Deus Homo*, II, xv, ed. Schmitt, *Anselmi opera*, ii. 115.

prayed the Father to forgive those who killed him.[1] No theologian had hitherto formulated the thesis of the possible innocence of Christ's crucifiers. Once the storm of anger had abated, attention was constructively focused upon Abelard's theory of the moral indifference of all human actions, even the killing of Christ, and upon the sense in which ignorance as such did not constitute sin unless it was positively willed.[2] They were led to agree with Abelard that actions on the whole are neither good nor bad, and Peter Lombard, for example, gave a place to this thesis in his *Sentences*. But they could not support the view that even the most scandalous acts were not intrinsically sinful or could be performed without prevarication. The Lombard argued that certain actions were in themselves evil and his view prevailed in the later twelfth century.[3]

There is much else of historical significance in Abelard's *Ethics*. Just as consent was seen to be the constituent feature of sin, so too inward sorrow for sin was seen to be the constituent feature of penance, and this interiorizing emphasis of Abelard led to his redefinition of the role of confession and of priestly absolution in the penitential scheme. Abelard denied neither the necessity for confession nor the power of the keys, but he interpreted their meaning in ways which his contemporaries disputed. Confession for Abelard did not mark the moment when divine forgiveness was granted, if sorrow and inner contrition had already preceded the still necessary act of confession.[4] As for the power of the keys, Abelard's argument, which in the present edition can be read for the first time in its entirety on consecutive pages, was subtle. Abelard distinguished the various gifts which Christ gave to his Apostles and suggested, not without hesitation, that the gift of the Spirit to remit or to retain sins (John 20: 22–3) was specially

[1] Cf. Luke 23: 34. Bernard of Clairvaux, *De baptismo*, c. 4 (*PL* 182. 1041–2). Cf. William of Saint-Thierry, *Disputatio adversus Abaelardum*, c. 13 (*PL* 180. 282B) and *Epistola* 326 (*PL* 182. 532C). Also L. Ott, *Untersuchungen zur theologischen Briefliteratur der Frühscholastik*, BGPTMA, xxxiv (1937), 539–47.

[2] Lottin, *Psychologie et morale*, iii. 18 et seq.

[3] Peter Lombard, *Sententiarum liber* II. xxxv. 2 et seq., especially II. xl, *cap. unicum* (2nd edn., Ad Claras Aquas, 1916), pp. 492 et seq., 518–22. And on this see my *School of Peter Abelard*, pp. 276–7.

[4] Cf. Anciaux, *La théologie du sacrement de pénitence*, pp. 176–82. Although Abelard stressed the remissive value of inner contrition, one of his disciples who wrote an *Enchiridion* (contained in the Bavarian State Library, Munich, Clm. 7698) consistently argued in favour of the practice of oral confession to a priest; see my *School of Peter Abelard*, pp. 168–70.

reserved to the worthy Apostles, excluding the traitor Judas and the unbelieving Thomas, and to those of their successors who imitated them in worthiness. Otherwise their successors merely received a power of declaring, accurately or inaccurately as the case might be, an existing divine judgement or of excommunicating and readmitting into the church. Abelard in no way eliminated the role of priests in the penitential process, but his redefinition of the nature of this role burned deeply into the minds of his contemporaries and successors.[1]

The *Ethics* may be enjoyed by modern readers who lack a special knowledge of the history of early scholasticism, and the notes which accompany the present text have largely been designed to provide a historical orientation where it is necessary. The text itself is bracing and exciting in its argumentation. It is also somewhat spicy, for Abelard had a vivid sexual imagination. Moreover, Abelard did not mince words when expressing his dissatisfaction with the quality of the prelates of his own day or with the contemporary nobility. In this way his work leads us back from the task of speculation and of introspection to the reappraisal of the real world of practical and social endeavour.

[1] Cf. L. Hödl, *Die Geschichte der scholastischen Literatur und der Theologie der Schlüsselgewalt*, i, BGPTMA, xxxviii. 4 (Münster, 1960), pp. 79–86; Anciaux, *La théologie du sacrement de pénitence*, pp. 286–93; D. E. Luscombe, *The school of Peter Abelard*, pp. 195, 224, 242, 248–9, 278–9, 297, 312–15.

# THE MANUSCRIPTS OF THE *ETHICA*

THE need for reliable editions of Abelard's writings is happily now being increasingly satisfied by modern scholars. All of Abelard's known logical writings have been edited or re-edited in the course of this century,[1] as has much of his correspondence[2] and poetry.[3] For his other mainly theological works, until very recently the reader has had to consult a series of editions which commenced in 1616 with the publication in Paris by A. Duchesne of *Petri Abaelardi . . . Opera.* Many of these editions were assembled together in volume 178 of J. P. Migne's *Patrologia latina,* and they formed the basis too of V. Cousin's collected edition published in

[1] B. Geyer, *Peter Abaelards Philosophische Schriften,* i. *Die Logica 'Ingredientibus',* BGPTMA, xxi. 1–3 (1919–27); ii. *Die Logica 'Nostrorum Petitioni Sociorum',* ibid. xxi. 4 (1933). M. dal Pra, *Pietro Abelardo. Scritti filosofici,* Nuova Biblioteca Filosofica, serie II, vol. 3 (Rome–Milan, 1954). L. M. de Rijk, *Petrus Abaelardus. Dialectica,* Wijsgerige Teksten en Studies, i (Assen, 1956). L. Minio-Paluello, *Twelfth Century Logic. Texts and Studies,* ii. *Abaelardiana Inedita* (Rome, 1959).

[2] J. T. Muckle, 'Abaelard's Letter of Consolation to a Friend (*Historia Calamitatum*)', *Medieval Studies,* xii (1950), 163–213; id., 'The Personal Letters between Abelard and Héloïse', ibid. xv (1953), 47–94; id., 'The Letter of Héloïse on the Religious Life and Abaelard's First Reply', ibid. xvii (1955), 240–81. J. T. Muckle, *The Historia Calamitatum and the Letters of Abaelard and Héloïse* (New York, 1947), has not been available to me. See also T. P. McLaughlin, 'Abaelard's Rule for Religious Women', *Medieval Studies,* xviii (1956), 241–92; J. Monfrin, *Abélard, Historia Calamitatum. Texte critique avec une introduction,* Bibliothèque des textes philosophiques (Paris, 1962). The *Epistula Petri Abaelardi contra Bernardum Abbatem* has been edited by J. Leclercq in *Études sur S. Bernard et le texte de ses écrits,* Analecta Sacri Ordinis Cisterciensis, ix. 1–2 (Rome, 1953), pp. 104–5, and by R. Klibansky, 'Peter Abailard and Bernard of Clairvaux', *Medieval and Renaissance Studies,* v (1961), 1–27, here pp. 6–7. Six other letters from Abelard (to the nuns of the Paraclete, to Bernard of Clairvaux, to Héloïse, on St. Denis, to a regular canon, and to the bishop of Paris) are to be found in *PL* 178 and in V. Cousin; other manuscript copies of some of these letters are now known. A new edition of the letters between Abelard and Héloïse is being prepared by Dr. R. W. Southern of Oxford.

[3] G. M. Dreves, *Petri Abaelardi Hymnarius Paraclitensis* (Paris, 1891), and *Analecta hymnica medii aevi,* xlviii (1905). W. Meyer, *Gesammelte Abhandlungen zur Mittellateinischen Rythmik,* i (Berlin, 1905), 340–74. G. Vecchi, *Pietro Abelardo. I 'Planctus'* (Modena, 1951). The *Carmen ad Astralabium filium* was edited by B. Hauréau in *Notices et extraits des manuscrits de la Bibliothèque nationale,* xxxiv. 2 (Paris, 1895).

two volumes in 1849 and 1859. Fortunately Migne and Cousin and their predecessors have been relatively reliable guides to Abelard's work. The Migne version of Abelard's writings is generally superior to that of the writings of his contemporary, Gilbert of Poitiers, whose thought, it has been said,[1] cannot be grasped at all accurately by using *PL* 64. *PL* 178, moreover, contains no nest of dubiously authentic writings; P. Glorieux in his tables *Pour révaloriser Migne* corrected only one attribution in *PL* 178, the so-called *Epitome theologiae christianae* which is now ascribed to Abelard's disciple Hermann rather than to Abelard himself, whereas for *PL* 175–7 Glorieux corrected no fewer than twenty-eight attributions of works to Abelard's contemporary, Hugh of Saint-Victor.[2]

None the less, in spite of the relative usefulness of Migne and Cousin, it has long been evident that Abelard's theological writings have stood in need of re-edition and many are now being re-edited by the Revd. E. M. Buytaert, O.F.M., in the series *Corpus Christianorum*. The minute inquiries of H. Ostlender,[3] J. Cottiaux,[4] N. Haring,[5] D. Van den Eynde,[6] and of Fr. Buytaert himself[7] have revealed in detail the continual effort of revision which Abelard applied to his *Theologia* in all its three main forms, namely, the *Theologia 'Summi boni'*, *Theologia christiana*, and *Theologia 'Scholarium'*. Thus, of the *Theologia 'Scholarium'* (the so-called *Introductio ad theologiam*) Migne produced only a version prepared

---

[1] By N. M. Haring, 'The Commentary of Gilbert, Bishop of Poitiers, on Boethius' Contra Eutychen et Nestorium', *Archives d'histoire doctrinale et littéraire du moyen âge*, xxix (1954), 241–357, here pp. 242–3; id., 'The Commentary of Gilbert of Poitiers on Boethius' De Hebdomadibus', *Traditio*, ix (1953), 177–211, here p. 178.

[2] 'Pour révaloriser Migne. Tables rectificatives', *Mélanges de science religieuse*. IX^e année (1952), *Cahier supplémentaire*, pp. 67–70.

[3] 'Die Theologia Scholarium des Peter Abaelard', *Aus der Geisteswelt des Mittelalters*, BGPTMA, Supplementband, iii. 1 (1935), pp. 262–81; *Peter Abaelards Theologia 'Summi boni'*, BGPTMA, xxxv. 2–3 (1939).

[4] 'La conception de la théologie chez Abélard', *Revue d'histoire ecclésiastique*, xxviii (1932), 247–95, 533–51, 788–828.

[5] 'A Third MS. of Peter Abelard's Theologia Summi boni (MS. Oxford, Bodleian Lyell, 49, ff. 101–128^v)', *Medieval Studies*, xviii (1956), 215–24.

[6] 'La "Theologia Scholarium" de Pierre Abélard', *Recherches de théologie ancienne et médiévale*, xxviii (1961), 225–41; 'Les rédactions de la "Theologia Christiana" de Pierre Abélard', *Antonianum*, xxxvi (1961), 273–99.

[7] 'An Earlier Redaction of the "Theologia Christiana" of Abelard', *Antonianum*, xxxvii (1962), 481–95; 'Critical Observations on the "Theologia Christiana" of Abelard', ibid. xxxviii (1963), 384–433.

by Abelard in the late 1130s, shortly before his prosecution and his second trial for heresy in 1140. But three earlier versions and one later version of this same '*Scholarium*' also exist. Similarly, with respect to Abelard's other theological works, many problems are now being solved. Fr. Van den Eynde has recently established a chronology for Abelard's Sermons[1] and his writings for Héloïse,[2] and has also considered his lost writings.[3] Further manuscript copies of Abelard's *Expositio in Hexaemeron*,[4] *Expositio in Epistolam Pauli ad Romanos*,[5] and *Dialogus inter Philosophum, Judaeum, et Christianum*[6] have become known. As for the *Sic et non*, the new edition by Fr. Buytaert will be most interesting, for the ten known medieval manuscripts of this work each contain a different sequence of chapters, and the choice and arrangement of the *auctoritates* within each chapter vary from manuscript to manuscript. And, as if this were not difficulty enough for Fr. Buytaert, the length and wording, as well as the placing, of the citations also vary from manuscript to manuscript.[7]

The case for a new edition of Abelard's *Ethica* is simple. The first edition of this work, made through the auspices of Bernard Pez[8] and reproduced in Migne, *PL* 178, cols. 633–78, is incomplete and rests upon only one manuscript (Bavarian State Library, Munich, lat. 14160). V. Cousin's second printed edition of the work is only slightly lengthier,[9] but, if read in conjunction with

---

[1] 'Le recueil des sermons de Pierre Abélard', *Antonianum*, xxxvii (1962), 17–54.

[2] 'Chronologie des écrits d'Abélard à Héloïse', *Antonianum*, xxxvii (1962), 337–49.

[3] 'Les écrits perdus d'Abélard', *Antonianum*, xxxvii (1962), 467–80.

[4] E. M. Buytaert, 'Abelard's *Expositio in Hexaemeron*', *Antonianum*, xliii (1963), 163–94.

[5] The MS. of this work (and reissued in *PL* 178. 783–978) is now apparently lost. The following MSS. are extant: Angers, Bibl. municipale 68, ff. 1ʳ–26ʳ; Vatican Library, *Reginensis* lat. 242, ff. 1ʳ–74ᵛ; Oxford, Balliol College 296, ff. 80ʳ–160ᵛ.

[6] A list is given by Buytaert, 'Abelard's Collationes', *Antonianum*, xliv (1969), 21. To it should be added a seventeenth-century transcript in the British Museum, Lansdowne 209.

[7] See Buytaert, 'The Greek Fathers in Abelard's "Sic et Non"', *Antonianum*, xli (1966), 413–53. To Buytaert's list of manuscripts there should be added Zürich, *Kantons- und Universitätsbibliothek* (*Stiftsbibliothek*) MS. Car. C. 162, ff. 23ʳ–38ᵛ.

[8] *Thesaurus anecdotorum novissimus*, tom. III, pars ii (Augustae Vindelicorum et Graecii, 1721), cols. 625–88.

[9] *Petri Abaelardi Opera*, ii (Paris, 1859), 593–642.

the fragment published in 1931 by C. Ottaviano,[1] is as complete a text, in point of length, as we are ever likely to have. However, these editors did not know all the extant manuscripts, and their printed texts lack the reliability that comes from a full examination and collation of the manuscripts. A new edition may help to remove uncertainties, both real and imagined, concerning Abelard's words and thought. Moreover, the sources and the quotations employed by Abelard merit a more thorough and helpful identification than they have yet received.[2]

Five extant copies made before 1500 are known to me. Two of these were made in the twelfth century and they are both now found in the Bavarian State Library in Munich. CLM 14160[3] A contains the *Ethica* on ff. 39ᵛ–67ʳ in a copy made by a single hand. The rubricator had added on f. 39ʳ a title: INCIPIT LIBER MAGISTRI PETRI ABELARDI QUI DICITUR SCITO TE IPSUM. Ff. 1ᵛ–39ʳ contain the *Sentences* of Abelard's disciple Hermann, here called by the rubricator on f. 2ʳ the SENTENCIE MAGISTRI PETRI ABELARDI. Ff. 68ʳ–157ʳ contain, according to the same rubricator on f. 68ʳ, the SENTENTIE MAGISTRI HUGONIS. From f. 68ʳ to f. 144ᵛᵃ this consists of a version of the *Summa Sententiarum* compiled by a disciple of Hugh of Saint-Victor who, among other achievements, vigorously controverted a number of the theological theses of Abelard.[4] The remaining folios of this section entitled the SENTENTIE MAGISTRI HUGONIS consist in reality of four pieces which are not identified by the copyist. Ff. 144ᵛᵃ–145ʳᵃ have a version of a part of the

---

[1] 'Frammenti abelardiani', *Rivista di cultura*, xii (1931), 425–45.

[2] Translations of the *Ethics* have been made in Italian by M. dal Pra, *Petrus Abaelardus. Conosci te stesso (Scito te ipsum) Etica*, Classici del pensiero, i (Vicenza, 1941); in French by M. de Gandillac in his *Œuvres choisies d'Abélard*, Bibl. philosophique (Paris, 1945), pp. 129–209; and in German by F. Hommel, *Nosce te ipsum. Die Ethik des Peter Abälard* (Wiesbaden, 1947). A Spanish translation is being prepared by Professor A. J. Capelletti of the Argentine. The English version by J. Ramsey McCallum, *Abailard's Ethics* (Oxford, 1935), is not reliable.

[3] For an earlier description of this manuscript see the *Catalogus Codicum Latinorum Bibliothecae Regiae Monacensis*, C. Halm *et alii*, tom. II, *pars* ii (Munich, 1876), pp. 137–8. A handwritten description by C. Sanftl, *Catalogus Veterum Codicum manuscriptorum ad S. Emmeram. Ratisbonae* (1809), part i, pp. 256, 273, 274–302, is available in the Bavarian State Library.

[4] The version found here consists of tract. I–VI (*PL* 176. 41–154C) and ends . . . *per inuocationem sancte trinitatis*. On medieval views of the authorship of the *Summa Sent.* see R. Baron, 'Note sur l'énigmatique "Summa Sententiarum"', *Recherches de théologie ancienne et médiévale*, xxv (1958), 26–42, especially pp. 37–8.

*Miscellanea* of Hugh of Saint-Victor, *lib.* iii, *tit.* xxiv.[1] F. 145^ra–b^
contains a short extract from Hugh's *De sacramentis* i. viii. 5
(*De discretione iudiciorum*).[2] Ff. 145^rb^–150^rb^ present under the
rubric *De sacris ordinibus* the second sermon of Ivo of Chartres.[3]
Ff. 150^va^–157^rb^ open with the rubric *De coniugio*. This is not, as
one might expect, *tractatus* VII of the printed version of the *Summa
Sententiarum*, but resembles in places Hugh's *De sacramentis* II.
xi and, to a lesser extent, his *De officiis ecclesiasticis* i. 28–30.[4]
Finally, ff. 157^v^–206^v^ contain a version of the *De claustro animae*
by Hugh of Fouilloy (d. 1172/3),[5] here called *dominus Hugo* (f.
157^v^), apparently in the belief, which long outlived the Middle
Ages, that the author may have been the Hugh who is already well
represented in this volume and whose *De meditando seu meditandi
artificio* follows immediately after, without title or attribution, on
ff. 206^va^–209^ra^.[6] The codex as a whole consists of twenty-six
quires of eight leaves each (all numbered, with the exception of
the twenty-sixth) and a twenty-seventh quire of four leaves, the
third of which is cancelled.

It was from this manuscript that B. Pez first had the *Ethica*
edited in 1721.[7] Pez found the volume at the abbey of Saint-
Emmeram in Regensburg and on the recto side of the flyleaf at the
front of the volume a twelfth-century inscription informs us that
it had lain there even in the century of its origin.[8] But the volume

---

[1] *Super tribus sceleribus . . . uel alie ciuitatibus.* Cf. *PL* 177. 647 BC; the printed
version is shorter.

[2] *Quatuor sunt iudicia . . . et confirmabit prescientiam.* Cf. *PL* 176. 309C–310A,
l. 10.

[3] QUIA CHRISTIANAM MILICIAM . . . *in diem* PROFICIAT. Cf. *PL* 162. 513A–519D.

[4] CUM OMNIA SACRAMENTA . . . *sancte ecclesie* DISPENSANDUM. Cf. *PL* 176.
479D–480D, 480D–481B, l. 4, 481C, l. 6 et seq. and *PL* 177. 396C et seq.

[5] Cf. *PL* 176. 1017–82. This manuscript version is divided into three parts.
Ff. 157^va^–181^vb^ contain what is book ii in *PL* 176, 1051B–1086D; ff. 181^vb^ et seq.
contain what is book iii in *PL* 176. 1086D–1104C. The third part, which ends on
f. 206^va^, is not in Migne: *Quod hypocrita in congregatione . . . quasi labiis murmura-
tionis laudat. Explicit liber domni hugonis de claustralibus.* This version resembles
that found in the Vienna MS. CVP. CCVI as described by M. Denis, *Codices
Manuscripti Theologici Bibliothecae Palatinae Vindobonensis*, I. i (Vienna, 1793),
cols. 643–5.                          [6] Cf. *PL* 176. 993–8.

[7] See above, p. xl n. 8. See also Pez's introduction, ibid., *tom.* III, *pars* i.
*Dissertatio isagogica*, pp. xix–xxii (only partly reproduced in *PL* 178. 631–4).
This introduction craftily censures Mabillon for being ungenerous in his atti-
tude concerning Abelard.

[8] *Iste liber pertinet ad sanctum Emmerammum. Lector scriptoris orans memorare
laboris. In hoc uolumine continentur magistri Petri abelardi libri duo de diuersis
diuine pagine sententiis.* A later ex libris inscription is found on f. 210^v^.

may well have been produced at Prüfening in the diocese of Regensburg, for, as A. Boeckler has observed, the inscription *Emmerammum* on the flyleaf has been added over an erasure, and the capital letters in the volume are in the style of the Prüfening school of illumination.[1] In the catalogue of books which Wolfger of Prüfening compiled before 1165, mention is made of a volume which seems very similar to the present Clm. 14160: *Sententiae Petri baiol. et liber eius qui dicitur scito teipsum et sent. m. Hugonis in uno uolumine.*[2] However, H. Weisweiler, writing in 1936,[3] reported an opinion advanced by Dr. L. Ott that Clm. 14160 is not identical with the manuscript recorded in the Prüfening catalogue because it contains a further work copied by the same scribe, namely the *Liber domini Hugonis de claustralibus* (ff. 157ᵛ et seq.), which would not have escaped the notice of a cataloguer. Ott's opinion, as reported here, rests on an argument from silence and on the assumption that Wolfger was not content with a partial summary of the contents of the manuscript; but it finds support in a catalogue made in 1347 and found now in Clm. 14397. Here we read on f. 7ᵛ that the *Liberia in Prufning* possessed among the *Libri Hugonis*: *Item sentencie magistri abelardi nomine scito te ipsum. et sentencie magistri hugonis in uno uolumine*, and on f. 16ʳ that the *Liberia Ecclesie S. Emmerammi. Ratᶻ.* possessed *Item duo libri domini hugonis. unus de quibus uariis. alter de claustralibus. Item duo libri magistri petri abelardi omnes in uno uolumine.* Subsequent catalogues of Saint-Emmeram mention only one manuscript,[4] but it is quite possible that Prüfening had produced two copies of the *Ethica*, one of which is now lost but was noted by Wolfger after the other, the present Clm. 14160, had gone to Saint-Emmeram.

The compiler of the extant codex clearly believed that the *Ethica*

---

[1] *Die Regensburg-Prüfeninger Buchmalerei des XII.–XIII. Jahrhunderts* (Munich, 1924), p. 120.

[2] G. Becker, *Catalogi Bibliothecarum Antiqui* (Bonn, 1885), p. 214 n. 144.

[3] *Das Schrifttum der Schule Anselms von Laon und Wilhelms von Champeaux in deutschen Bibliotheken*, BGPTMA, xxxiii. 1–2 (1936), p. 27.

[4] See the *Repertorium* made by the prior of Saint-Emmeram, Conrad Pleystainer (d. 1475), in Clm. 14675, f. 138ʳ and Menger's *Registrum* of the Saint-Emmeram library made in 1500 and also in Clm. 14675, f. 3ʳᵃ. Jean Mabillon noticed the manuscript at Saint-Emmeram in 1683, *Iter Germanicum* (Hamburg, 1717), pp. 63–4. See also Joannes Baptista (Kraus), *Bibliotheca Principalis Ecclesiae et Monasterii Ord. S. Benedicti ad S. Emmeramum Episc. et Martyr. Ratisbonae*, part i (1748), pp. 12–13, no. 64, and the handwritten *Catalogus* made in 1769 by Romanus Zirngibl, now in the Bavarian State Library, Cbm. Cat. 13, f. 2ʳ; finally see the *Catalogus* of Sanftl cited above.

and the Sentences ascribed to Peter Abelard, as well as writings by Hugh of Saint-Victor, merited a *de luxe* treatment. The illuminations are precious, the script bold and elegant, the parchment large and thick and of good quality. This volume testifies by its physical excellence to the fact that Abelard and Hugh were—to use Wolfger's phrase—*magistri moderni* of high repute.[1] R. L. Poole suggested that this volume originated among the innermost circle of Abelard's disciples.[2] Prüfening is not otherwise known to have had any connection with the followers of Abelard and only one *nota* sign has been added to the margins of the *Ethica*—on f. 44[r] where Abelard presented his theory of the moral indifference of human acts.[3] But it may well have been an enthusiastic admirer of Abelard who inserted at the beginning of this volume a fragment of a largely apocryphal outline of Master Peter's career. The writer, who claims for Abelard 'an unbelievable subtlety, an unheard-of memory and superhuman ability' and who credits him with having swiftly surpassed all the other masters of France in both dialectic and theology, shows himself familiar with anecdotes concerning Abelard.[4]

B    The other extant twelfth-century copy of the *Ethica* is CLM. 28363, ff. 103[r]–132[v]. This copy lacks a title and the name of the

[1] Earlier in his catalogue Wolfger named Hugh of Saint-Victor, Peter Damian, Gratian, Rupert of Deutz, Petrus Baiolardus et multi alii as *magistri moderni*, Becker, *Catalogi Bibliothecarum Antiqui* (Bonn, 1885), p. 209.

[2] *Illustrations of the History of Medieval Thought and Learning* (2nd edn., London, 1920), p. 314.

[3] See below, p. 22.

[4] This is written on f. 1[r] in a good twelfth-century hand. It was first printed by Pez, *Thesaurus anecdotorum novissimus, tom.* III, *pars* i (Augustae Vindelicorum et Graecii, 1721), p. xxii, and reprinted by Poole (*Illustrations*, pp. 314–15), who assessed its value (pp. 314–17). Pez, and therefore Poole, missed a final sentence which exists in the manuscript but which does not complete the intended biography: . . . *ad adipem. Nam processu temporis se usque adeo de lardo quadruuii potenter intromisit ut nos opera illius de geometricis et arithmeticis subtilitatibus usque hodie plura uideamus.* The biographer had just stated that Abelard attended lectures on the quadrivium given by Thierry; Poole inclined to believe the biographer on this point. Must we believe also this statement that Abelard wrote successful works on geometry and arithmetic? A passage in Abelard's *Dialectica* seems to contradict the biographer as regards arithmetic: . . . *etsi multas ab arithmeticis solutiones audierim, nullam tamen a me proferendam iudico, quem eius artis ignarum omnino recognosco,* ed. L. M. de Rijk, *Petrus Abaelardus. Dialectica* (Assen, 1956), p. 59. A complete text of this biography was published, without reference to Pez or to Poole, by L. Hödl, *Die Geschichte der scholastischen Literatur und der Theologie der Schlüsselgewalt*, I. Teil, BGPTMA, xxxviii. 4 (1960), pp. 79–86.

author is not given. It also lacks chapter headings and capitals; spaces were often left for these by the copyist but they were never filled; indeed the entering of the initials and headings almost wholly ceases after the first fifty folios of the codex. The text of the *Ethica* contained here is otherwise substantially the same as that printed by Pez, and both copies are of the same length. Minor variant readings as well as some peculiarities of spelling can, however, be found, and some folios have been misplaced.[1] This volume, which is all the work of a single scribe who wrote a small but clear hand, also contains on ff. 132ᵛ–135ᵛ a unique fragment of Abelard's *Apologia*.[2] Ff. 1ʳ–98ᵛ contain, again with some misplacement of folios, a version of the Victorine *Summa Sententiarum* (*PL* 176. 44A–174). On ff. 98ᵛ–100ʳ is found a letter by Walter of Mortagne, critic of Abelard and part author of the *Summa Sententiarum*; this is the only item in the volume which bears the name of its author.[3] It is followed on ff. 100ʳ–102ᵛ by various excerpts, some of which are Christological questions of the twelfth century.[4] Clm. 28363, unlike Clm. 14160, did not come to Munich from a Bavarian religious house. P. Ruf considered that this manuscript was copied in the late twelfth century, apparently in France; the manuscript seems to have been in Italy in the fourteenth or fifteenth century.[5] There are no inscriptions of provenance, and the manuscript may well have been the personal copy-book of an unknown *érudit*. The size of the writing area of the folios is only 12·1 × 6·6 cm. and there are 26 lines to a page.

The other surviving medieval copies of the *Ethica* were made in the fourteenth and fifteenth centuries. CLM. 18597 contains a  E fifteenth-century copy on ff. 4ʳ–51ᵛ which is very like the copies found in Clm. 14160 and Clm. 28363. A title is found on f. 4ʳ: *Incipit liber magistri petri Abelardi uel baiolardi. qui dicitur. Scito te ipsum*; this is written in the text hand. The manuscript mainly

---

[1] The reader should proceed from f. 103 to ff. 105, 106, 104, 109, 107, 108, 110, 111.

[2] P. Ruf and M. Grabmann, *Ein neuaufgefundenes Bruchstück der Apologia Abaelards*, Sitzungsberichte der Bayerischen Akademie der Wissenschaften, Philos.-hist. Abteilung, v (Munich, 1930). Ruf (here, pp. 5–9) gives a full description of this manuscript.

[3] The letter was printed by L. d'Achery, *Veterum aliquot scriptorum Spicilegium, tom.* II (2nd edn., Paris, 1681), 462–6. Cf. L. Ott, *Untersuchungen zur theologischen Briefliteratur der Frühscholastik*, BGPTMA, xxxiv (1937), pp. 162–87.    [4] See Ruf, *Ein neuaufgefundenes Bruchstück*, pp. 6–7.

[5] *Ein neuaufgefundenes Bruchstück*, pp. 5 and 8.

witnesses to the great harvest of ascetical and mystical literature, still mostly unpublished, which was produced and copied at Tegernsee in the mid fifteenth century and especially during the priorate of Bernhard von Waging, 1452–67 (d. 1472).[1] Ff. 52ʳ–60ʳ contain the *De discrecione inter peccatum mortale et ueniale* by Jerome, prior of Mondsee from 1463 to 1475 and formerly Johann de Werdea.[2] Ff. 64ʳ–195ʳ contain an anonymous work called *Lauachrum consciencie omnium sacerdotum*, in which are found examples taken from the lives of Parisian masters and students,[3] and which is accompanied on ff. 196ʳ–226ᵛ by an *Exposicio quedam misse*.[4] There follow on f. 227ʳ some prayers for use at Mass and on ff. 227ᵛ–276ᵛ an *Electula de origine et dignitate sacerdotum*.[5] Finally ff. 277ʳ–350ᵛ contain an *Electula seu formula de creacione ade et eue. Et de eorum lapsu. et eorum pena et penitencia*.[6] Abelard's *Ethica*, for all its attention to the problems of sin and of conscience, seems a strange companion of writings such as these, and indeed earlier readers were admonished about the perils of the work by means of warning notices placed in the manuscript. On f. 3ᵛ an anonymous student quoted from three of the letters concerning Abelard's teachings which St. Bernard of Clairvaux sent to Rome[7] and then added apropos of the *Ethica*: 'Legatur

---

[1] See M. Grabmann, 'Bernhard von Waging († 1472), Prior von Tegernsee, ein bayerischer Benediktiner-Mystiker des 15. Jahrhunderts', *Studien und Mitteilungen zur Geschichte des Benediktiner-Ordens*, lx (1946), 82–98, and S. Geiger, *Kloster Tegernsee. Ein Kulturbild* (Munich, 1936).

[2] *Vellem ego, O fautor amantissime . . . conscienciam ligat ad mortale.* This work appears to be inedited; see L. Glückert, 'Hieronymus von Mondsee (Magister Johannes de Werdea). Ein Beitrag zur Geschichte des Einflusses der Wiener Universität im 15. Jahrhundert', *Studien und Mitteilungen zur Geschichte des Benediktiner-Ordens und seiner Zweige*, xlviii (1930), 99–201, here p. 196.

[3] *Rogo omnes in hoc libello . . . eternaliter conregnare et gaudere. Qui cum deo patre . . . seculorum benedictus Amen.* Other copies of this work appear to exist in Clm. 3332, 3806, 3808, 4404, 5613, 5986, 7009, 7644, 11715, 15181, 17505, and 28489.

[4] *'Hoc facite in mea commemoracione'* (*Luc.* 22). *Unde missa est celebranda precipue . . . Deinde dicunt Ewangelium sancti Johannis In principio erat uerbum etc. Explicit lauacrum consciencie.* Other copies appear to exist in Clm. 11715 and 17505.

[5] *Hic primo ostenditur diccio christi . . . gaudium et uitam beatam per intercessionem . . . perducat nos omnipotens pater et filius et spiritus sanctus Amen.* Other copies appear to exist in Clm. 2778 (dated 1432) and 5976 (dated 1459).

[6] *Primo agitur de duabus potenciis deus . . . ad quod regnum celorum per ducat nos omnes deus . . . spiritus sanctus. Amen.* Other copies appear to exist in Clm. 2778, 2800 (dated 1468), 5976 (dated 1453).

[7] *Epist.* 188, 192, and 193 (*PL* 182. 351, 353C; 358C–359A; 359B). The student consulted for this purpose the Tegernsee copy of St. Bernard's letters; his

ergo caute.' On f. 4$^r$ the same student also drew upon the *Speculum hystoriale* (xxviii. 17) of Vincent of Beauvais to warn the reader that Abelard was a condemned master. Marginal notes on ff. 5$^r$, 8$^r$, 10$^r$, and 13$^r$, where Abelard's thesis that actions do not add to human merit or increase sin is presented, refer us to a small inserted leaf, f. 9, which contains a *Questio* perhaps added by the scribe and concerning the role of human actions in the commission of sins; reference is made at some length to the doctrine of Alexander of Hales in his commentary on book ii of the *Sentences* as well as to book ii, chapter 4 of the *Summa* of the Franciscan master Johannes Axtensis. This pleasant and well-executed copy was made on paper in 1469 (f. 51$^v$: *Explicit 1469*). The volume is throughout rubricated by one or more similar hands and the rubricator has numbered the folios beginning from f. 4. Many near-contemporary hands have been active in the margins. Most of the actual copying in the volume was done in 1470 by Oswaldus Nott of Tittmoning, a monk and the most prolific scribe of Tegernsee, who had come in 1449 with Bernhard von Waging from Indersdorf where both had been canons.[1] Nott generally copied ascetical writings. Abelard's *Ethica* is not in his hand, but the date (1469), paper, rubrication, and binding seem to unify the whole volume and to make it almost certain that the scribe of the *Ethica* was also a monk of Tegernsee. The work had certainly entered the library of Tegernsee by the time that a catalogue of books was compiled there in 1483/4 by Ambrosius Schwarzenbeck,[2] and the volume can be traced in the subsequent catalogues of

handwriting is found in the margins against the appropriate passages in Clm. 18211, ff. 47$^{va}$, 56$^{rb}$, 57$^{ra}$, 57$^{rb}$.

[1] See ff. 195$^r$, 226$^v$, 227$^r$, 276$^v$, 351$^r$. Nott copied here the *Lauacrum consciencie*, *Exposicio misse*, the prayers for Mass, *Electula de origine et dignitate sacerdotum*, and *Electula de creacione Ade*. His signature with the date, 1470, appears at the end of each of these works. See also V. Redlich, *Tegernsee und die deutsche Geistesgeschichte im 15. Jahrhundert* (Munich, 1931), Schriften zur bayerischen Landesgeschichte, Band ix, p. 193, who lists over 70 manuscripts copied by Nott; and P. Lindner, *Familia S. Quirini in Tegernsee. Die Äbte und Mönche der Benediktiner Abtei Tegernsee von den ältesten Zeiten bis zu ihrem Aussterben (1861)*, I. Teil (Munich, 1897), pp. 74–5.

[2] J. A. Schmeller, 'Ueber Bücherkataloge des XV. und früherer Jahrhunderte', *Serapeum*, ii (1841), 241–54, 257–71, 283–7, here p. 270. The original entry is in Clm. 1925, f. 84$^v$. The cataloguer took a favourable view of Abelard (*magister Parisiensis insignis*), but another hand, as if to correct the balance, added unfavourable matter concerning Abelard in the lower margin. Clm. 18597, f. 2$^r$ contains a fifteenth-century ex libris inscription of Tegernsee as well as a list of the contents of the present volume.

Tegernsee.[1] It was seen at Tegernsee by B. Pez, who did not, however, use it for his edition of the *Scito te ipsum* for the charming
reason that the codex was only three hundred years old.[2]

D   A second fifteenth-century copy on paper is found in MAINZ,
STADTBIBLIOTHEK, MS. LAT. 76, ff. 292ᵛ–320ᵛ. The text is introduced on f. 292ᵛ by a title written in the text hand: *Incipit. Scito
te te* (!) *ipsum*, but another hand, seemingly of the fifteenth century,
has added above this an identification of authorship: *Iste tractatus uidetur esse Petri abailardi doctoris parisiensis uerbo et scripto de
heresi conuicti a sancto bernhardo. Vide epistolam eius 187.*[3] The
chapter headings, which are all written by the text hand, are
frequently different in wording from those which we read in the
Pez edition as well as being greater in number. The text of the
*Ethica* ends on f. 320ᵛ at the point where the Pez edition also breaks
off, but the copyist continues without any indication of a change
of work. Under a new heading, *De reliquijs sexte etatis*, he presents
what seem to be concluding chapters from a book concerning the
eight epochs of history. The missing earlier part of this unidenti-
fied work had discussed the past in the light of 'Hebrew truth' and
of Jerome. Present here are five chapters pertaining to the future—
the coming of the Lord, the time of Antichrist, the day of judgement, and the seventh and eighth epochs of the future—and on
f. 325ʳ the unknown author concludes: *Ergo noster libellus de
uolubili ac fluctiuago* (?) *temporum lappsu descriptus oportunum de
eterna stabilitate ac stabili eternitate habeat finis. Finis huius libelli.*
Other works contained in this volume are the *De sacramentis* of
Hugh of Saint-Victor on ff. 1ʳ–292ʳ (*PL* 176. 173–618) and the
*Cura pastoralis* of Gregory the Great, here divided into fifty-six
chapters, on ff. 326ʳ–399ᵛ (*PL* 77. 13–128). Fourteen red leather
tabs are attached to the outer edges of as many folios and the
volume is stoutly bound in decorated white vellum mounted on
boards. The quires (thirty-two of twelve leaves, one of twenty, and
one of one) were originally numbered and some numbers have

---

[1] See the *Registrum* made in 1500–4, now Bavarian State Library, Cbm. Cat.
22, f. 191ʳ (*Scito teipsum Petri Abelardi. Caute legatur*); the Catalogue of 1610,
Cbm. Cat. 3, f. 344ᵛ; the Catalogue of 1682 of Chrysogonus Auceps, Cbm. Cat.
24, f. 293ʳ; and the Catalogue of 1730 of R. Krinner, Cbm. Cat. 24a.

[2] B. Pez, *Thesaurus anecdotorum novissimus*, tom. III, pars i. *Dissertatio
isagogica*, p. xxii.

[3] Perhaps Bernard's *Epist.* 188 (*PL* 182. 351–4) is meant; the present *Epist.*
187 does not mention the *Ethica*.

escaped the trimmer's knife. The writing area varies from 18·2 to 19 cm. by 12·8 to 14 cm.; there are usually 33 or 34 lines to the page. The whole volume was copied in the *studium* at Heidelberg in 1458 by Henry of Waldkirch (near Freiburg), who was then in his fiftieth year and who informs us of this on ff. 292$^r$ and 399$^v$. He was one among several scholars and students, such as Johannes Juff and Marcellus Geist, who came to the Charterhouse on Michaelsberg outside Mainz from Heidelberg bringing manuscripts. He had previously graduated as *baccalarius artium* in Vienna, at latest by 1438,[1] and he may be identifiable with Heinricus Waltkirchen de Tapfhein who had matriculated at Heidelberg in June 1428.[2] His hand appears in three other manuscripts of the Charterhouse, each containing much varied canonistic material and now in the Mainz Stadtbibliothek as MSS. lat. 70, 454 (dated 1453) and 467 (dated 1438 at Heidelberg). The ex libris of the Mainz Charterhouse appears in MS. 76 on the first (unnumbered) folio recto, and in the library the volume bore the number 122. The catalogue of the Charterhouse, Mainz Stadtbibliothek, MS. lat. 577, which was possibly prepared by Johannes Steinbach after 1466 and perhaps before 1470,[3] does not expressly mention Abelard's *Scito te ipsum*, perhaps because Nott had not given the author's name. But on ff. cɪɪɪ recto and cxɪx verso of the catalogue two manuscripts are mentioned which both contained the *De sacramentis* of Hugh and the *Cura pastoralis* of Gregory and which bore the classification marks respectively of E. iii. S and E. iii. T. These two manuscripts are again mentioned with the same classification marks in a later catalogue, made *c.* 1520[4] and now Mainz Stadtbibliothek, MS. lat. 576, on ff. 251$^v$ and 259$^r$ and also on 242, where in addition to the works of Hugh and Gregory both manuscripts are stated to contain Abelard's *Scito te ipsum*. E. iii. T is certainly the present MS. 76, for the cataloguer gives the opening words of the second folio (*que sit cautela*). It is just possible that E. iii. S, which does not appear to survive today, was a 'twin' of E. iii. T and not an error of duplication by both

---

[1] See H. Schreiber, *Die Bibliothek der ehemaligen Mainzer Kartause. Die Handschriften und ihre Geschichte*, Zentralblatt für Bibliothekswesen, Beiheft lx (Leipzig, 1927), 62.

[2] See G. Toepke, *Die Matrikel der Universität Heidelberg von 1386 bis 1662* (Heidelberg, 1884), i. 178.

[3] See H. Schreiber, *Die Bibliothek der ehemaligen Mainzer Kartause*, pp. 23–4.

[4] See H. Schreiber, *Die Bibliothek*, p. 41.

cataloguers; if so, it contained a copy of the *Ethica* which, like that of MS. 76, was not immediately identified as a work by Abelard.[1] MS. 76 entered the old university library in Mainz after the dissolution of the Charterhouse in 1781 and thence it came to the town library.[2]

C    OXFORD, BALLIOL COLLEGE MS. 296 contains on ff. 61$^r$–79$^v$ a version of the *Ethica* which was copied very regularly and carefully in the mid fourteenth century in a large hand and then illuminated reasonably modestly. The rubric on f. 61$^r$ reads: *Liber petri abaelardi qui intitulatur Scito teipsum.*[3] Near the bottom of f. 78$^v$, at the point where all other copies end, the words *Explicit iuxta exemplar* have been erased and the scribe continues to the bottom of this folio and on to f. 79 with a continuation, not found in Pez, which completes what is in fact a first book of the *Ethica* and which commences a second book, of which only the beginning is present here.[4] There can be no doubt that this continuation, which is not found in any other medieval manuscript of the *Ethica*, is by Abelard. The completion of the first book develops and clarifies the theses on the nature of the power of the keys which Abelard had introduced earlier in his chapter. The fragment of the second book makes the plan of the *Ethica* comprehensible, for the second book concerns virtue and goodness, whereas the first book had treated only of vice and sin. Just as in the first book Abelard focuses upon consent to evil and contempt of God as the essence of sin, so too the beginning of book ii focuses upon the will's readiness to obey God as the essence of good behaviour. Since f. 79 is an inserted leaf which upsets the quiring, it would appear that the original scribe found a longer version than the one

[1] The publication of these catalogues is greatly to be desired.
[2] This copy of the *Ethica* has previously been signalled by M. Bernards, 'Zur Überlieferung mittelalterlicher theologischer Schriften'. Neue Handschriften', *Recherches de théologie ancienne et médiévale*, xix (1952), 332 (who mistakenly makes the *Ethica* end on f. 325$^r$), and also by A. M. Landgraf, *Introducción à la historia de la litteratura teológica de la escolástica incipiente* (Barcelona, 1956), p. 106, and by M. Manitius, *Geschichte der lateinischen Literatur des Mittelalters* (Munich, 1931), iii. 112. I am most grateful to Dr. L. M. de Rijk for lending me his photostats of this manuscript before I could go to Mainz and to Dr. Darapsky of the Mainz Stadtarchiv for her help when I was there.
[3] A full and excellent description of this manuscript is given by R. A. B. Mynors, *Catalogue of the Manuscripts in Balliol College, Oxford* (Oxford, 1963), pp. 314–17.
[4] Mynors, *Catalogue*, p. 315. This fragment was edited by C. Ottaviano in *Rivista di cultura*, xii (1931), 442–5.

which he had been using and that he decided to add its ending to his already completed copy. This Balliol manuscript is further valuable by reason of the versions of three other works by Abelard which it contains. Ff. $1^r$–$60^v$ contain a unique copy of the final and longest version of the *Theologia 'Scholarium'*;[1] ff. $80^r$–$160^v$ contain the *Commentary* on the Epistle to the Romans in a version which seems similar to that printed by Duchesne and then by Migne but which, like the Vatican Library MS. *Reginensis lat.* 242, ff. $1^r$–$74^v$,[2] does not distinguish between a fourth and a fifth book. Ff. $161^r$–$189^v$ contain the *Dialogus*, here sensibly divided into two parts under the title of *Collationes*, the first *Collatio* being between the Philosopher and the Jew and the second between the Philosopher and the Christian; this copy, according to R. Thomas,[3] is longer than the printed version. Among other works contained in the Balliol manuscript are the commentary on Boethius' *De trinitate* by Abelard's opponent, Clarembald of Arras, the *Epitome Dindimi* by Hugh of Saint-Victor, and two spiritual pieces by Richard of Saint-Victor.[4] The manuscript may have come to Balliol College from the collection of William Gray, bishop of Ely, who died in 1478; it may have been copied in England.[5]

V. Cousin, introducing his edition of the *Ethica*, observed that the Pez edition was incomplete; in the *Commentary* on the Epistle to the Romans Abelard had reserved to the *Ethica* some questions which do not appear in the Pez edition.[6] Cousin was fortunately

---

[1] See H. Ostlender, 'Die Theologia Scholarium des Peter Abaelard', *Aus der Geisteswelt des Mittelalters*, BGPTMA, Supplementband iii. 1 (1935), pp. 275–9, and Mynors, *Catalogue*, pp. 314–15. This version was written 1139–40; see D. Van den Eynde, 'La "Theologia scholarium" de Pierre Abélard', *Recherches de théologie ancienne et médiévale*, xxviii (1961), 241.

[2] See A. Wilmart, *Bibliothecae Apostolicae Vaticanae Codices Manu Scripti*, I. *Codices Reginenses Latini* (Vatican City, 1937), pp. 578–9. H. Ostlender, 'Die Theologia Scholarium', p. 279 n. 79; W. Affeldt, 'Verzeichnis der Römerbriefkommentare der lateinischen Kirche bis zu Nikolaus von Lyra', *Traditio*, xiii (1957), 369–406, here p. 395; and A. M. Landgraf, *Introducción à la historia de la litteratura teológica de la escolástica incipiente* (Barcelona, 1956), p. 106, describe the Vatican version and the Balliol version as longer and shorter respectively.

[3] *Der philosophisch-theologische Erkenntnisweg Peter Abaelards im Dialogus inter Philosophum, Judaeum, et Christianum* (Bonn, 1966), p. 26 n. 19. Thomas is re-editing Abelard's *Dialogus*.

[4] For full details see Mynors, *Catalogue*, pp. 314–17.

[5] Mynors, *Catalogue*, p. 317 (on Gray see pp. xxiv–xlv).

[6] *Opera P. Abaelardi*, ii. 594. Cf. Abelard, *Expositio in Epistolam ad Romanos*, ii. 4; v. 13 (*PL* 178. 841D–842A, 950C–951A).

able to add a fragment of the second book[1] but he appears to have used for this purpose not the Balliol manuscript, of the existence of which he was certainly aware,[2] but a seventeenth-century copy-book in the Bodleian Library at Oxford containing extracts from the Balliol manuscript, namely MS. WOOD DONAT. 2.[3] This transcript contains, as regards book ii of the *Ethica*, only a fragment of the Balliol fragment. However, Cousin seems not to have had an adequate knowledge even of this transcript, for he missed the copy which is there made of the complete ending of book i. The Bodleian Library contains one other seventeenth-century transcript of the *Ethica*, presumably made from the Balliol copy, namely CORPUS CHRISTI COLLEGE MS. 318, ff. 48ʳ–86ᵛ.[4] The library of TRINITY COLLEGE, CAMBRIDGE, contains a third transcript of the seventeenth century, MS. o. 5. 14, which is certainly a copy of the Balliol *Ethica*.[5] The Oxford antiquary, Anthony Wood, informs

---

[1] *Opera P. Abaelardi*, ii. 642.

[2] Cousin referred to the Balliol MS. in editing the *Theologia* (*Opera P. Abaelardi*, ii. 2).

[3] Cousin, *Opera P. Abaelardi*, ii. 594, declared that he based his edition upon a manuscript noted in E. Bernard, *Catalogi Librorum MSS. Angliae et Hiberniae* (Oxford, 1697) as containing a fragment of a second book. The only manuscript so described there (*Catalogi*, i. 1, no. 8615, 7) is the present Bodleian Wood donat. 2 which contains excerpts from the *Ethica* on pp. 172–81, 186–7. It also contains excerpts from the *Theologia* on pp. 148–71 and 247. The excerpt from the *Ethica* from the Balliol MS. begins on p. 172 of the Wood MS.: *Ex libro petri Abaelardi qui intitulatur Scito teipsum siue Ethicus lib.* 1º and at a point shortly after the opening of the work. The fragment from the opening of the second book, which is found here on pp. 180–1, is the same as that printed by Cousin and is shorter than the Balliol fragment of book ii. On the Wood MS. see also H. O. Coxe, *Catalogi codicum manuscriptorum Bibliothecae Bodleianae*, i. (Oxford, 1858), 886: *Gerardi Langbainii Adversaria*, Cod. 23. Mynors therefore was not quite correct in thinking (*Catalogue of the Manuscripts in Balliol College*, p. 315) that Cousin used the Balliol MS.

[4] H. O. Coxe, *Catalogus codicum manuscriptorum qui in collegiis aulibusque Oxoniensibus hodie adservantur*, ii (Oxford, 1852), 161: *Ricardi Davis de Sandford Collectaneorum volumen secundum*, 16. This copy omits some passages of the *Ethica* and bears many annotations.

[5] M. R. James, *The Western Manuscripts in the Library of Trinity College, Cambridge*, iii (Cambridge, 1902), 317, and E. Bernard, *Catalogi Librorum Manuscriptorum Angliae et Hiberniae*, ii. 1 (Oxford, 1698), p. 191, nos. 6086–7. This manuscript belonged to Thomas Gale (1635?–1702), who was at Trinity College from 1655 to 1672; it was given by his son Roger (d. 1744) to Trinity College. The *Ethica* is here divided into the same chapters as those into which the Balliol MS. was divided in the seventeenth century by the same hand. The Trinity MS. also contains Abelard's *Collationes ex Bibliotheca S. Jacobi*. In fact this transcript of the *Dialogus* is from the Balliol MS. also and not from the Jacobean MS., now London, British Museum, Royal 11. A. V, ff. 99ʳ–109ᵛ. Landgraf, *Introducción à la historia de la litteratura teológica de la escolástica*

us that his cousin, Henry Jackson, formerly Fellow of Corpus Christi College, Oxford (1586–1662), had copied Abelard's *Ethica* 'out of Sir Robert Cotton's library'.[1] Jackson's exemplar was probably the Balliol manuscript which wandered somewhat peculiarly in his lifetime and narrowly escaped being acquired for Cotton's library.[2] I do not know whether Jackson's work survives as one of the transcripts just mentioned or is now lost.

These transcripts were all made by English scholars before the appearance of the Pez edition but after the publication of Abelard's works by A. Duchesne in 1616 in a volume from which the *Ethica*, by reason of the absence of extant French copies, was missing. The Trinity College transcript actually contains on its title-page a list, drawn up perhaps by Thomas Gale, of works by Abelard which had not appeared in the Duchesne edition of 1616, but which were extant in English libraries. This knowledge of the available English manuscripts had not been regained in Cousin's day and it is unfortunate both that Cousin only partially used what was the least complete of three similar transcripts of the *Ethica* and that no scholar in England in the seventeenth century proceeded from a transcription to a printed edition of this work. In 1931 C. Ottaviano writing in the *Rivista di cultura* printed the inedited fragments of the Balliol *Ethica*.[3] Ottaviano's contribution is not wholly reliable. R. Blomme in his excellent study of Abelard's doctrine of sin also utilized, apparently in ignorance of Ottaviano's article, the further fragments found in the Balliol manuscript.[4]

The five medieval manuscripts which are described above represent the total number of extant copies of the *Ethica* made before 1500 and known to me. All these texts have personal characteristics, but the only major differentiating feature lies in

*incipiente* (Barcelona, 1956), p. 112, erroneously describes the Trinity MS. as a MS. from Abelard's school.

[1] 'He had completed all Peter Aebaelard's his Ethicka out of Sir Robert Coton's library; but when the war came and he began to dote the designe failed ... He was an excellent scholman', *The Life and Times of Anthony Wood, antiquary, of Oxford, 1632–1695, described by Himself collected from his diaries and other papers by Andrew Clark*, i (Oxford, 1891), 441.

[2] Mynors, *Catalogue of the Manuscripts in Balliol College*, p. 317 and also p. li.

[3] 'Frammenti abelardiani', *Rivista di cultura*, xii. 442–5. Ottaviano did not explain why Cousin's supplement was so incomplete.

[4] *La Doctrine du péché*, 2ᵉ partie, pp. 101–294. L. Hödl used Ottaviano's edn. in *Die Geschichte der scholastischen Literatur und der Theologie der Schlüsselgewalt*, I. Teil, BGPTMA, xxxviii. 4 (1960), pp. 79–86.

the additional passages which are contained in the Balliol manuscript. And on one matter all these copies fully agree: even though Abelard refers in his *Commentary* on Romans to his *Ethica*,[1] the surviving manuscripts of the *Ethica* never themselves use this word as a title. The only title found in the manuscripts is *Scito te ipsum*.

If, as all agree, Abelard's *Ethica* represents a brilliant moment in the development of medieval ethical thought, then the lack of a larger number of surviving manuscripts may seem disappointing. From the twelfth century itself only two copies survive and nowhere in modern France can a copy from any medieval century be found today. The survival or loss of manuscripts is, however, largely a matter of hazard. The *Ethica*, moreover, did not belong to the class of work which became indispensable in the schools, in the manner of the *Sentences* of Peter Lombard or the *Decretum* of Gratian. It was a personal and provocative treatise which contained uncommon theological opinions and which did not belong to an established or developing literary genre. It neither sought to compile systematically all the materials needed for ethical discussion nor to integrate moral theology with the other branches of contemporary theological inquiry. Even in 1139, shortly before Abelard's condemnation at Sens, William of Saint-Thierry complained to Bernard of Clairvaux and to Bishop Geoffrey of Chartres that he could not obtain copies of Abelard's *opuscula*, especially the *Sic et non* and the *Scito te ipsum*: 'I fear that just as they are monstrous in their titles, so too are they monstrous in their teaching, but, men say, they have shunned the light and, even when looked for, are not found.'[2] Likewise of the *Theologia* William revealed that he had encountered it only by chance.[3] R. L. Poole suggested that the *Ethica* might have had an esoteric reputation.[4] Certainly the milieu of William and that of Abelard were different from each other. Yet the high quality of the early copy found in Clm. 14160 does not in itself lend weight to the suggestion that this work 'shunned the light'. This version was made to be admired and it is accompanied by other non-Abelardian works which have no esoteric flavour. None the less, the scarcity of surviving twelfth-century copies is a fact. The three copies of the fourteenth

---

[1] *PL* 178. 842A, 951A, and 959D.
[2] *Epist.* 326 (*PL* 182. 532D–533A).
[3] *Epist.* 326 (*PL* 182. 531C).
[4] *Illustrations of the History of Medieval Thought and Learning* (2nd edn., London, 1920), p. 314.

and fifteenth centuries testify, however, to a continuing appeal exercised by the work some two or three hundred years after the impulses which had promoted the early scholastic theological movement had changed.

We must now examine further the textual characteristics of the five medieval copies and determine how they are related to each other.

A  The text in Clm. 14160 is divided by rubricated headings written by the scribe. The use of capitals and punctuation is careful. Important capitals are often placed in the margin and drawn in red and sometimes also in green or they contain a red vertical line drawn through them. The first letter of all is particularly well drawn and some attempt at giving variety to subsequent initials is made. Many other capitals, smaller in size, are helpfully placed, although many introduce a clause within a sentence. Nearly all interrogatory sentences terminate with a question mark ⁊ Sensible and regular use is made of the stop, both within and at the end of sentences. But the scribe makes sparing use, within sentences or between sentences which are not greatly divided from one another, of a variety of medial signs ⁖ ⁘ : ⁏ The last shown of these is sometimes used to preface a quotation or an *exemplum*. The scribe made few mistakes; occasional correction marks appear in the margin and the scribe seems to have vetted his own copy. His hand is clear to read and his spelling is quite regular. He often distinguishes between *e* and *ae* which he writes, except in one instance, as *ę*. But *e* does sometimes replace *ę*, especially in word-endings and in some other words such as *haec* and *caelum*. Moreover, the scribe always shortens this vowel in words beginning with *prae-* and in some other words, of which the modern successors remain shortened, e.g. *premium, demones, quaerat*.

E  The text of Clm. 18597 is also divided by headings written in the scribe's hand and throughout the copy resembles that found in A. The opening letter of the work is rather fancifully drawn and all rubrications appear to be by the copyist. Major initials and the headings are rubricated; capitals have a red vertical stroke drawn through them. Page numbers are also provided by the scribe. The punctuation is clear and simple. The question mark ⁓ is regularly

found. Full stops are seldom used and capitals indicate where a sentence is begun. Within a sentence a medial stop is provided or a short vertical stroke in black ink is drawn. This scribe worked in haste. Mistakes of transcription abound and some of them are howlers, but the most common are simple omissions of single words (on average once every two hundred or so words), the mis-reading or mis-spelling of single words in the exemplar, and the omission or repetition of single letters or of syllables within words. Many small corrections are made *au courant*, but another corrector appears in about half a dozen places.

AE   A is a more valuable copy than E, but both closely resemble each other and together they form our first group of manuscripts.

B   The text of Clm. 28363 has no headings, and many unfilled spaces have been left without titles or capitals. Paragraph marks announce the beginnings of some sections of the work. In one place (p. 48, l. 30) what appears as a heading in other manuscripts is here inserted awkwardly into the concluding phrase of the pre-vious section; probably, therefore, the scribe's exemplar already had chapter headings. Some sections begin on a new line and leave space for a capital letter where other manuscripts proceed without interruption. There is no colouring in this manuscript. The punctuation is not reliable; question marks are found but some full and medial stops are misplaced. The scribe's writing, which is normally regular but compressed, becomes larger and rounder at p. 96. He seems to have been his own corrector, but he also seems not to have executed his review of the text beyond the opening passages and there is a very large number of slips and minor omissions. His spelling is very inconsistent. He drops *h* frequently, e.g. *erbis, orrendum*. But as frequently he adds *h*, e.g. *trihumpha-mus, habraam*. Double consonants are frequently reduced to single consonants, e.g. *dixiset*, and single consonants are often doubled, e.g. *ippsa*. The diphthong *-ae* appears in this spelling in a few places, but is more frequently written as *ę*.

C   The text of Balliol 296 lacks chapter headings and is divided by blue and red paragraph marks added after the copying was done. It is rubricated somewhat fitfully. Capital letters are of various

sizes; sometimes a minuscule letter in heavier ink is used to start a section. The punctuation by full and medial stops is assiduous. Superficially the copy gives every appearance of being a good one. Omissions are not annoyingly frequent. There are a few marginalia: a *nota*, perhaps written by the scribe, appears at p. 12, l. 14 and a hand is drawn at p. 22, l. 22 and again at p. 26, l. 28. A contemporary corrector, who is not the scribe, has taken pains to review the text; some of his now erased marks are detectable in the margin. The scribe himself has also frequently erased words and replaced them.

In view of the fact, already noted above, that two differing exemplars of the *Ethica* were available to this copyist, the question has to be raised whether some of these corrections were made necessary by a collation with the second and longer exemplar. This question cannot be conclusively answered. There are places in the text where C seems to abandon AE to follow BD. Thus at p. 88, l. 20 the scribe of C wrote *anima* as in AE, but later the first two letters of this word were marked for erasure and in the margin the word *antea*, which is found in BD, was added. Similarly on p. 86, l. 13 the scribe wrote *aut*, a mistake found in AE, but the corrector has added *e* in an attempt to produce *ante* as in BD. On p. 4, ll. 31–2 the manuscripts read: *Quid est enim iste* (*hic* BC) *consensus nisi dei contemptus*, but in both B and C *dei* is an added word and in B it is added after *contemptus*. On p. 64, l. 2, where ADE have *conuerti* and where B has *conueniens asignacio*, in C *conueniens assignacio* is added over an erasure, but I cannot tell whether the word was originally *conuerti*.

However, on p. 8, l. 13 *unde* is found in ADE but not in B. In C it is added above the line and here C may be thought to be moving away from B to ADE, but the scribe of C might equally well be correcting his own temporary aberration. Similarly on p. 32, ll. 11–14 ADE read: *intentio iubentis excusat ipsum qui precipit fieri quod tamen minime conuenit fieri . . . Vt ergo breui conclusione supradicta colligam.* In BC the phrase *quod tamen minime conuenit fieri* is misplaced after *breui* but in C the scribe realized his mistake and rewrote the phrase in the margin facing the place where it should rightly appear. On p. 72 AE read: *timor penam habet quem perfecta karitas foris mittit.* BD read *quam* for *quem*; this may be smoother grammatically but it is not in accordance with 1 John 4: 18. C reads *timor penam habet et perfecta caritas foris mittit timorem.*

This could be an attempt by C to make an exemplar like BD more faithful to St. John's meaning, but it could equally be an attempt to improve the style of an exemplar close to AE.

BC Although one cannot say whether C in its corrections and in its recourse to a second and differing exemplar was leaving a manuscript of the B type to follow one like A or vice versa, BC none the less, in the main, hunt together differently from AE. We may speak of two main text traditions, but in no instance of variation between the two traditions does Abelard's actual teaching seem to evolve. Most of the variants are of slight importance and show BC or BCD substituting a different word from one found in ADE or AE, e.g. *hic* for *iste*, *sicut* for *quemadmodum*, *dico quod* for *dico quia*, *asseris* for *dicis*, *ueniant* for *perueniant*, and so on. Some of the variants concern the selection and placing of words in a sentence as the following examples show:

*contemptus creatoris est* AE / *creatoris contemptus est* BCD (p. 6, ll. 2–3);

*punit (punire* B) *innocentem. Debet ergo punire illum qui puniri (quem punire* B) *non debet. Debet utique quia quod ille non meruit hic secundum legem iuste agit* BC / *punire innocentem debet qui puniri non debet. Itaque punire debet, licet non meruerit cum tamen lege precipiente hoc iuste iudex peragit* ADE (p. 40, ll. 1–3);

*iniungi ei in quo nulla culpa precessit* ADE / *iniungi ei ubi culpa non precessit* BC (p. 40, l. 4).

It is possible that some of these variants reflect the different states in which Abelard parted with his text to his copyists, but it is also possible that all these variants result from the reformulations of copyists.[1] To speak, as others have done, of different 'editions' of the *Ethica* would seem to me to be very bold.[2] It is true that the additional ending to the text found in C, together with its

---

[1] Some observations upon the texts of other works by Abelard are made in my *School of Peter Abelard*, pp. 95–6.

[2] B. Geyer, *Patristische und scholastische Philosophie* in Ueberweg–Heinze, *Grundriß der Geschichte der Philosophie*, II. Neubearbeitung (Berlin, 1927), p. 216; J. Cottiaux, 'La conception de la théologie chez Abélard', *Revue d'histoire ecclésiastique*, xxviii (1932), 252; H. Ostlender, 'Die Theologia Scholarium des Peter Abaelard', *Aus der Geisteswelt des Mittelalters*, BGPTMA, Supplementband iii. 1 (1935), p. 279 n. 79; N. d'Olwer, 'Sur la date de la Dialectica d'Abélard', *Revue du moyen âge latin*, i (1945), 383; J. de Ghellinck, *Le mouvement théologique du XII^e siècle* (2nd edn., Bruges, 1948), p. 151, and A. M. Landgraf, *Introducción à la historia de la litteratura teológica de la escolástica incipiente* (Barcelona, 1956), p. 106, all state that the *Ethica* underwent revision.

direct criticism of contemporary enemies of truth, may represent a latter-day addition, made at the time of the council of Sens, to a text which had already found copyists. But it is, surely, just as plausible to conjecture that a copyist, whose version lies behind A, B, D, and E, abruptly abandoned his task because of the increasingly controversial and unorthodox tone of the argument at this point in the book or for another unknowable reason.

It would not be easy to decide whether one of these two groups AE or BC is on balance superior. Many variants are indifferent in value. Many are preferable to others. For example, BC confuse Abelard's meaning in the following sentence: *Non itaque concupiscere mulierem sed concupiscentie consentire peccatum est, nec uoluntas concubitus sed uoluntatis consensus (uoluntas consensus BC) dampnabilis est* (pp. 12–14). On the other hand, from time to time BC and BCD offer better readings, e.g.:

  *cum diximus (dicimus AE) 'uicia' premisimus 'animi'* (p. 2, l. 5);

  *Omnis quippe pugna quam non dum experti sumus grauius sustinetur (sustinemus ADE) et amplius formidetur (formidamus ADE)* (p. 36, ll. 11–13).

The preferable readings do not belong consistently to one of the text traditions nor to one tradition rather than to the other.

D  The text of Mainz 76, like AE, is divided by headings. Henry of Waldkirch, the scribe, has used red ink to underline some prominent nouns (e.g. *psalmiste, augustinus*) and to underline the headings. His major capitals are drawn with a certain flourish. The punctuation is simple. Henry uses no stops or interrogation signs but frequently indicates pauses by a short vertical line placed between words. To begin a sentence he often draws a short vertical stroke through the first letter. A feature of his spelling is a tendency to write a double consonant where a single one might be expected, e.g. *consenssus*. Another feature, a Germanic trait, is the use of the *w* in place of *u*, e.g. *perswasio*. On the whole this scribe is fairly reliable. On about five occasions he omitted a few words and there are a few errors, e.g. *prestari* for *patri* (p. 10, l. 18), *non* for *ut* (p. 74, l. 22); sometimes he abbreviated or excessively too fancifully and he could be careless in writing minims. But he corrected his text as he was writing and again as he rubricated. There are no marginalia.

D offers few helpful readings that cannot be found in other manuscripts. Its peculiarity is that it sometimes hunts with BC and sometimes with AE and one has the impression that the scribe's exemplar did so too. A further peculiarity of D is that, although like AE it presents chapter headings, in eleven cases these are differently worded and on four occasions the titles are unique to this manuscript (see below pp. 16, 42, 68, 76).

ABCDE There are, then, two main groups of manuscripts, AE and BC, but D belongs to neither in particular. The two groups do not differ in any serious respect but are divided by a mass of minor and irritating variants. Neither is consistently or clearly superior to the other. Sometimes BC and BCD seem to be markedly better than ADE or AE; sometimes it seems as if someone, either Abelard himself or a student, might have been touching up an earlier rough draft from which copies had already been made, but the faults of AE and ADE could just as well have crept in at an early stage in the copying tradition.

In themselves these considerations may seem unimportant and fussy. But the habit of revising his texts is very characteristic of Abelard and the understanding of this habit in the case of the *Logica* and the *Theologia* has proved exceedingly fruitful in revealing major phases in the history, not only of Abelard's opinions, but of twelfth-century thought in general. As a result, there is a strong temptation to presume that, where the manuscripts of Abelard's other works differ between themselves, recensions may be enumerated and Abelard himself may be held responsible for the changes in his texts. In all probability, however, the verbal differences between the surviving manuscripts of the *Ethica* are historically insignificant and do not permit us to conclude that Abelard proceeded to a second recension of this work.[1]

### THIS EDITION

The choice of a base manuscript for the following edition is a little difficult to make since the textual relationships between the manuscripts are so blurred. C is a strong candidate and C alone carries the text to the very end of book i and the beginning of book ii.

---

[1] I am most grateful to Dr. B. Scott of the Queen's University, Belfast, for supporting me in this conclusion.

However, I have preferred A, that is, the manuscript used by Pez, mainly because it seems to me to require less frequent emendation by recourse to the other manuscripts than would C and also because A, like D and E, offers the convenience, such as it is, of chapter headings which are wholly missing in C and which were not inserted in B. However, I have drawn readily upon BC where improvements can be made and upon C to continue beyond the end of ABDE.

In the apparatus a selection of variants is shown, principally to illustrate the relationships between the two main groups of manuscripts and to mark the places where A is not followed. The spelling of A and, towards the end, of C is retained. Where A sometimes uses the vowel ę I have consistently presented *ae*. Inconsistency in this respect was common in the mid twelfth century, although the shorter vowel *e* has already firmly replaced *ae* in many uses and in these cases I have not resorted to the longer form. The indeterminate practice of A testifies in a modest way to changes in the history of the Latin language. The punctuation of A has had to be supplemented and therefore modernized, since it is too light and insufficiently helpful for modern readers. There appears to be no reason to think that Abelard punctuated his work as carefully as an Eadmer[1] or an Orderic,[2] and the scribe of A has left a copy which can be read, as perhaps Abelard meant the *Ethics* to be read, at a brisk pace and with a minimum of pauses.

[1] See R. W. Southern, *The Life of St. Anselm by Eadmer* (London–Edinburgh, 1962), pp. xxv–xxxiv.
[2] See M. Chibnall, *The Ecclesiastical History of Orderic Vitalis* (Oxford, 1969), ii, pp. xl–xlii.

# PETER ABELARD'S
## *ETHICS*

# INCIPIT. LIBER. MAGISTRI. PETRI. ABELARDI. QUI DICITUR. SCITO. TE IPSUM.[a]

MORES dicimus animi uicia uel uirtutes quae nos ad mala uel bona[b] opera pronos efficiunt. Sunt autem uicia seu bona non tantum animi sed etiam corporis, ut debilitas corporis uel fortitudo quam uires appellamus, pigredo uel uelocitas, claudicatio uel rectitudo, 5 cecitas uel uisio. Vnde ad differentiam talium cum diximus[c] 'uicia' premisimus 'animi'. Haec autem uicia scilicet animi contraria sunt uirtutibus, ut iniusticia iusticiae, ignavia constantiae, intemperantia temperantiae.[1]

## De uicio animi quod ad mores pertinet[d]

10 Sunt autem[e] animi quoque nonnulla uicia seu bona quae a moribus seiuncta[f] sunt, nec uitam humanam uituperio[g] uel laude dignam efficiunt, ut hebitudo animi uel uelocitas ingenii, obliuiosum uel memorem esse, ignorantia uel scientia. Quae quidem omnia cum eque reprobis ut bonis eueniant,[h] nichil ad morum 15 compositionem pertinent nec turpem uel honestam efficiunt uitam. Vnde bene cum superius[i] premisissemus 'animi uicia', ad exclusionem talium subiunximus, 'que ad mala opera pronos efficiunt', id[j] est, uoluntatem inclinant ad aliquid quod minime conuenit fieri uel dimitti.[2]

## 20 Quid distet inter peccatum et uicium inclinans ad malum[k]

Non est autem huiusmodi animi uicium idem quod peccatum, nec peccatum idem quod actio mala. Verbi gratia, iracundum esse, hoc est, pronum uel facilem ad irae perturbationem, uicium est et mentem inclinat ad aliquid impetuose et irracionabiliter gerendum, 25 quod minime conuenit. Hoc autem uicium in anima est, ut uide-

 [a] Liber petri Abaelardi qui intitulatur. Scito teipsum C; Incipit. Scito te teipsum (!) D; Incipit liber magistri petri Abelardi uel baiolardi, qui dicitur. Scito te ipsum E; *om.* B    [b] bona uel mala BC    [c] dicimus AE [d] *This title is missing in* BC    [e] autem *om.* BCD    [f] disiuncta BC [g] uituperacione B    [h] conueniant BCD    [i] superius cum BCD    [j] hoc BCD    [k] *This heading appears in* AE. *In* D *it reads* Quid distet uicium inclinans a malo a peccato

# THE BEGINNING OF THE BOOK OF MASTER PETER ABELARD WHICH IS CALLED *KNOW THYSELF*

WE consider morals to be the vices or virtues of the mind which make us prone to bad or good works. However, there are vices or goods not only of the mind but also of the body, such as bodily weakness or the fortitude which we call strength, sluggishness or swiftness, limpness or being upright, blindness or vision. Hence to distinguish these, when we said 'vices' we added 'of the mind'. Now these vices, that is of the mind, are contrary to the virtues, as injustice is to justice, sloth to constancy, intemperance to temperance.[1]

## Of vice of the mind which concerns morals

There are also, however, some vices or good things of the mind which are separate from morals and do not make human life worthy of blame or praise, such as dullness of mind or quickness of thinking, forgetfulness or a good memory, ignorance or learning. Since all these befall the wicked and the good alike, they do not in fact belong to the composition of morality nor do they make life base or honourable. Hence rightly when above we presented 'vices of the mind' we added, in order to exclude such things, 'which make us prone to bad works', that is, incline the will to something which is not at all fitting to be done or to be forsaken.[2]

## The difference between sin and vice inclining to evil

Mental vice of this kind is not, however, the same as sin nor is sin the same as a bad action. For example, to be irascible, that is, prone or ready for the emotion of anger, is a vice and inclines the mind impetuously or unreasonably to do something which is not at all suitable. However, this vice is in the soul, so that in fact it is

---

[1] Cf. Abelard, *Dialogus* (PL 178. 1642A, 1643D). Also Boethius, *In Categorias Aristotilis*, iv, *De oppositis* (PL 64. 264-83).
[2] Rom. 1: 28.

licet facilis[a] sit ad irascendum, etiam cum non mouetur[b] ad iram, sicut claudicatio, unde claudus dicitur homo, in ipso est quando etiam[c] non ambulat claudicando, quia uicium adest etiam cum actio deest.

Sic et multos ad luxuriam sicut ad iram natura ipsa 5 uel complexio corporis pronos efficit,[1] nec tamen in ipso hoc[d] peccant quia tales sunt, sed pugnae materiam ex hoc habent ut per temperantiae uirtutem de se ipsis triumphantes coronam percipiant, iuxta illud Salomonis,[2] 'Melior est patiens uiro forti et qui dominatur animo suo expugnatore urbium.' Non enim religio ab 10 homine uinci, sed a uicio turpe existimat. Illud quippe bonorum quoque hominum est, in hoc a bonis[e] declinamus. Hanc nobis uictoriam commendans Apostolus ait,[3] 'Non[f] coronabitur quis, nisi legitime certauerit.' Certauerit, inquam, non tam hominibus quam uiciis resistendo, ne nos uidelicet in consensum pertrahant 15 prauam. Quae, et si homines cessent, inpugnare nos non cessant, ut tanto periculosior eorum[g] pugna sit quanto frequentior, et tanto uictoria clarior quanto[h] difficilior. Homines uero[i] quantumcumque preualeant, nichil uitae nostrae turpitudinis ingerunt, nisi[j] cum more uiciorum et quasi nobis in uicia conuersis,[k] turpi 20 nos consensui subiciunt. Illis[l] corpori dominantibus, dum liber animus fuerit nichil de uera libertate periclitatur, nichil obscenae seruitutis incurrimus. Non enim homini seruire sed uicio turpe est, nec corporalis seruitus sed uiciorum subiectio animam deturpat. Quicquid enim bonis pariter et malis commune est, nichil ad 25 uirtutem uel uicium refert.

## Quid sit animi uicium et quid proprie dicatur peccatum[m]

Vitium itaque est quo ad peccandum proni efficimur, hoc est, inclinamur ad consentiendum ei quod non conuenit, ut illud scilicet faciamus aut dimittamus. Hunc uero consensum proprie 30 peccatum nominamus, hoc est, culpam animae qua dampnationem meretur, uel apud deum rea statuitur. Quid est enim iste[n] consensus nisi Dei contemptus[o] et offensa ipsius? Non enim Deus ex dampno sed ex contemptu offendi potest. Ipse quippe est

---

    [a] facilis *om.* AE        [b] commouetur BCD            [c] etiam quando BCD
[d] hoc ipso CD; hoc *om.* B      [e] nobis ADE      [f] Nec BC        [g] eius BC
[h] quanto: uero *add.* BC        [i] uero *om.* BC      [j] non AE        [k] conuersi
ABCDE      [l] Illud AE; et illis C      [m] *This heading appears in A (where the word*
uicium *is omitted) and* E; *in* D *it runs*: Quid animi preditum uicium et quid
proprye dicatur peccatum et quid sit peccatum      [n] hic BC      [o] dei contemptus ADE; *in* C dei *has been added*; *in* B dei *has been added after* contemptus

---

[1] Abelard here thinks of vice as a natural predisposition or innate human characteristic. In his *Dialogus* Abelard considers vice both in this way (*PL* 178. 1659BC)

ready to be angry even when it is not moved to anger, just as the limpness for which a man is said to be lame is in him even when he is not walking limply, because the vice is present even though the action is not. So too nature itself or the constitution of the body makes many prone to luxury just as it does to anger,[1] yet they do not sin in this because that is how they are, but through this they have the material for a struggle so that triumphing over themselves through the virtue of temperance they may obtain a crown. As Solomon said:[2] 'The patient man is better than the valiant: and he that ruleth his spirit than he that taketh cities.' For religion does not consider it base to be beaten by man but by vice. The former happens in fact to good men too; in the latter we turn away from good things. The Apostle commends this victory to us, saying:[3] 'He will not be crowned except he strive lawfully.' Strive, I say, in resisting vices rather than men, lest they entice us into wrongful consent; even if men cease, vices do not cease to assault us, and their attack is so much more dangerous for being more constant and victory is so much more brilliant for being more difficult. But however much men prevail over us, they bring no turpitude into our lives unless after the manner of the vices and having, as it were, converted us to vices they submit us to a shameful consent. When they command our bodies, so long as the mind remains free, true freedom is not in peril and we do not fall into an indecent subjection. For it is shameful to serve vice, not man; subjection to vices soils the soul, bodily servitude does not. For whatever is common to good and bad men alike is of no importance to virtue or vice.

## What is mental vice and what is properly said to be sin

And so vice is that by which we are made prone to sin, that is, are inclined to consent to what is not fitting so that we either do it or forsake it. Now this consent we properly call sin, that is, the fault of the soul by which it earns damnation or is made guilty before God. For what is that consent unless it is contempt of God and an offence against him? For God cannot be offended against through harm but through contempt. He indeed is that supreme

and as a disposition which is deliberately acquired (1651CD); at the beginning of the second book of the *Ethica* (below, p. 128) virtue is considered to be acquired through application and not to be innate.

[2] Prov. 16: 32.                                           [3] 2 Tim. 2: 5.

summa illa potestas quae dampno aliquo non minuitur, sed contemptum sui ulciscitur. Peccatum itaque nostrum contemptus
creatoris est,[a] et peccare est creatorem contempnere, hoc est, id
nequaquam facere propter ipsum quod credimus propter ipsum
5 a nobis esse faciendum, vel non dimittere propter ipsum quod
credimus esse dimittendum.[1] Cum itaque peccatum diffinimus
abnegatiue, dicentes scilicet non facere uel non dimittere quod
conuenit, patenter ostendimus nullam esse substantiam peccati
quod in non esse potius quam esse subsistat,[b] ueluti si tenebras
10 diffinientes dicamus absentiam lucis ubi lux habuit[c] esse.[2]

   Sed fortassis inquies, quia et uoluntas mali operis peccatum est,
quae nos apud Deum reos constituit, sicut uoluntas boni operis
iustos facit, ut quemadmodum uirtus in bona uoluntate,[d] ita
peccatum in mala uoluntate[e] consistat, nec in non esse tantum,
15 uerum etiam in esse sicut et[f] illa. Quemadmodum[g] enim uolendo
facere quod Deo credimus placere ipsi placemus, ita uolendo
facere quod Deo credimus displicere ipsi displicemus, et ipsum
offendere siue contempnere uidemur. Sed dico quia[h] si diligentius
adtendamus, longe aliter de hoc sentiendum est quam uideatur.
20 Cum enim nonnunquam peccemus absque omni mala uoluntate,
et cum ipsa mala uoluntas refrenata, non extincta, palmam resi-
stentibus pariat, et materiam pugnae et gloriae coronam[i] conferat,[3]
non tam ipsa peccatum quam infirmitas quaedam iam necessaria
dici debet. Ecce enim aliquis est innocens in quem crudelis domi-
25 nus suus per furorem adeo commotus est, ut eum euaginato ense
ad interimendum persequatur,[j] quem ille diu fugiens et quan-
tumcunque potest sui occisionem[k] deuitans, coactus tandem et
nolens occidit eum[l] ne occidatur ab eo. Dicito mihi quicumque es,
quam malam uoluntatem habuerit in hoc facto. Volens siquidem
30 mortem effugere uolebat propriam uitam conseruare. Sed numquid
haec uoluntas mala erat? Non, inquies, haec[m] arbitror, sed illa quam
habuerit[n] de occisione domini persequentis. Respondeo, Bene[o] et
argute dicis, si uoluntatem possis[p] assignare in eo quod asseris.[q]
Sed, iam ut dictum est, nolens et coactus hoc[r] fecit, quod quantum

---

        a creatoris est contemptus BCD          b subsistit BD          c ? habet BC
d uoluntate bona BC          e uoluntate *om.* BCD          f in CD          g Sicut
BC          h quod BC          i gloriam corone BCD          j prosequitur B; pro-
sequatur D          k ocissionem sui B; occasionem sui C; occisionem sui D; sui
occisione E          l cum occidit BCD          m hoc BC          n habebat BCD          o Bene
respondeo B; Bene responde(s: *added by corrector*) C          p posses ADE
q dicis BC          r nolens hoc et coactus BD; nolens hoc coactus fecit C

---

   [1] Blomme (*La doctrine du péché*, pp. 154–8) considers that sin, as described
by Abelard, need not be a formal or express contempt of God, but a recognition
that what is done is opposed to the divine will. Anselm of Laon (*Sententia*,

power who is not impaired by any harm but who avenges contempt of himself. And so our sin is contempt of the Creator and to sin is to hold the Creator in contempt, that is, to do by no means on his account what we believe we ought to do for him, or not to forsake on his account what we believe we ought to forsake.[1] So, by defining sin negatively, that is to say, as not doing or not forsaking what is fitting, we plainly show there is no substance of sin; it subsists as not being rather than being, just as if in defining darkness we say it is the absence of light where light used to be.[2]

But perhaps you will say that the will to do a bad deed is also sin and makes us guilty before God, even as the will to do a good deed makes us just, so that just as virtue consists in a good will, so sin consists in a bad will and not only in not being but also, and like virtue, in being. For just as we please God by willing to do what we believe to please him, so we displease him by willing to do what we believe to displease him and we seem to offend him or hold him in contempt. But I say that if we consider this more carefully, our conclusion should be very different from what it seems. For since we sometimes sin without any bad will and since that bad will when restrained but not extinguished procures a prize for those who resist it and brings the material for a struggle and a crown of glory,[3] it ought not to be called sin so much as a weakness which is now necessary. For consider: there is an innocent man whose cruel lord is so burning with rage against him that with a naked sword he chases him for his life. For long that man flees and as far as he can he avoids his own murder; in the end and unwillingly he is forced to kill him lest he be killed by him. Tell me, whoever you are, what bad will he had in doing this. If he wanted to escape death, he wanted to save his own life. But surely this was not a bad will? You say: not this, I think, but the will he had to kill the lord who was chasing him. I reply: that is well and cleverly said if you can show a will in what you claim. But, as has already been said, he did this unwillingly and under

no. 87, ed. Lottin, *Psychologie et morale*, v. 76) had attempted to distinguish various senses in which contempt of God could occur.

[2] In the *Ethica* Abelard has little to say of sin as not-being because he is seeking a 'moral' definition of sin (as Blomme, *La doctrine du péché*, puts it) and a psychological understanding of moral imputability. By contrast the school of Anselm of Laon had been preoccupied with the ontological nature of sin and evil; see Blomme, *La doctrine du péché*, pp. 9–14. But see also Abelard, *Sic et non, cap.* 143: 'Quod peccatum actus sit, non res, et contra' (*PL* 178. 1588–90).

[3] Cf. 1 Peter 5: 4.

potuit uitam incolomen<sup>a</sup> distulit, sciens quoque ex hac inter-
fectione uitae sibi periculum imminere. Quomodo ergo illud
uoluntarie fecit, quod cum ipso etiam uitae suae periculo commisit?

5   Quod si respondeas ex uoluntate id quoque esse factum, cum
ex uoluntate scilicet mortem euadendi, non dominum suum occi-
dendi, constet in hoc eum esse inductum, nequaquam id refelli-
mus, sed, ut iam dictum est, nequaquam uoluntas ista tamquam
mala est improbanda, per quam ille, ut dicis, mortem euadere,
10  non dominum uoluit occidere,<sup>b</sup> et tamen deliquit consentiendo,
quamuis coactus timore mortis, iniustae interfectioni quam eum
potius ferre quam inferre oportuit. Gladium quippe accepit<sup>c</sup> per
se, non traditum sibi habuit a potestate. Vnde<sup>d</sup> Veritas,[1] 'Omnis',
inquit, 'qui acceperit gladium gladio peribit.' 'Qui<sup>e</sup> acceperit',
15  inquit, 'gladium' per presumptionem, non cui traditus est ad
exercendam ulcionem. 'Gladio peribit', hoc est, dampnationem
atque animae suae occisionem ex hac temeritate incurrit. Voluit
itaque, ut dictum est, ille mortem euadere, non dominum occidere. Sed quia in occisione consensit in qua non debuit, hic eius
20  iniustus consensus qui occisionem precessit, peccatum fuit.[2]

Quod siquis forte dicat, quia uoluit interficere dominum suum
propter hoc ut mortem euaderet, non ideo simpliciter inferre
potest quia uoluit eum occidere. Veluti si dicam alicui quia uolo
ut habeas cappam meam propter hoc ut des mihi quinque solidos,
25  uel libenter eam pro precio isto fieri tuam uolo, non ideo concedo
quod eam tuam esse uelim.<sup>f</sup> Sed et<sup>g</sup> siquis in carcere constrictus
uelit filium suum ibi pro se ponere ut redemptionem suam per-
quirat, numquid ideo simpliciter concedimus<sup>h</sup> quod filium suum

---

<sup>a</sup> uitam incollumen B; uita incolumi C; uita incolomi D      <sup>b</sup> interficere
BCD        <sup>c</sup> accipit A        <sup>d</sup> unde *om.* B; *add.* C *above the line*        <sup>e</sup> Qui
. . . peribit *om.* ADE        <sup>f</sup> eam uelim tuam esse BD; uelim eam suam esse
C        <sup>g</sup> et *om.* BC        <sup>h</sup> concedemus BC

---

[1] Matt. 26: 52. Cf. Abelard, *Sic et non, cap.* 156: 'Quod nulla de causa liceat
Christianis quemquam interficere, et contra' and *cap.* 157: 'Quod liceat homines
interficere et non' (*PL* 178. 1606–9).

[2] The school of Anselm of Laon thought that sin, since it was not a substance,
was 'an evil will' or 'a will which diverged from the Creator'; for references see
Blomme, *La doctrine du péché*, pp. 10–12. Against such a view Abelard here
argues, but in other writings he too was ready to speak of sin in this way, e.g.
in his *Expositio* of Romans, ii (*animae culpa et contemptus Dei, id est praua
uoluntas nostra*; *PL* 178. 866B), and iv (942B); also in the *Dialogus* (1634B). The
example of the servant who kills unwillingly is also given in the *Expositio* of
Romans, iii (894C–895A). In the *Ethica* the term 'will' generally denotes desire
or concupiscence, not the act of decision, consent, disposition, or of endurance in
respect of the undesirable. On this see Blomme, *La doctrine du péché*, pp. 167

compulsion; as far as he could he deferred injury to life; he was also aware that by this killing he would put his own life in danger. So how did he do willingly what he committed with danger to his own life as well?

If you reply that that too was done out of will, since it is agreed that he was led to this out of a will to avoid death, not to kill his lord, we do not confute that at all but, as has already been said, that will is in no way to be derided as bad through which he, as you say, wanted to evade death, not to kill the lord. And yet although he was constrained by fear of death, he did do wrong in consenting to an unjust killing which he should have undergone rather than have inflicted. In fact he took the sword himself; no power had handed it to him. Whence Truth says:[1] 'All that take the sword shall perish by the sword.' 'He who takes the sword', he says, by presumption, not he to whom it has been granted for the purpose of administering vengeance, 'shall perish by the sword', that is, he incurs by this rashness damnation and the killing of his own soul. And so he wanted, as has been said, to avoid death, not to kill the lord. But because he consented to a killing to which he ought not to have consented, this unjust consent of his which preceded the killing was a sin.[2]

If perhaps someone says that he wanted to kill his lord for the sake of avoiding death, he cannot therefore simply infer that he wanted to kill him. For example, if I were to say to someone: 'I want you to have my cap for this reason, that you give me five *solidi*' or 'I gladly want it to become yours at that price', I do not therefore concede that I want it to be yours. Moreover if anyone held in prison wants to put his son there in his place so that he may seek his own ransom, surely we do not therefore simply concede that he wants to put his own son in prison—something which he is

---

et seq. In his *Expositio* of Romans, iii (893D–895C) Abelard distinguished between *uelle* as *uoluptas | desiderium | delectatio* and as *approbare*. Earlier Anselm of Canterbury had distinguished the power of the soul to will, the affection of the will, and the use of the will in his *De concordia*, q. iii, c. 11 (ed. Schmitt, *Anselmi opera*, ii. 279–84).

William of Saint-Thierry in his *Disputatio*, cap. 12 (*PL* 180. 282A) criticized Abelard's thesis concerning sin and will. See also the anonymous *Capitula Haeresum*, cap. 13 (*PL* 182. 1054AB). At the council of Sens Abelard was condemned for teaching *Quod neque opus neque uoluntas . . . peccatum sit, Capitulum* 19, ed. J. Leclercq in *Revue bénédictine*, lxxviii (1968), 104. See also Blomme, *La doctrine du péché*, pp. 262–74. In his *Confessio fidei* Abelard claimed that this teaching was alien to him (*PL* 178. 107–8).

in carcere[a] mittere uelit, quod cum magnis lacrimis et cum[b]
multis gemitibus sustinere cogitur? Non utique talis ut ita dicam
uoluntas, quae in magno dolore animi[c] consistit, dicenda est
uoluntas, sed potius passio. Et tale est quia hoc uult propter illud,
5 tamquam si diceretur, quia[d] quod non uult tolerat propter aliud[e]
quod desiderat. Sic et infirmus uri uel secari uelle dicitur ut sanetur
et martires pati ut ad Christum perueniant,[f] uel Christus ipse ut
nos eius saluemur passione, non tamen ideo simpliciter concedere
cogimur ut hoc[g] uelint. Nusquam enim passio esse potest nisi ubi
10 contra uoluntatem aliquid fit, nec quisquam in eo patitur ubi
suam implet uoluntatem et quod fieri eum oblectat. Et certe
Apostolus qui ait,[1] 'Cupio dissolui et esse cum Christo', id[h] est,
ad hoc mori ut ad eum perueniam,[i] ipse alibi commemorat,[j][2]
'Nolumus exspoliari sed superuestiri, ut absorbeatur mortale a
15 uita.' Quam etiam sententiam a Domino dictam beatus Augustinus
meminit ubi Petro dixit,[3] 'Extendes manus tuas et alius te cinget
et ducet quo tu non uis.' Qui etiam iuxta infirmitatem humanae
naturae assumptam Patri ait,[4] 'Si possibile est transeat a me calix
iste, uerumtamen non sicut ego uolo sed sicut tu.' Magnam quippe
20 mortis passionem anima eius naturaliter formidabat, nec uoluntarium ei esse poterat quod penale sciebat. De quo cum alibi
scriptum sit,[5] 'Oblatus est quia ipse uoluit', aut secundum diui-
nitatis naturam accipiendum est in cuius uoluntate fuit illum
assumptum hominem pati, aut 'uoluit' dictum est pro 'disposuit'
25 iuxta illud Psalmistae,[6] 'Quaecumque uoluit fecit.' Constat itaque
peccatum non numquam committi sine mala penitus uoluntate,
ut ex hoc liquidum sit quod peccatum est uoluntatem non dici.

Equidem,[k] inquies, ita est ubi coacti peccamus, sed non ita ubi
uolentes, ueluti si tale quid committere uelimus, quod nequaquam
30 debere a nobis committi[l] scimus. Ibi quippe mala illa uoluntas et
peccatum idem esse uidetur. Verbi gratia,[m] uidet aliquis mulierem,
et in concupiscentiam incidit, et delectatione carnis mens eius[n]

---

[a] carcere BC      [b] cum *om.* BCD      [c] animi dolore BCD      [d] quia:
hoc *add.* BCD      [e] illud BC      [f] ueniant BC      [g] hec BD      [h] hoc
BC      [i] transeam BCD      [j] ait BC      [k] Et quidem BCD      [l] a
nobis debere committi BD; a nobis committi debere C      [m] causa BCD
[n] tocius C; cicius B

---

[1] Phil. 1: 23.
[2] 2 Cor. 5: 4.
[3] John 21: 18. Cf. Augustine, *In Iohannis Euangelium Tractatus CXXIII*. 5

driven to endure with floods of tears and with many sighs? At any
rate such a will which consists in great grief of mind is not, I would
say, to be called will but rather suffering. That he wills this on
account of that is the equivalent of saying that he endures what he
does not will on account of the other things which he desires. Thus
the sick man is said to want a cauterization or an operation in order
to be healed and martyrs to suffer in order to come to Christ or
Christ himself in order that we may be saved by his suffering. Yet
we are not therefore compelled to concede simply that they want
this. On no occasion can there be suffering except where something
is done against will nor does anyone suffer where he fulfils his
will and gains delight in doing so. Certainly the Apostle who says:[1]
'I desire to be dissolved and to be with Christ', that is, to die for the
purpose of coming to him, himself observes elsewhere:[2] 'We would
not be unclothed but clothed upon, that that which is mortal may
be swallowed up by life.' The blessed Augustine also remembers
this thought which the Lord expressed when he said to Peter:[3]
'Thou shalt stretch forth thy hands, and another shall gird thee
and lead thee whither thou wouldest not.' In the weakness which he
had assumed of human nature the Lord also said to the Father:[4]
'If it be possible, let this chalice pass from me. Nevertheless, not
as I will but as thou wilt.' His soul naturally dreaded the great
suffering of death and what he knew to be painful could not be
voluntary for him. Although it is written of him elsewhere:[5] 'He
was offered because it was his own will', this is either to be understood according to the nature of the divinity in whose will it was
that the assumed man should suffer, or 'it was his will' means 'it
was his plan' as it does when the Psalmist says:[6] 'He hath done all
things whatsoever he would.' So it is evident that sometimes sin
is committed entirely without bad will; it is therefore clear from
this that what is sin is not to be called will.

Certainly, you will say, that is so where we sin under constraint,
but not where we do so willingly, as for instance if we want to
commit something which we know should not be done by us at all.
There indeed that bad will and the sin seem to be the same. For
example, someone sees a woman and falls into concupiscence and
his mind is affected by the pleasure of the flesh, so that he is

(*CCL* 36, p. 679, or *PL* 35. 1968–9). This passage is cited by Abelard in *Sic et
non, cap.* 83 (*PL* 178. 1468AB).
⁴ Matt. 26: 39.         ⁵ Isa. 53: 7.              ⁶ Ps. 113B: 3.

tangitur, ut ad turpitudinem coitus accendatur. Haec ergo uoluntas
et turpe desiderium quid aliud, inquis,[a] est quam peccatum?
Respondeo, Quid si ista uoluntas temperantiae uirtute[b] refrenetur
nec tamen extinguatur,[c] ad pugnam permaneat et ad certamen
5 persistat nec deficiat uicta.[d] Vbi enim pugna si pugnandi desit
materia aut unde premium grande si non sit quod toleremus graue?
Cum certamen defuerit, non iam superest pugnare sed premium
percipere. Hic autem pugnando certamus ut alibi certaminis
triumphatores coronam percipiamus.[e] Vt uero[f] pugna sit, hostem
10 esse conuenit qui resistat, non qui prorsus deficiat. Haec[g] uero
est nostra uoluntas mala[h] de qua triumphamus cum eam diuinae
subiugamus, nec eam prorsus extinguimus, ut semper habeamus
contra quam dimicemus.
Quid enim magnum pro Deo facimus si nichil nostrae uolun-
15 tati aduersum toleramus, sed magis quod uolumus implemus?
Quis etenim nobis grates habeat si in eo quod pro ipso nos facere
dicimus, uoluntatem nostram inpleamus? Aut quid,[i] inquies,
apud Deum meremur ex eo quod uolentes[j] aut inuiti agimus?
Nichil[k] certe, respondeo, cum ipse animum potius quam actionem
20 in remuneratione penset, nec quicquam ad meritum actio addat,
siue de bona siue de mala uoluntate prodeat,[l] sicut postmodum
ostendemus. Cum uero uoluntatem eius nostrae preponimus, ut
illius potius quam nostram sequamur, magnum apud eum meritum obtinemus, iuxta illam Veritatis perfectionem,[1] 'Non ueni
25 facere uoluntatem meam sed[m] eius qui misit me.' Ad quod et nos[n]
exhortans ait,[2] 'Siquis uenit ad me et non odit patrem et matrem
adhuc autem et animam suam, non est me dignus', hoc est, nisi
suggestionibus eorum uel propriae renunciet uoluntati et pre-
ceptionibus[o] meis se omnino subiciat. Si[p] ergo patrem odire non
30 perimere iubemur, ita et uoluntatem nostram ut non eam sequamur, non ut funditus eam destruamus. Qui enim ait,[3] 'Post concupiscentias tuas non eas et a uoluntate tua auertere', precepit nos[q]
concupiscentias nostras non inplere, non penitus eis carere. Illud
quippe uiciosum est, hoc autem[r] infirmitati nostre impossibile. Non

---

[a] inquies BD      [b] per temperancie uirtutem BCD      [c] extinguatur: ut
*add.* BCD      [d] nec deficiat uicta AE: nec deficiat sed uicta succumbat BCD
[e] certaminis triumphatores coronam percipiamus: coronemur BC      [f] ubi
CD      [g] Hic BCD      [h] mala uoluntas BCD      [i] At quid B; at quit
D; Ad quod C      [j] nolentes BD      [k] Nichil: est *add. in marg.* BC
[l] procedat BCD      [m] sed: uoluntatem *add.* BCD      [n] etiam exortans nos

incited to the baseness of sexual intercourse. Therefore, you say, what else is this will and base desire than sin?

I answer that if that will is restrained by the virtue of temperance but is not extinguished, it remains for a fight and persists in struggling and does not give up even when overcome. For where is the fight if the material for fighting is lacking? Or whence comes the great reward if what we endure is not hard? When the struggle is over, it no longer remains to fight but to receive the reward. Here, however, we strive by fighting, so that elsewhere as winners of the struggle we may receive a crown. But in order that there be a fight, it is evident that there must be an enemy who resists, not one who actually gives up. This surely is our bad will, over which we triumph when we subdue it to the divine will, but we do not really extinguish it, so that we always have it to fight against.

Indeed, what great thing do we for God if we support nothing against our will but rather discharge what we will? And who has thanks for us if in what we say we are doing for him we fulfil our own will? But what, you will say, do we gain before God out of what we do whether willingly or unwillingly? I reply: nothing, certainly, since he considers the mind rather than the action when it comes to a reward, and an action adds nothing to merit whether it proceeds from a good or a bad will, as we shall later show. But when we put his will before our own so as to follow his rather than ours, we obtain great merit with him according to that perfectness of Truth:[1] 'I came not to do my own will but the will of him that sent me.' Exhorting us to this he says:[2] 'If any man come to me and hate not his father and mother, yea and his own life also, he is not worthy of me', that is, if he does not renounce their suggestions or his own will and subject himself completely to my precepts. If therefore we are ordered to hate but not to destroy a father, so too our will; we are not to follow it but neither are we to destroy it completely. For he who said:[3] 'Go not after thy lusts: but turn away from thy own will', taught us not to fulfil our lusts, but not to be entirely without them. The former is vicious, but the latter is not

BC; eciam nos exortans D [o] precibus B; preceptis E [p] Sicut BD; Dicit C [q] nos concupiscentias nostras AE; nos concupiscentias quidem nostras BC; nos quidem concupiscencias nostras D [r] iam BCD

[1] John 6: 38. [2] Luke 14: 26. Cf. Matt. 10: 37.
[3] Ecclus. 18: 30.

itaque concupiscere mulierem sed concupiscentiae consentire peccatum est, nec uoluntas concubitus sed uoluntatis consensus[a] dampnabilis est.[1]

Quod de luxuria diximus, hoc et de gula uideamus. Transit
5 aliquis iuxta ortum alterius, et conspectis delectabilibus fructibus in concupiscentiam eorum incidit, nec tamen concupiscentiae suae consentit, ut inde aliquid furto uel rapina auferat,[b] quamquam delectacione cibi in magnum desiderium mens eius sit accensa. Vbi autem desiderium ibi procul dubio uoluntas consistit. Desi-
10 derat itaque fructus illius esum in quo delectationem esse non dubitat. Ipsa quippe[c] suae infirmitatis natura compellitur id desiderare quod inscio domino uel non permittente non licet accipere. Desiderium ille reprimit, non extinguit, sed[d] quia non trahitur ad consensum, non incurrit peccatum.[2]

Quorsum autem ista? Vt denique pateat in talibus ipsam quo-
15 que uoluntatem uel desiderium faciendi quod non licet nequa-quam dici peccatum, sed ipsum potius, ut diximus, consensum. Tunc uero consentimus ei quod non licet, cum nos ab eius per-petratione nequaquam retrahimus parati penitus, si daretur facultas,[e] illud perficere.[3] In hoc itaque proposito quisquis reperi-
20 tur reatus perfectionem incurrit nec operis effectus super additus ad peccati augmentum[f] quicquam addit, sed iam apud Deum eque reus est qui ad hoc peragendum quantum ualet nititur, et quantum in se est illud peragit, ac si, ut beatus Augustinus meminit,[4] in opere quoque ipso esset deprehensus.

---

    [a] uoluntas consensus BC    [b] tollat BCD    [c] quippe *om.* BC    [d] et BC; sed . . . peccatum *om.* D    [e] facultas daretur BCD    [f] augmen-tum peccati BCD

---

    [1] Earlier in his *Expositio* of Romans, iii (*PL* 178. 888AB) Abelard had written that the introduction of the Law had revealed that concupiscence and not one's deeds is sin. In the *Ethica* Abelard refines his thought; see Blomme, *La doc-trine du péché*, pp. 188–90. For the same doctrine see Augustine, *Expositio quarumdam propositionum ex Epistola ad Romanos*: 'Non enim in ipso desiderio prauo, sed in nostra consensione peccamus' (*PL* 35. 2066), but see also Augustine, *Enarratio in Psalmum L*, n. 3: 'Inest peccatum, cum delectaris; regnat, si con-senseris' (*CCL* 38, p. 601, or *PL* 36. 587). Anselm of Canterbury had written of the appetites of the flesh: 'non eos sentire, sed eis consentire peccatum est', *De conceptu uirginali et de originali peccato, cap.* 4 (ed. Schmitt, *Anselmi opera*, ii. 144); see too Anselm's *De moribus* and the *Dicta Anselmi*, c. 17 (ed. F. Schmitt and R. Southern, *Memorials of Saint Anselm* (Oxford, 1969), pp. 85 and 175). In the school of Anselm of Laon the same attitude broadly prevailed; see Anselm of Laon, *Sententia*, no. 85, and *Sententiae*, nos. 218 and 450 from Anselm's school as well as *Sententia*, no. 278 of William of Champeaux (ed. Lottin, *Psychologie et morale*, v. 73–4, 138–9, 303, 222). Like Abelard, the *Enarrationes in Euangelium Matthaei* (of the school of Laon) regard the suggestion of sin as not a sin but as the *materia pugnandi et uictoriae* (*cap.* 5, *PL* 162. 1294). The theme

possible for our weakness. So sin is not lusting for a woman but consenting to lust; the consent of the will is damnable, but not the will for intercourse.[1]

What we have said with respect to luxury, let us consider with respect also to gluttony. Someone passes through another man's garden and seeing delightful fruits he falls into longing for them; however, he does not consent to his longing so as to remove something from there by theft or robbery, even though his mind has been incited to great desire by the pleasure of food. But where desire is, there undoubtedly is will. And so he desires to eat of that fruit in which he is certain there is pleasure. In fact by the very nature of his infirmity he is compelled to desire what he is not allowed to take without the knowledge or the permission of the lord. He represses his desire; he does not extinguish it, but because he is not drawn to consent, he does not incur sin.[2]

Now where does this lead us? It shows in short that in such things also the will itself or the desire to do what is unlawful is by no means to be called sin, but rather, as we have stated, the consent itself. The time when we consent to what is unlawful is in fact when we in no way draw back from its accomplishment and are inwardly ready, if given the chance, to do it.[3] Anyone who is found in this disposition incurs the fullness of guilt; the addition of the performance of the deed adds nothing to increase the sin. On the contrary, before God the man who to the extent of his power endeavours to achieve this is as guilty as the man who as far as he is able does achieve it—just as if, so the blessed Augustine reminds us,[4] he too had also been caught in the act.

of consent was, then, familiar to thinkers in the twelfth century and earlier; see Blomme, *La doctrine du péché*, pp. 46 et seq., 117 et seq., 270–1, 306 et seq.

Abelard's thesis on concupiscence was attacked by William of Saint-Thierry, *Disputatio*, *cap.* 13 (*PL* 180. 282BC) and *Epist.* 326 (*PL* 182. 532B). See too the anonymous *Capitula Haeresum*, *cap.* 13 (*PL*. 182. 1054AB). The thesis was condemned at the council of Sens, although Abelard denied the charge in his *Confessio fidei* (*PL* 178. 107–8). See Blomme, *La doctrine du péché*, pp. 262–74.

[2] Abelard's distinction here between desire and the consent to desire is an improvement upon his thought in the *Expositio* of Romans, ii (*PL* 178. 862B), where Eve's original sin is said to have been her concupiscence, and in *Epistola* VIII where the appetite for food is decried (ed. T. P. McLaughlin, 'Abelard's Rule for Religious Women', *Medieval Studies*, xviii (1956), 278; or *PL* 178. 297CD). Cf. Augustine, *De sermone Domini in monte*, i. 12, n. 34 (*CCL* 35, pp. 36–7, or *PL* 34. 1246).

[3] Cf. Augustine, *De sermone Domini in monte*, i. 12, n. 33 (*CCL* 35, p. 36, or *PL* 34. 1246).

[4] Augustine, *De libero arbitrio*, i. 3, n. 8 (*CSEL* lxxiv, p. 8, or *PL* 32. 1225).

Cum autem uoluntas peccatum non sit et non numquam inuiti, ut diximus, peccata committamus, nonnulli tamen omne peccatum uoluntarium esse[a] dicunt, in quo et quandam differentiam peccati a uoluntate inueniunt, cum aliud uoluntas aliud uolun-
5 tarium dicatur, hoc est, aliud uoluntas aliud quod per uoluntatem committitur.[1] At uero si peccatum dicimus quod proprie dici peccatum[b] prefati sumus, hoc est, contemptum Dei siue consensum in eo quod credimus propter Deum dimittendum, quomodo dicimus[c] peccatum esse uoluntarium, hoc est, nos uelle Deum
10 contempnere, quod est peccare, uel deteriores fieri aut dignos dampnatione effici?[d] Quamuis enim uelimus facere id quod[e] debere puniri scimus uel unde puniri digni simus,[f] non tamen puniri uolumus, in hoc ipso manifeste iniqui[g] quod hoc uolumus facere quod est iniquum, nec tamen penae quae iusta[h] est subire uolumus
15 equitatem. Displicet pena quae iusta est, placet actio quae est iniusta. Sepe etiam contingit ut cum uelimus concumbere cum ea quam scimus coniugatam, specie illius illecti, nequaquam tamen adulterari cum ea uellemus quam esse coniugatam nollemus.[2] Multi e contrario sunt qui uxores potentum ad gloriam suam eo
20 magis appetunt quia talium uxores sunt quam si essent innuptae, et magis adulterari quam fornicari cupiunt,[i] hoc est, magis quam minus excedere. Sunt quos omnino piget in consensum concupiscentiae vel malam uoluntatem trahi, et hoc ex infirmitate carnis uelle coguntur quod nequaquam uellent uelle. Quomodo ergo
25 hic consensus quem habere non uolumus uoluntarius dicetur, ut secundum quosdam, uelut[j] dictum est, omne peccatum dicamus uoluntarium, profecto non uideo nisi uoluntarium intelligamus[k] ad exclusionem necessarii, cum uidelicet nullum peccatum ineuitabile sit, uel uoluntarium dicamus quod[l] ex aliqua procedat[m]
30 uoluntate. Nam et si[n] ille qui coactus dominum suum occidit, non habuit uoluntatem in occisione, id tamen ex aliqua commisit uoluntate cum uidelicet mortem euadere uel differre uellet.[3]

Sunt[o] qui non mediocriter moueantur cum audiant nos dicere

| | | |
|---|---|---|
| [a] esse uoluntarium BCD | [b] peccatum dici BCD | [c] dicemus BCD |
| [d] effici dampnacione BC | [e] quo A | [f] sumus BE | [g] inquit CD |
| [h] iuxta B *and* ? C | [i] appetunt BC | [j] ut B; sicut C; vel ut D |
| [k] intelligamus: dicamus et intelligamus D | [l] quia BCD | [m] procedit |

BC     [n] et si: et BC     [o] *The scribe of* D *prefaces this section with a heading:* Cur exteriora meritis non addant. *In* B *a space appears to have been provided by the scribe for a heading which was not inserted*

[1] Cf. Augustine, *Retractationes*, i. 13, n. 5 (*PL* 32. 603–4). Both in the earlier *Expositio* of Romans, iii (*PL* 178. 894C–895A) and in the final version of his *Theologia 'Scholarium'*, iii (Cousin, *Opera P. Abaelardi*, ii. 145) Abelard himself wrote that every sin is voluntary, i.e. freely chosen; now in the *Ethica* he

Now, although will is not sin and, as we have said, we sometimes commit sins unwillingly, yet some say that every sin is voluntary, and they find a certain difference between sin and will, since will is said to be one thing and what is voluntary is said to be something different, that is, will is one thing but what is committed through the will is another.[1] But if we call sin what we have previously said is properly called sin, that is, contempt of God or consent to that which we believe should be forsaken on God's account, how do we say that sin is voluntary, that is, our own willing to offer the contempt of God which is sin or to become worse or to be made worthy of damnation? For although we may want to do that which we know ought to be punished or for which we may deserve to be punished, we do not, however, want to be punished. Obviously we are wicked in this, that we want to do what is wicked, yet we do not want to submit to the fairness of a just punishment. The punishment which is just is displeasing; the action which is unjust is pleasing. Moreover, it often happens that when we want to lie with a woman whom we know to be married and whose looks have enticed us, yet we by no means want to be adulterous with her— we would prefer that she was unmarried.[2] There are, on the other hand, many men who for their own renown desire the wives of the mighty more keenly because they are married to such men than they would if they were unmarried; they want to commit adultery rather than fornication, that is, to transgress by more rather than by less. There are people who are wholly ashamed to be drawn into consent to lust or into a bad will and are forced out of the weakness of the flesh to want what they by no means want to want. Therefore I certainly do not see how this consent which we do not want to have may be called voluntary with the result, as has been said, that we should, according to some, call every sin voluntary, unless we understand voluntary to exclude the element of necessity, since clearly no sin is unavoidable, or unless we call voluntary that which proceeds from will. For even if he who killed his lord under constraint did not have the will to kill, yet he did it out of will, since in fact he wanted to avoid or to defer death.[3]

There are people who may be considerably disturbed when they

refines and alters his position. See Blomme, *La doctrine du péché*, pp. 182 et seq. Also Abelard, *Sic et non, cap.* 145: 'Quod aliquando peccamus nolentes et contra' (*PL* 178. 1591D–1594B).

[2] Cf. Abelard, *Expositio* of Romans, iii (*PL* 178. 895AB).

[3] Cf. Abelard, *Expositio* of Romans, iii (*PL* 178. 894C–895A).

operationem peccati nichil addere ad reatum uel ad dampnationem apud deum. Obiciunt quippe quod in actione peccati quaedam delectatio sequatur quae peccatum augeat, ut in coitu uel esu illo quem diximus. Quod quidem non absurde dicerent,[a] si carnalem
5 huiusmodi delectationem peccatum esse conuincerent,[b] nec tale quid committi posse nisi peccando. Quod profecto si recipiant,[c] utique nemini licet hanc carnis delectationem habere. Vnde nec coniuges immunes sunt a peccato cum hac sibi carnali delectatione[d] concessa permiscentur, nec ille quoque qui esu delectabili sui
10 fructus uescetur.[e1] Essent etiam in culpa quilibet infirmi qui ad recreationem[f] ut de infirmitate conualescant suauioribus cibis fouentur, quos nequaquam sine delectatione sumunt, uel si sumerent non prodessent. Denique et Dominus, ciborum quoque creator sicut et corporum, extra culpam non esset, si tales eis[g]
15 sapores immitteret qui necessario ad peccatum sui delectatione uescentes[h] cogerent. Quomodo enim ad esum nostrum talia conderet uel esum eorum concederet, si haec nos edere sine peccato inpossibile esset? Quo modo etiam in eo quod est concessum dici potest committi peccatum? Nam et illa quae quandoque illicita
20 fuerunt atque prohibita, si postmodum concedantur et sic licita fiant, iam omnino absque peccato committuntur, ut[i] esus carnium suillarum,[j2] et pleraque alia Iudeis quondam interdicta, nunc uero nobis concessa. Cum itaque uidemus Iudeos quoque ad Christum conuersos huiusmodi cibis quos[k] lex[l] interdixerat libere uesci,
25 quomodo eos inculpabiles[m] defendimus, nisi quia iam eis hoc a Deo esse concessum asserimus? Si ergo in esu tali olim eis prohibito sed nunc concesso, ipsa concessio peccatum excusat et contemptum Dei remouet, quis quempiam in eo peccare dicat quod ei licitum diuina concessio fecit? Si ergo concubitus cum uxore uel
30 esus etiam delectabilis cibi a primo die nostrae creationis, quo in paradyso sine peccato uiuebatur,[n] nobis concessus[o] est, quis nos in hoc peccati arguat si concessionis metam non excedamus?

---

    [a] diceres BC; dicerent *om.* D          [b] conuinceres C; B *appears here to read* conuinctas *or* coniunctas          [c] recipias C; respicias B; recipiunt E          [d] uoluptate carnis B; carnali uoluptate C; carnali uoluptati D          [e] uesceretur BCD          [f] recreationem: sui *add.* BC          [g] ei CD          [h] nescientes ADE          [i] ut: est *add.* BC          [j] suille carnis BC          [k] que BC          [l] lex: eis *add.* BCD          [m] in hoc a culpa B; a culpa in hoc C          [n] uidebatur AE          [o] concessus nobis BCD

---

    [1] In the *Sic et non, cap.* 130 and in the *Problemata Heloissae,* no. 42 (*PL* 178.

hear us say that the doing of sin adds nothing to guilt or to damnation before God. They object that in the action of sin a certain
pleasure may follow which increases the sin, as in sexual intercourse, or in that eating which we mentioned. They would not in
fact say this absurdly if they were to prove that carnal pleasure of
this sort is sin and that such a thing cannot be committed except
by sinning. If they really admit this, it is definitely not lawful for
anyone to have this fleshly pleasure. Therefore, spouses are not
immune from sin when they unite in this carnal pleasure allowed
to them, nor is he who enjoys the pleasurable consumption of his
own fruit.[1] Also, all invalids would be at fault who relish sweeter
foods to refresh themselves and to recover from illness; they certainly do not take these without pleasure or if they did so, they
would not benefit. And lastly the Lord, the creator of foods as well
as of bodies, would not be beyond fault if he put into them such
flavours as would necessarily compel to sin those who eat them
with pleasure. For how would he produce such things for our
eating or allow their eating if it were impossible for us to eat them
without sin? And how can sin be said to be committed in that which
is allowed? For what were at one time unlawful and prohibited acts,
if they are later allowed and thus become lawful, are now committed wholly without sin, for example the eating of swine's flesh[2]
and many other things formerly forbidden to Jews but now permitted to us. And so when we see Jews converted to Christ also
freely eating foods of this sort which the Law had forbidden, how
do we defend them from blame if not by our claim that this is now
granted to them by God? So if in such eating once forbidden but
now conceded to them the concession itself excuses sin and re-
moves the contempt of God, who will say that anyone sins in that
which a divine concession has made lawful to him? If therefore to
lie with a wife or even to eat delicious food has been allowed to us
since the first day of our creation which was lived in Paradise
without sin, who will accuse us of sin in this if we do not exceed
the limit of the concession?

---

1560–3, 723–30) Abelard presents authorities who discuss the morality of conjugal relations. In *Epistola* VIII Abelard wrote that although marriage (*nuptiae*)
and the use of food and drink are morally indifferent, conjugal relations (*copulae
nuptialis usus*) do not entirely lack sin (ed. T. P. McLaughlin, 'Abelard's
Rule for Religious Women', *Medieval Studies*, xviii (1956), 278; or *PL* 178.
298A).

² Cf. Isa. 65: 4, 66: 17; 1 Macc. 1: 50.

Sed rursum inquiunt[a] quia coniugalis quidem coitus et delectabilis cibi esus ita concessus est ut delectatio ipsa non concedatur,
sed ut ista omnino sine delectatione agantur. Sed profecto si ita
est, sic[b] fieri sunt concessa quomodo ea[c] nullatenus fieri possunt,
5 nec racionabilis fuit permissio quae ita[d] fieri concessit quomodo ea[e]
certum est non posse fieri. Qua insuper ratione lex ad matri-
monium olim cogebat ut unusquisque semen relinqueret in
Israel, uel[f] Apostolus coniuges debitum inuicem[g] soluere com-
pellit,[1] si haec[h] nullatenus absque peccato fieri possunt?[i] Quomodo
10 in hoc debitum dicit ubi iam necessario est peccatum? Aut
quomodo quis ad hoc agendum[j] est cogendus, in quo peccando
Deum sit offensurus? Ex his, ut arbitror, liquidum est nullam
naturalem carnis delectationem peccato asscribendam esse, nec
culpae tribuendum in eo nos delectari, quo cum peruentum sit
15 delectationem necesse est sentiri.[2] Veluti siquis religiosum aliquem
uinculis constrictum inter feminas iacere compellat, et ille molli-
ciae lecti, et circumstantium feminarum contactu in delectationem, non in consensum, trahatur, quis hanc delectacionem quam
natura fecit necessariam[k] culpam appellare presumat?
Quod si obicias, ut quibusdam uidetur, delectationem carnis in
20 concubitu quoque legitimo peccatum[l] imputari, cum David dicat,[3]
'Ecce enim in iniquitatibus conceptus sum',[m] et Apostolus cum
dixisset,[4] 'Iterum reuertimini in id[n] ipsum ne[o] temptet uos Satanas
propter incontinenciam uestram', adiungat,[5] 'Hoc autem secundum indulgentiam dico non secundum inperium', magis nos
25 auctoritate quam ratione uidentur constringere, ut ipsam scilicet
carnis delectationem peccatum fateamur. Non enim in fornicatione sed in matrimonio Dauid conceptum fuisse constat nec
indulgentia, hoc est uenia, ut asserunt, intercedit, ubi culpa penitus absistit. Quantum uero mihi uidetur, quod ait Dauid in ini-
30 quitatibus uel peccatis fuisse se[p] conceptum, nec addidit quorum,
generalem originalis peccati maledictionem induxit qua uidelicet
unusquisque ex culpa propriorum parentum dampnationi subici-
tur, iuxta illud quod alibi scriptum est, 'Nemo mundus a sorde,

---

| | | | |
|---|---|---|---|
| [a] inquies BC | [b] ita BC | [c] ea *om.* BCD | [d] sic ea BC [e] eam |
| AE [f] uelut BC | [g] inuicem debitum BCD | | [h] hoc BCD [i] possit |
| BC; posset D | [j] agendum *om.* BCD | | [k] necessariam facit BC |
| [l] peccato BC | [m] sum: etc. *add.* BCD | | [n] id *om.* BC [o] ne . . . |
| uestram BCD: etc. tandem AE | [p] se fuisse BCD | | |

---

[1] 1 Cor. 7: 3.
[2] Abelard was criticized on this point by William of Saint-Thierry, *Disputatio*, cap. 12 (*PL* 180. 282A–C), and *Epistola* 326̄ (*PL* 182. 532B), and by the
compiler of the *Capitula Haeresum*, cap. 13 (*PL* 182. 1054AB). In his *Confessio
fidei* (*PL* 178. 107–8) he denied that he had advocated the proposition con-

Yet again they say that marital intercourse and the eating of delicious food are in fact conceded in such a way that the pleasure itself is not conceded; they should be performed wholly without pleasure. But assuredly if this is so, they are allowed to be done in a way in which they cannot be done at all and it was an unreasonable permission which allowed them to be done in a way in which it is certain that they cannot be done. Besides, by what reason did the law once prescribe marriage so that everyone should leave his seed in Israel or the Apostle urge spouses to pay their debt to one another,[1] if these cannot be done at all without sin? In what way does he speak here of debt where now necessarily there is sin? Or how is one to be compelled to do what in sinning will offend God? It is clear, I think, from all this that no natural pleasure of the flesh should be imputed to sin nor should it be considered a fault for us to have pleasure in something in which when it has happened the feeling of pleasure is unavoidable.[2] For example, if someone compels a religious who is bound in chains to lie between women and if he is brought to pleasure, not to consent, by the softness of the bed and through the contact of the women beside him, who may presume to call this pleasure, made necessary by nature, a fault?

But if you object that, as it seems to some, carnal pleasure in legitimate intercourse is also to be considered a sin, since David says:[3] 'For, behold, I was conceived in iniquities', and since the Apostle when he said:[4] 'Return together again, lest Satan tempt you for your incontinency' adds:[5] 'But I speak this by indulgence, not by commandment', the pressure upon us to say that this carnal pleasure itself is sin seems to come from authority rather than from reason. For it is known that David had been conceived not in fornication but in matrimony and, as they say, indulgence, that is, pardon, does not occur where fault is wholly absent. In my view, however, David's statement that he had been conceived in iniquities or in sins—he did not add whose they were —represents the general curse of original sin by which everyone is subjected to damnation because of the fault of his parents, in accordance with what is written elsewhere: 'No one is free from

demned at the council of Sens which asserted *Quod neque opus neque uoluntas neque concupiscentia neque delectatio quae mouet eam peccatum sit, nec debemus eam uelle extingui, Capitulum* 19, ed. J. Leclercq, in *Revue bénédictine*, lxxviii (1968), 104.

[3] Ps. 50: 7.          [4] 1 Cor. 7: 5.          [5] 1 Cor. 7: 6.

nec infans unius diei si sit uita eius super terram'.[1] Vt enim
beatus meminit Hieronimus[2] et manifesta ratio habet, quamdiu
anima in infantili aetate constituta est peccato caret. Si ergo a
peccato munda est, quomodo sordibus peccati inmunda est nisi
5 quia hoc de culpa, illud intelligendum est de pena? Culpam quippe
non habet ex contemptu Dei, qui quidem quid[a] agere debeat
nondum racione percipit, a sorde tamen peccati priorum parentum
immunis non est a qua iam penam contrahit, etsi[b] non culpam, et
sustinet in pena quod illi commiserunt in culpa. Sic[c] cum ait
10 Dauid in iniquitatibus uel peccatis se esse conceptum, generali[d]
sententiae dampnationis ex culpa propriorum[e] parentum se con-
spexit esse subiectum, nec tam ad proximos parentes quam ad
priores haec delicta retorsit.

Quod uero Apostolus indulgentiam dixit, non ita, ut uolunt, est
15 accipiendum ut indulgentiam permissionis ueniam dixerit[f] peccati.
Tale quippe est quod ait, 'secundum indulgentiam, non secundum
inperium', ac si diceret, secundum permissionem non secundum
coactionem. Si enim uolunt coniuges et pari consensu decreuerint,
abstinere possunt penitus ab usu carnis, nec per inperium ad eum
20 sunt cogendi. Quod si non decreuerint, indulgentiam habent, hoc
est permissionem, ut a uita perfectiore in usum declinent laxioris
uitae. Non ergo Apostolus hoc loco indulgentiam intellexit[g]
ueniam peccati, sed permissionem laxioris uitae[h] pro euitatione
fornicationis, ut inferior uita peccati magnitudinem preueniret,
25 et minor esset in meritis, ne maior fieret in peccatis.

Haec autem ad hoc[i] induximus, ne quis uolens forte[j] omnem
carnis delectationem esse peccatum, diceret ex actione ipsum
peccatum augeri, cum quis uidelicet consensum ipsum animi in
exercitium duceret operationis, ut non solummodo consensu
30 turpitudinis, uerum etiam maculis contaminaretur actionis, tamquam si animam contaminare[k] posset quod exterius in corpore
fieret.[3] Nichil ergo[l] ad augmentum peccati pertinet qualiscumque operum executio, et nichil animam nisi quod ipsius est
coinquinat,[m] hoc est consensum quem solummodo peccatum esse[n]

---

[a] qui quidem quid AE; quicquid B; quia quid C; quod D?    [b] si B; set
C    [c] Sic: et *add.* BC; eciam *add.* D    [d] generalis BCD    [e] priorum
BC *and* ? D    [f] dicunt BC    [g] indulsit C; indulxit B    [h] uite laxioris
BCD    [i] ad hoc *om.* CE    [j] forte uolens BCD    [k] inquinare BC
[l] igitur BC    [m] inquinat BCD    [n] esse peccatum BCD

---

[1] Job 14: 4–5 (Septuagint version). This quotation appears, with similar
wording, in St. Jerome, *Commentariorum in Jonam liber, cap.* iii (*PL* 25. 1140D),
and *Commentariorum in Hiezechielem lib.* vi, *cap.* xviii (*CCL* 75, p. 228, or *PL*
25. 169A), and also in Origen, *Commentariorum in Epistolam Pauli ad Romanos
lib.* v (*PGL* 14. 1012C). Abelard attributes it to Jerome in his *Sic et non, cap.* 108
(*PL* 178. 1502C), and to Origen in the *Sic et non, cap.* 144 (1591A).

uncleanness nor is the one-day-old child if he is alive upon earth.'[1]
For as the blessed Jerome has mentioned,[2] and as manifest reason
holds, as long as the soul exists in the age of infancy it lacks sin.
If therefore it is clean from sin, how is it soiled with the uncleanness
of sin unless the former is to be understood with respect to fault,
the latter with respect to punishment? One who does not yet see
through reason what he should do has no fault arising from contempt of God, but he is not free of the stain of earlier parents and
thence he already contracts punishment, but not fault, and he
sustains in his punishment what they committed in their fault. So
when David says he was conceived in iniquities or in sins, he saw
that he was subjected to a general sentence of damnation by virtue
of the fault of his own parents and he referred these crimes back
less to his immediate parents than to earlier ones.

However, what the Apostle calls indulgence is not to be interpreted, as they want, as if he had meant this indulgence of
permission to be the pardon of a sin. In fact what he says, 'by
indulgence, not by commandment', means 'by permission, not
by compulsion'. For if spouses want and have decided with equal
consent, they can abstain altogether from carnal relations and
they should not be driven into them by authority. But if they have
not taken this decision, they have the indulgence, that is, the permission to turn aside from the more perfect life into the practice
of a laxer life. In this place, therefore, the Apostle did not mean
by indulgence pardon for sin but permission for a laxer life for the
sake of avoiding fornication, so that a lower life might prevent a
magnitude of sin and one might be smaller in merits lest one become
greater in sins.

Now we have mentioned this lest anyone, wishing perhaps
every carnal pleasure to be sin, should say that sin itself is increased by action when one carries the consent given by the mind
into the commission of an act and is polluted not only by shameful
consent but also by the blemishes of an action—as if an exterior
and corporeal act could contaminate the soul.[3] The doing of deeds
has no bearing upon an increase of sin and nothing pollutes the soul
except what is of the soul, that is, the consent which alone we have

[2] St. Jerome, *Commentariorum in Hiezechielem lib.* iv, cap. xvi (*CCL* 75,
p. 168, or *PL* 25, 130). Also cited by Abelard in his *Expositio* of Romans, ii
(*PL* 178. 868A).
[3] Cf. Abelard, *Epistola* VIII (ed. T. P. McLaughlin, 'Abelard's Rule for
Religious Women,' *Medieval Studies*, xviii (1956), 276; or *PL* 178. 295B–296A).

diximus, non uoluntatem[a] eum precedentem uel actionem operis
subsequentem.[1] Et si enim uelimus uel faciamus quod non conuenit, non ideo tamen peccamus, cum haec frequenter sine peccato contingant, sicut e conuerso consensus sine istis, sicut iam ex
5  parte monstrauimus, de uoluntate quidem sine consensu in eo qui
incidit in concupiscentiam uisae mulieris siue alieni fructus[b] nec
tamen ad[c] consensum pertractus est, de consensu uero malo sine
mala uoluntate[d] in illo qui inuitus dominum suum interfecit.

De his autem quae fieri non debent quam sepe absque peccato
10  fiant, cum per uim scilicet aut ignorantiam committantur,[e] neminem latere arbitror.[2] Veluti si qua uim passa cum uiro alterius
concubuerit, uel aliquis quoquomodo deceptus cum ea dormierit
quam uxorem putauit, uel eum per errorem occiderit quem a se
tamquam a iudice occidendum[f] credidit. Non est itaque peccatum
15  uxorem alterius concupiscere uel cum ea concumbere sed magis
huic concupiscentiae uel actioni consentire. Quem profecto consensum concupiscentiae lex concupiscentiam uocat cum ait,[3] 'Non
concupisces.' Non enim concupiscere[g] quod uitare non possumus
uel in quo, ut dictum est, non peccamus prohiberi debuit, sed
20  assentire illi. Sic et illud intelligendum est quod ait Dominus,[4]
'Qui uiderit mulierem ad concupiscendum eam', hoc est, qui
uiderit sic[h] ut in concupiscentiae consensum incidat, 'iam mechatus
est in corde suo', etsi non mechatus sit[i] in opere, hoc est, iam
peccati reatum habet, etsi adhuc[j] effectu caret.

25  Et si diligenter consideremus ubicumque opera sub precepto
uel prohibitione concludi uidentur, magis haec[k] ad uoluntatem[5]
uel consensum operum quam ad ipsa opera referenda sunt, alioquin nichil quod ad meritum pertineat sub precepto poneretur
et tantominus preceptione sunt digna quantominus in nostra

    [a] in uoluntate AE        [b] uel fructus alieni BC        [c] in BCD        [d] con-
cupiscentia AE        [e] comittatur B; committitur C; committamus E        [f] occidendum: esse *add.* BC        [g] concupisces AE        [h] sic uiderit BCD        [i] sit
mechatus BC        [j] adhuc: peccati *add.* BC        [k] hoc ADE

[1] Abelard's thesis that the execution of sin does not increase the sin committed
in consent was questioned by Walter of Mortagne in his *Epistola ad Abaelardum*
(ed. H. Ostlender in *Florilegium Patristicum*, xix (Bonn, 1929), 40); by William
of Saint-Thierry in the *Disputatio, cap.* 12 (*PL* 180. 282AB) and in *Epistola* 326
(*PL* 182. 532B); and also by the compiler of the *Capitula Haeresum, cap.* 10
(*PL* 182. 1052D–1053A). See too Bernard of Clairvaux, *Epistola* 188 (*PL* 182. 353C).
At the council of Sens Abelard was condemned for teaching *quod propter
opera nec melior nec peior efficiatur homo, Capitulum* 12, ed. J. Leclercq in
*Revue bénédictine*, lxxviii (1968), 104. In his *Confessio fidei* (*PL* 178. 107–8)
Abelard confined himself to stating that a good will does not lose its merit when
one is hindered from proceeding to action. Hugh of Saint-Victor, *De Sacramen-
tis*, ii. 14. 6 (*PL* 176. 560C–564A) maintained that good actions increase the merit

called sin, not the will which precedes it nor the doing of the deed which follows.[1] For even though we will or do what is not fitting, we do not therefore sin, since these things often happen without sin, just as conversely consent occurs without them. This we have already partly shown for the will which lacks consent, in the case of the man who fell into longing for a woman he had seen or for fruit which did not belong to him and yet is not brought to consent, and for evil consent without evil will, in the case of him who killed his lord unwillingly.

Moreover, I think everyone knows how often things that should not be done are done without sin, when, that is, they are committed under coercion or through ignorance,[2] as for example if a woman is force to lie with another woman's husband or if a man who has been tricked in some way or other sleeps with a woman whom he thought to be his wife or kills in error a man whom he believed he, as a judge, should kill. And so it is not a sin to lust after another's wife or to lie with her but rather to consent to this lust or action. This consent to covetousness the Law calls covetousness when it says:[3] 'Thou shall not covet.' In fact, what had to be forbidden was not the coveting of what we cannot avoid or in which, as has been said, we do not sin, but the assenting to that. What the Lord said has similarly to be understood:[4] 'Whosoever shall look on a woman to lust after her', that is, whosoever shall look in such a way as to fall into consent to lust, 'hath already committed adultery in his heart', although he has not committed the deed of adultery, that is, he is already guilty of sin although he is still without its outcome.

If we carefully consider also all the occasions where actions seem to come under a commandment or a prohibition, these must be taken to refer to the will[5] or to consent to actions rather than to the actions themselves, otherwise nothing relating to merit would be put under a commandment and what is less within our power

earned by the will. On evil action in Abelard's thought see Blomme, *La doctrine du péché*, pp. 198–207, 261 n. 1.

[2] Blomme, *La doctrine du péché*, p. 201, observes that as the argument proceeds Abelard moves away from considering illicit acts which can be performed without sin and more clearly poses the indifferent moral character of all acts.

[3] Deut. 5: 21.

[4] Matt. 5: 28. Cf. Augustine, *De sermone Domini in monte*, i. 12, n. 33 (*CCL* 35, p. 36, or *PL* 34. 1246).

[5] Abelard here seems to use the word 'will' in the sense of consent; usually in the *Ethica* 'will' means the natural power of willing and not the will of approval.

potestate sunt constituta. Multa quippe sunt a<sup>a</sup> quibus operari
prohibemur, uoluntatem uero semper et consensum in nostro
habemus arbitrio. Ecce Dominus ait,[1] 'Non occides, Non falsum
testimonium dices.' Quae si de operatione tantum, ut uerba
5 sonant, accipiamus, nequaquam reatus interdicitur nec culpa sic<sup>b</sup>
prohibetur, sed actio culpae. Non enim hominem occidere peccatum est, nec concumbere cum aliena uxore, quae non numquam<sup>c</sup>
absque peccato committi possunt. Neque enim ille qui falsum
testimonium uult dicere uel etiam<sup>d</sup> in dicendo consentit, dum-
10 modo illud<sup>e</sup> non dicat, quacumque de causa reticens, reus legis
efficitur si prohibitio huiusmodi de opere, sicut uerba sonant,
accipiatur. Non enim dictum est ut non uelimus falsum testimonium dicere uel ne in dicendo consentiamus, sed solummodo
ne dicamus. Aut cum lex prohibet ne sorores nostras ducamus
15 uel eis permisceamur,[2] nemo est<sup>f</sup> qui hoc preceptum seruare
possit, cum sepe quis<sup>g</sup> sorores suas recognoscere nequeat,<sup>h</sup> nemo
inquam, si de actu potius quam de consensu prohibitio fiat. Cum
itaque accidit ut quis per ignoranciam ducat sororem suam, numquid transgressor precepti est quia facit quod facere lex<sup>i</sup> pro-
20 hibuit? Non est, inquies, transgressor quiat ransgressioni non
consensit in eo quod<sup>j</sup> ignoranter egit. Sicut ergo transgressor non
est dicendus qui facit quod prohibetur, sed qui consentit in hoc
quod constat esse prohibitum, ita nec prohibitio de opere sed de
consensu est accipienda, ut uidelicet cum dicitur 'ne<sup>k</sup> facias hoc
25 uel illud', tale sit 'ne consentias in hoc uel<sup>l</sup> illo faciendo', ac si
dicatur, 'ne scienter hoc presumas'. Quod et beatus diligenter considerans Augustinus, omne preceptum<sup>m</sup> uel prohibicionem ad karitatem seu<sup>n</sup> cupiditatem potius quam ad opera reducens ait, 'Nichil
precipit lex nisi karitatem et nichil prohibet nisi cupiditatem.'[3]
30 Vnde et Apostolus,[4] 'Omnis lex', inquit, 'in uno sermone comple-
tur, diliges proximum tuum sicut te ipsum.' Et rursum,[5] 'Pleni-
tudo<sup>o</sup> legis est dilectio.' Nichil quippe ad meritum refert utrum
elemosinam indigenti tribuas, et te paratum tribuere karitas
faciat et presto sit uoluntas cum desit facultas, nec in te remaneat
35 facere quod potes quocumque prepediaris casu. Constat quippe

---

<sup>a</sup> a *om.* BC    <sup>b</sup> sic *om.* C; hic BD    <sup>c</sup> non numquam . . . possunt
ADE; nonumquam . . . non possunt *add.* B; nunquam . . . fieri non possunt C
<sup>d</sup> etiam *om.* BC    <sup>e</sup> id BCD    <sup>f</sup> est *om.* ADE    <sup>g</sup> sepe quis B;
nemo ACDE    <sup>h</sup> nequeat B; queat ACD; querat E    <sup>i</sup> lex facere BC
<sup>j</sup> quod: in quo BC    <sup>k</sup> nec BC    <sup>l</sup> uel: in *add.* BCD    <sup>m</sup> peccatum
BC    <sup>n</sup> uel BC    <sup>o</sup> Plenitudo: ergo *add.* BC

---

[1] Deut. 5: 17, 20.
[2] Cf. Deut. 27: 22; Lev. 20: 17.

is less worthy of being commanded. There are in fact many things by which we are restrained from action yet we always have dominion over our will and consent. Behold, the Lord says:[1] 'Thou shalt not kill', 'Thou shall not bear false witness.' If, following the sound of the words, we take these to refer only to the deed, guilt is by no means forbidden nor is fault thereby, but the action of a fault is prohibited. Truly, it is not a sin to kill a man nor to lie with another's wife; these sometimes can be committed without sin. If a prohibition of this kind is understood, according to the sound of the words, to refer to the deed, he who wants to bear false witness or even consents to speaking it, as long as he does not speak it, whatever the reason for his silence, does not become guilty according to the Law. For it was not said that we should not want to bear false witness or that we should not consent to speaking it, but only that we should not speak it. The Law forbids us to take our sisters or to commingle with them,[2] but there is no one who can keep this ordinance, since one is often unable to recognize one's sisters—no one, I mean, if the prohibition refers to the act rather than to consent. And so when it happens that someone through ignorance takes his sister, he is not surely the transgressor of an ordinance because he does what the Law has forbidden him to do? He is not a transgressor, you will say, because in acting ignorantly he did not consent to transgression. Therefore, just as he is not to be called a transgressor who does what is forbidden, but he who consents to that which it is evident has been prohibited, so the prohibition is not to be applied to the deed but to the consent, so that when it is said 'do not do this or that' the meaning is 'do not consent to do this or that', just as if it were said 'do not venture this knowingly'. The blessed Augustine carefully considered this and reduced every commandment or prohibition to charity or cupidity rather than to deeds, saying: 'The Law ordains nothing except charity and prohibits nothing except cupidity.'[3] Hence also the Apostle says:[4] 'All the Law is fulfilled in one word: Thou shalt love thy neighbour as thyself.' And again:[5] 'Love is the fulfilling of the Law.' It does not in fact matter to merit whether you give alms to the needy; charity may make you ready to give and the will may be there when the opportunity is missing and you no longer remain able to do so, whatever the cause preventing you.

---

[3] Augustine, *De doctrina christiana*, iii. 10, n. 15 (*CCL* 32, p. 87, or *PL* 34. 71).
[4] Gal. 5: 14.  [5] Rom. 13: 10.

opera quae fieri conuenit aut minime eque a bonis sicut a malis
hominibus geri, quod intentio sola separat. In eodem quippe facto,
ut predictus doctor meminit,[1] in quo uidemus Deum Patrem et
Dominum Ihesum Christum,[a] uidemus et[b] Iudam proditorem.
5 Facta quippe est a Deo Patre traditio Filii, facta est et a Filio,
facta est et a proditore illo, cum et Pater Filium tradidit et Filius
se ipsum, ut meminit[c2] Apostolus, et Iudas magistrum. Fecit ergo
proditor quod et Deus,[d] sed numquid ille[e] bene fecit? Nam et si[f]
bonum, non utique bene uel quod ei prodesse debuerit. Non enim
10 quae fiunt, sed quo animo fiant pensat Deus,[g3] nec in opere sed
in intentione meritum operantis uel laus consistit. Sepe quippe
idem a diuersis agitur, per iusticiam unius et per nequitiam alterius,
ut si unum reum duo suspendant, ille quidem zelo iusticiae, hic
antiquae odio inimiciciae, et cum sit suspensionis eadem actio, et
15 utique quod bonum est fieri et quod iusticia exigit agant, per[h]
diuersitatem tamen intentionis idem a diuersis fit, ab uno male,
ab altero bene.[4]

Quis denique ipsum[i] diabolum nichil facere ignoret, nisi quod
a Deo facere permittitur, cum uel iniquum punit pro meritis uel
20 ad purgationem uel exemplum patientiae iustum aliquem permittitur affligere? Sed quia id quod agere eum Deus permittit, nequicia sua stimulante agit, sic[j] potestas eius bona dicitur uel etiam
iusta ut uoluntas eius semper sit iniusta. Hanc enim a Deo accipit,
illam a se habet. Quis etiam electorum in his quae ad opera
25 pertinent ypocritis potest adequari?[k] Quis tanta sustinet uel agit
amore Dei quanta illi[l] cupiditate humanae laudis? Quis denique
nesciat non numquam ea quae Deus prohibet fieri recte geri uel
esse facienda, sicut e contrario nonnulla quandoque precipit
quae tamen fieri minime[m] conuenit? Ecce enim non nulla nouimus[n]

---

[a] Christum *om.* BCD    [b] etiam BCD    [c] apostolus meminit BC
[d] Deus: fecit *add.* BCD    [e] ideo BCD    [f] Nam et si ADE; aut si BC
[g] pensat deus: pensanda sunt BC    [h] per . . . male. ab altero bene AE;
per . . . bene ab altero bene D; pro diuersitate tamen intencionis idem a diuersis fit (set C) male et bene BC    [i] ipsum: quoque *add.* BCD    [j] sicut
BCD    [k] ypocritas potest adequare BC    [l] ille BD; illa C    [m] minime
fieri BC    [n] eius nouimus CD

---

[1] Augustine, *In Epistolam Joannis ad Parthos Tractatus VII*, cap. iv, no. 7
(*PL* 35. 2032–3). Cf. Augustine, *Enarrationes in Psalmos*, lxv. 7 and xciii. 28
(*CCL* 39, pp. 846, 1328–9, or *PL* 36. 793 and 37. 1214–15). Also, Abelard,
*Expositio* of Romans, i, and *Dialogus* (*PL* 178. 827D–828A, 1678A).
[2] Rom. 8: 32, Gal. 2: 20.
[3] Cf. Augustine, *De sermone Domini in monte*, ii. 13, n. 46 (*CCL* 35, p. 137, or
*PL* 34. 1289); also Abelard, *Expositio* of Romans, i and v (*PL* 178. 801B, 959B),
*Ethica*, below, p. 40, and *Dialogus* (1677C). Augustine's phrase was familiar in
the school of Laon; cf. cod. Alençon 26, f. 119[va] (cited by Blomme, *La doctrine*

It is indeed obvious that works which it is or is not at all fitting to
do may be performed as much by good as by bad men who are
separated by their intention alone. In fact, as the same Doctor has
observed,[1] in the same deed in which we see God the Father and
the Lord Jesus Christ we also see Judas the betrayer. The giving
up of the Son was certainly done by God the Father; and it was
done by the Son and it was done by that betrayer, since both the
Father delivered up the Son and the Son delivered up himself, as
the Apostle observed,[2] and Judas delivered up the Master. So the
betrayer did what God also did, but surely he did not do it well?
For although what was done was good, it certainly was not well
done nor should it have benefited him. For God thinks not of
what is done but in what mind it may be done,[3] and the merit
or glory of the doer lies in the intention, not in the deed. In fact the
same thing is often done by different people, justly by one and
wickedly by another, as for example if two men hang a convict,
that one out of zeal for justice, this one out of a hatred arising from
an old enmity, and although it is the same act of hanging and
although they certainly do what it is good to do and what justice
requires, yet, through the diversity of their intention, the same
thing is done by diverse men, by one badly, by the other well.[4]

Who, finally, may be unaware that the devil himself does nothing
except what he is allowed by God to do, when either he punishes a
wicked man for his faults or is allowed to strike a just man in order
to purge him or to provide an example of patience? But because
on the prompting of his own wickedness he does what God allows
him to do, so his power is said to be good or even just, while his
will is always unjust. For he receives the former from God; the
latter he holds of himself. Moreover, in respect of works, who among
the elect can be compared with hypocrites? Who endures or does
out of love of God as much as they do out of greed for human
praise? Who lastly may not know that what God forbids to be done
is sometimes rightly performed or should be done, just as conversely he sometimes ordains some things which, however, it is not
at all fitting to do? For consider, we know of some miracles of his
that when by them he healed illnesses, he forbade that they should

---

*du péché*, p. 75) and *Sententia*, no. 423 (ed. Lottin, *Psychologie et morale*, v. 292),
where, as here, it accompanies Augustine's discussion of Judas. Cf. also Seneca,
*De beneficiis*, i. 6. 1.
    [4] Cf. Abelard, *Dialogus* (PL 178. 1677D; also 1652B).

eius miracula quibus cum infirmitates curauerit reuelari prohibuit,
ad exemplum scilicet humilitatis, ne quis forte de gratia sibi collata
simili[a] gloriam appeteret. Nec tamen minus illi qui beneficia illa
susceperant publicare illa cessabant, ad honorem scilicet eius qui
5 et illa fecerat, et reuelari[b] prohibuerat.[c] De qualibus scriptum est:[1]
'Quanto eis precipiebat ne dicerent, tanto plus[d] predicabant' etc.
Numquid tales reos transgressionis iudicabis qui contra preceptum
quod acceperant egerunt atque hoc etiam scienter? Quid[e] eos
excuset a transgressione nisi quia nichil egerunt per contemptum
10 precipientis, quod ad honorem ipsius facere decreuerunt? Dic
obsecro, si precepit[f] Christus quod precipiendum non[g] fuit, aut si
illi dimiserunt quod tenendum fuit. Fuit bonum precipi, quod non
fuit bonum fieri. Vtique et in Abraham accusabis dominum, cui
primum precepit de immolando filio quod postmodum ipse in-
15 hibuit. Numquid non bene precepit Deus id fieri quod non erat
bonum fieri? Si enim bonum quomodo postea prohibitum? Si
autem idem et bonum fuit precipi et bonum prohiberi nec enim
quicquam absque racionabili causa fieri Deus permittit, nec dum
facere consentit, uides quia sola intentio precepti, non actio facti,
20 Deum excusat cum id bene precepit[h] quod non est bonum fieri.
Non enim Deus ad hoc[i] intendebat[j] uel agi precipiebat[k] ut
Abraham filium immolaret, sed ut ex hoc maxime obedientia eius
et constantia fidei uel amoris in eum probaretur, et in exemplo
nobis relinqueretur. Hoc quippe[l] patenter et Dominus ipse post-
25 modum profitetur cum ait,[2] 'Nunc cognoui quod timeas Dominum',[m] ac si aperte diceret, ad hoc istud tibi[n] precepi ad quod te
paratum exhibuisti ut ab aliis facerem cognosci quod ante secula
de te ipse[o] cognoueram. Recta igitur haec intentio Dei fuit[p] in
facto quod rectum non fuit, et sic[q] recta prohibitio eius in illis quae
30 diximus quae ad hoc prohibuit, non ut prohibitio teneretur, sed ut
uitandae inanis[r] gloriae nobis infirmis exempla darentur. Precepit
itaque Deus quod fieri bonum non fuit, sicut e contrario prohibuit

[a] simili collata sibi BC     [b] reuelare BD     [c] prohibebat BC     [d] ne
dicerent tanto plus A; ne diceret tanto plus E; ne deberent tanto plus D; tanto
magis plus B; tanto magis C     [e] Quis AE     [f] precipit BC     [g] non
*om.* BC     [h] precipit BCE     [i] ad hoc deus CD     [j] attendebat B
[k] disposuerat B; disposuerit C     [l] enim BC     [m] deum BCD     [n] hoc
istud tibi ADE; istud B; hoc tibi istud C     [o] ipso BD     [p] fuit dei BC
[q] si AE     [r] inanis *om.* BC

be revealed, as an example, that is, of humility, lest someone who had a similar grace granted to him should perhaps seek prestige. None the less they who had received those benefits did not stop publicizing them in honour, of course, of him who had both worked them and had prohibited their revelation. Of such it was written:[1] 'The more he charged them that they should not tell, so much the more did they publish it', etc. Surely you will not judge such men guilty of transgression for acting contrary to the command which they had received and for even doing this knowingly? What will excuse them from transgression if not the fact that they did nothing through contempt of him who commanded; they decided to do this in honour of him. Tell me, I ask you, if Christ ordained what should not have been ordained or if they repudiated what should have been kept? What was good to be commanded was not good to be done. You at any rate will reproach the Lord in the case of Abraham, whom at first he commanded to sacrifice his son and later checked from doing so. Surely God did not command well a deed which it was not good to do? For if it was good, how was it later forbidden? If, moreover, the same thing was both good to be commanded and good to be prohibited—for God allows nothing to be done without reasonable cause nor yet consents to do it—you see that the intention of the command alone, not the execution of the deed, excuses God, since he did well to command what is not a good thing to be done. For God did not urge or command this to be done in order that Abraham should sacrifice his son but in order that out of this his obedience and the constancy of his faith or love for him should be very greatly tested and remain to us as an example. And this indeed the Lord himself subsequently avowed openly when he said:[2] 'Now I know that thou fearest the Lord', as if he were saying expressly: the reason why I instructed you to do what you showed you were ready to do was so that I should make known to others what I myself had known of you before the ages. This intention of God was right in an act which was not right, and similarly, in the things which we mentioned, his prohibition was right which prohibited for this reason, not so that the prohibition should be upheld but so that examples might be given to us weaklings of avoiding vainglory. And so God enjoined what was not good to be done, just as

[1] Mark 7: 36.
[2] Gen. 22: 12.

quod fieri bonum fuit,[a] et sicut ibi excusat eum intentio ita et
hic eos qui preceptum opere non impleuerunt. Sciebant quippe
non ob hoc eum precepisse ut teneretur, sed ut predictum exemplum preponeretur. Salua itaque uoluntate iubentis non eum con-
5 tempserunt, cuius uoluntati se non esse contrarios intellexerunt.
Si ergo opera magis quam intentionem[b] pensemus, uidebimus
non numquam contra preceptum Dei non solum uelle fieri, uerum
etiam fieri aliquid et hoc scienter sine ullo reatu peccati, nec malam
uoluntatem uel actionem ideo esse dicendam quia preceptum
10 Dei non seruat in opere, cum a uoluntate precipientis non discrepat eius intentio cui preceptio fit. Sicut[c] enim intentio iubentis
excusat ipsum qui precipit[d] fieri quod tamen minime conuenit
fieri, ita et eum cui fit preceptio excusat karitatis intentio.
Vt ergo breui[e] conclusione supradicta colligam, quatuor sunt
15 quae premisimus ut ab inuicem ipsa diligenter distingueremus,
uicium scilicet animi quod ad peccandum pronos efficit, ac postmodum ipsum peccatum quod in consensu mali uel contemptu[f]
Dei statuimus, deinde mali uoluntatem malique operationem.[g]
Sicut autem non idem est uelle quod uoluntatem implere, ita non
20 idem est peccare quod peccatum perficere. Illud quippe de consensu
animi quo peccamus, hoc de effectu operationis est accipiendum,
cum uidelicet illud in quo prius consensimus opere implemus.
Cum ergo[h] peccatum uel temptationem tribus modis dicimus[i]
peragi, suggestione scilicet, delectatione, consensu,[1] ita est intelligendum, quod ad operationem peccati per hec tria frequenter
25 deducimur sicut in primis contigit parentibus. Persuasio quippe
diaboli precessit, cum ex gustu uetitae arboris immortalitatem
promisit. Delectatio successit cum mulier uidens lignum pul-
chrum et ipsum intelligens suaue ad uescendum in concupiscentiam eius exarsit cibi uoluptate quam credebat correpta. Quae
30 cum reprimere concupiscentiam deberet ut preceptum seruaret,
consentiendo in peccatum tracta est. Quod etiam peccatum cum

---

[a] fieri bonum fuit ADE; fuerit bonum fuit B; bonum fuit fieri C    [b] intentionem: dei *add.* BCD    [c] Sic AE    [d] precipit . . . conuenit fieri:
precipit hoc fieri B. *In* C *the words* quod tamen minime conuenit fieri *appear*
*in the margin*    [e] *After* breui *in* B *and* C *the words* quod tamen minime
conuenit (*om.* B) fieri *follow, having been misplaced by the scribe, but in* C
*the scribe realized his mistake, crossed out the phrase, and rewrote it in the margin*
supra    [f] contemptum BC *and* ?D    [g] malique operationem A;
operacionemque mali E; deinde mali operacionem B; denique mali operacionem CD    [h] ergo: dicimus *add.* BCD    [i] dicimus *om.* BCD

---

[1] Cf. Augustine, *De sermone Domini in monte*, i. 12, n. 34 (*CCL* 35, pp. 36–8,
or *PL* 34. 1246–7); Gregory the Great, *XL Homiliarum in Euangelia lib.* i,
*Hom.* xvi (*PL* 76. 1135) and *Moralia*, iv. 27, n. 49 (*PL* 75. 661B).

conversely he prohibited what was good to be done; and just as the intention excuses him in the one case, so too in this case it excuses those who have not fulfilled the command in practice. They knew indeed that he had not made the command on this account, that it should be observed, but so that the example that has been mentioned should be set forth. While not violating the will of him who commands, they did not offer contempt to him to whose will they understood that they were not opposed.

If therefore we think of deeds rather than the intention, we shall not only see that sometimes there is a will to do something against God's commandment but also that it is done and knowingly so without any guilt of sin. So, when the intention of him to whom the command is made does not differ from the will of the commander, one should not speak of an evil will or an evil action simply because God's commandment is not kept in a deed. Just as intention excuses the commander who commands to be done what is however not at all fitting to be done, so also the intention of charity excuses him to whom the command is made.

To bring the above together in a brief conclusion, there are four things which we have put forward in order carefully to distinguish them from each other, namely the vice of the mind which makes us prone to sinning and then the sin itself which we fixed in consent to evil or contempt of God, next the will for evil and the doing of evil. Just as, indeed, to will and to fulfil the will are not the same, so to sin and to perform the sin are not the same. We should understand the former to relate to the consent of the mind by which we sin, the latter to the performance of the action when we fulfil in a deed what we have previously consented to. When we say that sin or temptation occurs in three ways, namely in suggestion, pleasure, and consent,[1] it should be understood in this sense, that we are often led through these three to the doing of sin. This was the case with our first parents. Persuasion by the devil came first, when he promised immortality for tasting the forbidden tree. Pleasure followed, when the woman, seeing the beautiful fruit and understanding it to be sweet to eat, was seized with what she believed would be the pleasure of the food and kindled a longing for it. Since she ought to have checked her longing in order to keep the command, in consenting she was drawn into sin. And although she ought to have corrected the sin through repentance in order to deserve pardon, she finally completed it in deed.

per penitentiam deberet corrigere ut ueniam mereretur, ipsum denique consummauit in opere, et ita tribus gradibus ad perpetrandum peccatum incessit. Sic et nos frequenter non ad peccandum sed ad peccati perpetrationem hisdem passibus[a] peruenimus,

5 suggestione scilicet, hoc est, exhortatione alicuius nos exterius[b] incitantis ad aliquid agendum quod non conuenit. Quod quidem agere si delectabile[c] nouerimus ante ipsum etiam factum ipsius facti delectatione mens nostra corripitur et in ipsa cogitatione per delectationem temptamur. Cui uidelicet delectationi dum assen-

10 timus per consensum peccamus. His tandem tribus ad operationem peccati peruenimus.

Sunt qui suggestionem carnis, etiam si persona suggerens desit, comprehendi nomine suggestionis uelint, ueluti si quis uisa muliere in concupiscentiam eius incidat.[1] Sed haec profecto

15 suggestio nichil aliud quam delectatio uidetur esse dicenda. Quam quidem delectationem[d] quasi necessariam[e] factam et ceteras huiusmodi quas non peccatum esse[f] supra meminimus humanam temptationem Apostolus uocat cum ait,[2] 'Temptatio uos non apprehendat[g] nisi humana, fidelis autem Deus qui non patietur

20 uos temptari supra id quod potestis, sed faciet cum temptatione etiam prouentum, ut possitis sustinere.' Temptatio autem generaliter dicitur quaecumque inclinatio animi ad aliquid agendum[h] quod non conuenit, siue illa[i] uoluntas sit siue consensus. Humana uero temptatio dicitur sine qua iam humana infirmitas uix aut

25 numquam subsistere potest, ut concupiscentia carnalis uel delectabilis cibi desiderium. A quibus se liberari postulabat[j] qui dicebat,[3] 'De necessitatibus meis erue me Domine',[k] hoc est de his temptationibus concupiscentiarum quae quasi naturales ac necessariae iam factae sunt,[l] ne ad consensum pertrahant, uel uita ista

30 plena temptationibus finita prorsus eis careat. Quod ergo ait Apostolus, 'Temptatio uos non apprehendat nisi humana', consimilis sententia est ac[m] si diceret, Si inclinatur animus ex delectatione quae est, ut diximus, humana temptatio, non usque ad consensum pertrahat in quo peccatum consistit. Quod quasi

35 aliquis quereret qua nostra uirtute concupiscentiis istis possemus resistere, 'Fidelis', inquit,[n] 'Deus qui non patietur uos

[a] passionibus AE    [b] exterius *om.* BC    [c] delectabile: esse *add.* BCD
[d] delectationem: iam *add.* BCD    [e] necessaria B; necessario C    [f] esse
peccatum BCD    [g] apprehendit BC    [h] gerendum BC    [i] ulla BC
[j] postulabat: ille *add.* BC    [k] domine *om.* BCD    [l] sunt facte BCD
[m] tamquam BD    [n] inquit . . . temptari AE; inquit deus etc. B; inquit
est deus etc. C; inquit etc. D

---

[1] Cf. Anselm of Laon, *Sententia*, no. 85; also *Sententia*, no. 450 of the

And so she proceeded to carry through the sin in three stages. Likewise we also frequently arrive by these same steps not at sinning but at the carrying through of sin, namely by suggestion, that is, by the encouragement of someone who incites us externally to do something which is not fitting. And if we know that doing this is pleasurable, even before the deed our mind is seized with the pleasure of the deed itself and in the very thought we are tempted through pleasure. When in fact we assent to this pleasure through consent, we sin. By these three we come at last to the execution of the sin.

There are those who would like carnal suggestion to be included in the term suggestion, even if there is no person making a suggestion—for instance, if someone on seeing a woman falls into lust for her.[1] But this suggestion, it seems, should really be called nothing other than pleasure. Indeed this pleasure, which has become almost necessary, and others of its kind which, we observed above, are not sin, are called by the Apostle human temptation when he says:[2] 'Let no temptation take hold on you, but such as is human. And God is faithful, who will not suffer you to be tempted above that which you are able; but will also make issue with temptation, that you may be able to bear it.' Now, temptation is generally said to be any inclination of the mind, whether a will or consent, to do something which is not fitting. But human temptation, such as carnal concupiscence or the desire for delicious food, is said to be that without which human infirmity can now scarcely or can never survive. He asked to be set free from these who said:[3] 'Deliver me from my necessities, O Lord', that is, from these lustful temptations which have now become almost natural and necessary, lest they lead to consent; alternatively, let me really be free of them at the end of this life full of temptations. So, what the Apostle says, 'Let no temptation take hold on you, but such as is human', is as an opinion very like saying: 'If the mind is inclined by pleasure which is, as we have said, human temptation, let it not lead as far as consent, in which sin consists.' He says, as if someone were asking by what virtue of ours we can resist those lusts: 'God is faithful who will not suffer you to be tempted', that

school of Anselm (ed. Lottin, *Psychologie et morale*, v. 73, 303). Abelard may be said to rejoin here Gregory the Great, *Moralia*, iv. 27, n. 49: 'fit enim suggestio per aduersarium, delectatio per carnem' (*PL* 75. 661B).
[2] 1 Cor. 10: 13.                                                                 [3] Ps. 24: 17.

temptari.' Tamquam si diceret, De ipso potius est confidendum
quam de nobis presumendum, qui nobis auxilium promittens in
omnibus uerax est promissis, quod est eum fidelem esse ut ei
scilicet de omnibus adhibenda sit fides. Tunc uero nos non patitur
5 temptari supra id quod possumus, cum per misericordiam suam
ita hanc temptationem humanam temperat ut non plus ad peccatum premat quam perferre possimus ei uidelicet resistendo. Tunc
autem insuper hanc ipsam temptationem nobis conuertit ad com-
modum, dum per eam sic nos exercet ut deinceps cum occurrerit
10 minus grauare possit, et iam minus impetum hostis timeamus[a]
de quo iam triumphauimus et perferre nouimus. Omnis quippe
pugna quam non dum experti sumus grauius sustinetur[b] et amplius
formidetur;[c] cum uero in consuetudinem uictoribus uenerit, pariter
uirtus eius et metus[d] euanescit.

15                          *De suggestionibus demonum*[e]

Sunt autem suggestiones non solum hominum, sed et[f] demonum, quia et isti non numquam ad peccatum[g] nos incitant non
tam uerbis quam factis. Periti quippe[h] naturae rerum tam ingenii
subtilitate quam longa experientia, unde et demones, hoc est,
20 scientes sunt appellati,[1] nouerunt uires rerum naturales unde ad
libidinem uel ad ceteros impetus humana infirmitas facile possit
commoueri. Sic et in languorem, Deo permittente, nonnumquam
aliquos mittunt ac postmodum supplicantibus sibi remedia con-
ferunt, et frequenter cum cessant ledere curare creduntur. Deni-
25 que in Egypto multa contra Moysen mirabiliter operari per magos
sunt permissi,[2] ea quidem naturali ui rerum quam nouerant non
tam eorum quae faciebant creatores dicendi quam composito-
res, ueluti siquis, iuxta documentum Virgilii,[3] tunsa[i] carne tauri,
apes inde[j] fieri laborando efficeret, non tam apum[k] creator quam
30 naturae preparator dicendus esset. Ex hac itaque rerum peritia
quam habent in earum naturis demones nos in libidinem uel[l]
ceteras animi[m] passiones commouent, quacumque arte nobis
ignorantibus eas admouendo,[n] sive in gustu siue in stratu[o] eas
ponendo uel quolibet modo eas interius uel exterius[p] collocando.

----

[a] senciamus BC          [b] sustinemus ADE          [c] formidamus ADE
[d] metus: eius *add.* BC      [e] ADE; *in B a space has been provided by the scribe,*
*perhaps for a heading*      [f] etiam BCD      [g] ad peccatum non nunquam
BCD      [h] quippe: et *add.* BC      [i] tonsa BCD      [j] inde . . . efficeret
ADE; inde procederent B; inde (?) produceret C      [k] apium BCD      [l] uel:
in *add.* BC      [m] anime BC      [n] admonendo D *?* C      [o] tactu *Cousin*
[p] exterius uel interius BC

is as if to say: 'Rather than rely on ourselves we should trust in him who, promising help for us, is true in all his promises', that is, he is faithful, so in everything faith should clearly be put in him. Then indeed he does not allow us to be tempted above that which we are able, since he moderates this human temptation with his mercy, so that it does not press us into sin by more than we are able to bear in resisting it. However, he then in addition turns this very temptation to our advantage when he trains us by it, so that eventually when it occurs it can bother us less and so that we should now have less fear of the attack of an enemy over whom we have already triumphed and whom we know how to manage. Every struggle which we have not hitherto experienced is borne more severely and is dreaded more. But when it comes regularly to the victorious, its power and its dread alike vanish.

### *Of the suggestions of demons*

Suggestions are made not only by men but also by demons, because they too sometimes incite us to sin, less by words than by deeds. By their subtle talent as much as by their long experience they are certainly experts in the nature of things and for this are called demons, that is, knowledgeable;[1] they know the natural powers of things by which human weakness may easily be stirred to lust or to other impulses. Sometimes by God's leave they send some into languor and then provide the remedies for those who beseech them, and when they cease to afflict they are often thought to cure. In Egypt they were in the end allowed through the magicians to do many things marvellously against Moses,[2] in reality by the natural power of things which they knew. They should not be called creators of what they have made so much as compositors; for instance, if anyone, following the example in Virgil,[3] having pounded the flesh of a bull should by his labour bring about from this the making of bees, he should be called not so much a creator of bees as a preparer of nature. And so, by this expertise which they have with the natures of things, demons provoke us to lust or to other passions of the mind, bringing them by every possible stratagem while we are unawares, whether setting them in taste or in bed or placing them by no matter what means inside or

---

[1] Cf. Isidore, *Etymologiae*, VIII. xi. 15–16, ed. W. M. Lindsay, vol. i (Oxford, 1911).      [2] Cf. Exod. 7.      [3] *Georgics*, iv. 281 et seq.

Multe quippe sunt in herbis uel seminibus uel tam arborum quam
lapidum naturis uires ad commouendos uel pacandos[a] animos
nostros aptae,[b] quas qui diligenter nossent[c] hoc[d] agere facile
possent.[e1]

5          *Cur opera peccati magis quam ipsum puniatur*[f]

Sunt etiam[g] qui non mediocriter mouentur, cum audiunt nos
dicere opus peccati non proprie peccatum dici, uel quicquam non[h]
addere ad peccati augmentum,[i] cur grauior satisfactio penitentibus iniungatur de operis effectu quam de culpae reatu. Quibus
10 quidem hoc primum respondeo cur non precipue mirentur pro eo
quod[j] non numquam magna satisfactionis instituitur pena ubi
nulla intercesserit culpa, et eos quandoque punire debeamus
quos innocentes scimus. Ecce enim pauper aliqua mulier infan-
tulum habet lactentem nec tantum indumentorum habet ut et
15 paruulo in cunis et sibi sufficere possit. Miseratione itaque infan-
tuli commota, eum sibi apponit ut propriis insuper foueat pannis,
et tandem infirmitate eius ui naturae superata, opprimere cogitur
quem amore summo amplectitur. 'Habe', inquit Augustinus,
'karitatem, et fac quicquid uis.'[2] Quae tamen pro satisfactione
20 cum ad episcopum uenerit, grauis ei pena iniungitur, non pro
culpa quam commiserit,[k] sed ut ipsa deinceps uel ceterae feminae
in talibus prouidendis cautiores reddantur.[3] Non numquam etiam
contingit aliquem ab inimicis suis apud iudicem accusari, et tale
quid illi imponi unde illum innocentem esse iudex cognoscit.[1]
25 Quia tamen illi instant[m] et audientiam in iudicio postulant, sta-
tuto die causam ingrediuntur, testes proferunt licet falsos ad
eum quem accusant conuincendum. Quos tamen testes cum nequaquam iudex manifestis de causis refellere possit, eos suscipere lege

[a] aplicandos B      [b] apte *om.* BC     [c] nosset BC     [d] hec BCD
[e] posset BC     [f] ADE     [g] etiam *om.* BC     [h] etiam BCD     [i] augmentum peccat: BCD     [j] quod . . . pena AE; nunquam magnam satisfactionis institui penam B; non nunquam magnam satisfaccionis institui penam C;
quod non nunquam magnam satisfactionis institui penam D     [k] comiserat
B; commisit C     [l] agnoscit B; agnoscat C; cognoscat E     [m] constant B

[1] William of Saint-Thierry, who did not possess the *Ethica*, knew a passage
in the lost *Liber Sententiarum* (which is probably the work of an anonymous
disciple of Abelard) where the devil is said to produce a stone or a herb, which
has the power of exciting a passion, when he wishes to suggest lust or anger,
*Disputatio, cap.* lv (*PL* 180. 281A–C). William commented that Abelard must
have been flippant in teaching this. None the less William proceeded with the
accusation; see *Epistola* 326 (*PL* 182. 532B) and Bernard of Clairvaux, *Epistola*
190 (*PL* 182. 1062B). At the council of Sens Abelard was condemned for teaching
*quod diabolus immittat suggestiones per appositionem lapidum siue herbarum,*

outside us. There are certainly many forces in herbs or seeds or in the natures of trees as much as of stones which are suitable for provoking or soothing our minds; those who carefully learn to know them can easily do this.[1]

## Why works of sin are punished rather than sin itself

There are also those who are considerably troubled, when they hear us say that a work of sin is not properly called sin or that it does not add anything to increase a sin, as to why a heavier satisfaction is imposed on penitents for doing a deed than for being guilty of a fault. To these I answer first: why do they not chiefly wonder about the fact that sometimes a large penalty of satisfaction is instituted where no fault has occurred? And why ought we sometimes to punish those whom we know to be innocent? For, consider, some poor woman has a suckling baby and lacks clothing adequate to provide for the little one in the cradle and for herself. And so, stirred by pity for the baby she takes him to herself to keep him warm with her own rags, and finally in her weakness overcome by the force of nature, she unavoidably smothers the one she clasps with the utmost love. 'Have charity', says Augustine, 'and do whatever you wish.'[2] However, when she comes before the bishop for satisfaction, a heavy punishment is imposed upon her, not for the fault which she committed but so that subsequently she or other women should be rendered more cautious in providing for such things.[3] Occasionally also it happens that someone is accused by his enemies before a judge, and that a certain imputation is made about him by which the judge knows he is innocent. However, because they insist and demand a hearing at a trial, they commence the suit on the appointed day, produce witnesses, albeit false ones, to convict him whom they accuse. Since the judge can in no way rebut these witnesses with plain reasons, he is compelled by law to

---

*Capitulum* 15, ed. J. Leclercq, in *Revue bénédictine*, lxxviii (1968), 104. He did not reply to the accusation in his *Confessio fidei* (PL 178. 105–8).

[2] Augustine, *In Epistolam Joannis ad Parthos Tractatus* VII, *cap.* 8 (PL 35. 2033): 'Dilige et quod uis fac.'

[3] Blomme, *La doctrine du péché*, p. 202 n. 1, illustrates the penitential and canonical context of this punishment, but he is surely mistaken in seeing in this *exemplum* an objection by Abelard to crudely objective methods of judgement employed by ecclesiastics. This, and the following example, are introduced to show the reasonableness on the human level of imposing even unfair punishments; God and men differ in their methods of judgement.

compellitur, et eorum probatione suscepta punit[a] innocentem.
Debet ergo punire illum qui puniri non debet. Debet utique quia
quod ille non meruit hic secundum legem iuste agit. Ex his itaque liquet non numquam penam racionabiliter iniungi ei in[b] quo
5 nulla culpa precessit. Quid igitur mirum si ubi culpa precesserit,
operatio subsecuta penam augeat apud homines in[c] hac uita, non
apud Deum in futura? Non enim homines de occultis, sed de
manifestis iudicant,[d] nec tam culpae reatum quam operis pensant
effectum. Deus uero solus qui non tam quae fiunt, quam quo
10 animo fiant[e] adtendit, ueraciter in intentione nostra reatum pensat et uero iudicio culpam examinat. Vnde et probator cordis et
renum dicitur[1] et in abscondito uidere.[2] Ibi enim maxime uidet
ubi nemo uidet, quia in puniendo peccatum non opus adtendit sed
animum, sicut nos e conuerso non animum quem non uidemus,
15 sed opus quod nouimus. Vnde sepe per errorem uel per legis, ut
diximus, coactionem innocentes punimus uel noxios absoluimus.
Probator et[f] cognitor cordis et renum dicitur Deus, hoc est,
quarumlibet intentionum ex affectione animae uel infirmitate seu
delectatione carnis prouenientium.

20          *De peccatis spiritalibus uel carnalibus*[g]

   Cum enim omnia peccata sint animae tantum, non carnis, ibi
quippe culpa et contemptus Dei esse potest ubi eius noticia et
ratio consistere habet.[h] Quaedam tamen peccata spiritualia, quaedam carnalia dicuntur, hoc est, quaedam ex uiciis animae,
25 quaedam ex carnis infirmitate prouenientia.[3] Et quamuis concupiscentia solius sit animae sicut et uoluntas, non enim concupiscere
uel desiderare aliquid nisi uolendo possumus, concupiscentia
tamen carnis sicut et concupiscentia spiritus dicitur. 'Caro enim',
ait Apostolus,[4] concupiscit aduersus spiritum et spiritus aduer-
30 sus carnem', hoc est, anima ex delectatione quam habet in carne
quaedam appetit quae tamen iudicio rationis refugit uel non[j] ap-
petenda censet.

    [a] punit (punire B) . . . qui puniri (quem punire B) . . . agit BC; punire in-
nocentem debet qui puniri non debet. Itaque punire debet licet non meruerit,
cum tamen lege precipiente hoc iuste iudex peragit ADE        [b] in . . . precessit ADE; ubi culpa non precessit BC        [c] homines in: homines quidem
in B; homines quid etiam C        [d] iudicare possunt BC        [e] fiunt CD
[f] et AE; id est BCD        [g] ADE (spiritualibus *in* D)        [h] posset B
[i] apostolus ait BCD        [j] non *om.* AE

[1] Jer. 20: 12.                              [2] Cf. Ezek. 8: 12.

recognize them and, having accepted their proof, he punishes the innocent man. Thus he ought to punish him who ought not to be punished. He ought at any rate because he transacts justly according to law what the other man has not deserved. It is clear from these examples that sometimes a punishment is reasonably inflicted on a person in whom no fault went before. So what is surprising if, where a fault has preceded, the subsequent action increases the punishment with men in this life, not with God in the future? For men do not judge the hidden but the apparent, nor do they consider the guilt of a fault so much as the performance of a deed. Indeed God alone, who considers not so much what is done as in what mind it may be done, truly considers the guilt in our intention and examines the fault in a true trial. Whence he is said to be both the prover of the heart and the reins[1] and to see in the dark.[2] For he particularly sees there where no man sees, because in punishing sin he considers not the deed but the mind, just as conversely we consider not the mind which we do not see but the deed which we know. Whence often we punish the innocent or absolve the culpable through error or, as we have said, through the compulsion of the law. God is said to be the prover and the judge of the heart and the reins, that is, of all the intentions which come from an affection of the soul or from a weakness or a pleasure of the flesh.

### Of spiritual or carnal sins

Since all sins are uniquely of the soul, not of the flesh, there can certainly be fault and contempt of God where knowledge of him and where reason dwell. Yet some sins are called spiritual, some carnal, that is, some come from the vices of the soul, some from the weakness of the flesh.[3] And although concupiscence, like will too, is only of the soul—for we cannot lust after or desire anything except by willing—yet there is said to be concupiscence of the flesh as well as concupiscence of the spirit. 'For', the Apostle says,[4] 'the flesh lusteth against the spirit and the spirit against the flesh', that is, the soul, by reason of the pleasure which it has in the flesh, seeks some things which, however, it shuns in the judgement of reason, or which it thinks should not be sought.

---

[3] Cf. Gregory the Great, *Moralia*, xxxi. 45, n. 88 (*PL* 76. 621).
[4] Gal. 5: 17.

*Cur Deus dicatur inspector cordis et renum*[a][1]

Iuxta igitur haec duo,[b] concupiscentiam carnis et concupiscentiam animae quae premisimus, probator cordis et renum dictus
est[c] Deus, hoc est, inspector intentionum uel consensuum inde
5 prouenientium.[2] Nos uero qui hoc[d] discutere ac diiudicare non
ualemus, ad opera maxime[e] iudicium nostrum conuertimus, nec
tam culpas quam opera punimus, nec in aliquo tam quod eius
animae nocet quam quod aliis nocere possit uindicare studemus,
ut magis publica preueniamus dampna quam singularia corriga-
10 mus,[f] iuxta quod et Dominus Petro ait,[3] 'Si peccauerit in te frater
tuus, corripe illum inter[g] te et ipsum solum.' Quid est 'peccauerit in te' quasi non in alium, ut magis iniurias nobis quam aliis
illatas corrigere uel uindicare debeamus? Absit. 'Si[h] peccauerit
in te' dixit cum manifeste agit unde te per exemplum corrumpere
15 possit. Quasi enim in se tantum peccat cum culpa eius occulta eum
solum reum constituit, non ad reatum alios quantum in se est per
exemplum trahit. Et si enim desunt[i] qui malam eius actionem
imitentur uel etiam[j] cognouerint, actio tamen ipsa magis quam
animi culpa castiganda est apud homines, quia plus offensae con-
20 trahere potuit et perniciosius per exemplum fieri quam culpa
latens animi. Omne namque quod in communem perniciem uel
in publicum redundare potest incommodum castigatione maiori
est puniendum,[k] et quod contrahit maiorem offensam, grauiorem
inter nos promeretur penam et maius hominum scandalum maius
25 inter homines incurrit supplicium, etsi leuior precessit[l] culpa.
Ponamus enim aliquem coitu suo mulierem aliquam corrupisse
in aecclesia.[m] Quod cum ad aures populi delatum fuerit, non
tantum de uiolatione feminae ac ueri templi Dei quantum de
infractione corporalis templi[n] commouentur, cum tamen grauius
30 sit in mulierem quam in parietes presumere, et homini quam loco
iniuriam inferre. Et incendia domorum maiori pena uindicamus

---

[a] AE; et renum *om.* D      [b] igitur haec duo AE; hec igitur duo B; ergo
hec duo D; hunc igitur C      [c] dicitur BC      [d] hec BCD      [e] maxima
AE      [f] corrigamus: Si peccauerit in te frater *add.* D *as a rubricated heading*
[g] inter . . . solum ADE: etc. BC      [h] Si AE: Sed BCD      [i] desint BC
[j] eam BCD      [k] preueniendum BCD      [l] precesserit BCD      [m] in
ecclesia corrupisse (corripuisse D) BCD      [n] confractione corporalis templi
B; corporalis templi fraccione C

---

[1] Cf. Prov. 24: 12, Ps. 7: 10, Jer. 11: 20, 17: 10, 20: 12, etc.
[2] Blomme, *La doctrine du péché*, pp. 128–44, shows that the two closely
related terms 'intentio' and 'consensus' are used in the *Ethica* for different

*Why God is said to be the inspector of the heart and the reins*[1]

According to these two which we have presented—concupiscence of the flesh and concupiscence of the soul—God has been said to be the prover of the heart and the reins, that is, the inspector of the intentions or the consents coming thence.[2] We, however, who are not capable of discussing and assessing this, direct our judgement particularly to deeds, and we punish not so much faults as deeds, and we strive to avenge in someone less what harms his soul than what can harm others, in order to prevent public rather than individual injuries and in accordance with what the Lord said to Peter:[3] 'If thy brother shall offend against thee, go and rebuke him between thee and him alone.' What is 'offend against thee'? Does it imply 'not against someone else', with the result that we should correct or avenge injuries caused to us rather than those caused to others? God forbid. He said: 'If he shall offend against thee', since plainly what he does may be able to corrupt you by way of example. But if he sins in himself alone, since his fault is hidden it made him alone guilty and does not intrinsically by example lead others to guilt. Indeed, although there be none to imitate his bad action or even to know of it, yet that action should be chastised before men rather than the fault of the mind, because it was able to cause more wrong and become more pernicious by example than a hidden fault of the mind. For whatever can redound to the common ruin or public detriment should be punished with greater correction, and what causes greater wrong deserves among us a heavier penalty, and the greater the scandal with men the greater the punishment which it incurs among men, even though a lighter fault has preceded it. For let us suppose that someone has corrupted a certain woman by having sexual intercourse in a church. When this has been brought to people's ears, they are disturbed not so much by the violation of a woman and a true temple of God as by the infraction of the physical temple, although it is more serious to take advantage of a woman than of a building and to inflict damage on a man rather than on a place. Yet we punish the burning of houses with a greater penalty

purposes. 'Intentio' is the unique determinant of the badness or goodness of a projected action; 'consensus' denotes the approval of an anterior desire and is usually employed by Abelard as the constitutive element of sin, whereas 'intentio' is usually used to indicate the earning of merit.

[3] Matt. 18: 15.

quam in peracta fornicatione,[a] cum longe apud Deum haec illis
habentur[b] grauiora.

Et haec quidem non tam iusticiae debito quam dispensationis
aguntur temperamento, ut, quemadmodum diximus, publica
5 preueniendo dampna communi consulamus utilitati. Sepe igitur
minima[c] peccata maioribus penis uindicamus, non tam aequitate
iusticiae adtendentes quae culpa precesserit quam discretione
prouidentiae cogitantes quanta hinc contingere possit incommoditas,[d] si leuiter puniantur.[e] Culpas itaque animi diuino reseruantes
10 iudicio, effecta earum de quibus iudicare habemus prosequimur
nostro, dispensationem[f] in talibus, hoc est, prouidentiae quam
diximus rationem magis quam aequitatis adtendentes puritatem.
Deus uero unius cuiusque penam secundum culpae quantitatem
disponit. Et quicumque ipsum equaliter contempnunt, equali
15 postmodum pena[g] puniuntur, cuiuscumque conditionis aut profes-
sionis sint.[h] Si enim monachus et laicus in consensum fornicationis pariter ueniant, et mens quoque laici in tantum sit accensa
ut neque ipse, si monachus esset, pro reuerentia Dei ab ista tur-
pitudine desisteret, eandem quam monachus penam meretur. Sic
20 et de illis sentiendum est quorum alter manifeste peccans multos
scandalizat, ac per exemplum corrumpit, alter uero, cum occulte
peccet, soli sibi nocet. Si enim[i] qui occulte peccet[j] in eodem quo
ille proposito et pari contemptu Dei existit,[k] ut quod alios non
corrumpit fortuitu magis eueniat quam ipse propter Deum dimit-
25 tat, qui nec sibi ipsi propter Deum temperat, profecto pari reatu
apud Deum constringitur. Solum quippe animum in remuneratione
boni uel mali, non effecta operum, Deus adtendit, ne quid de culpa
uel de bona uoluntate nostra proueniat pensat, sed ipsum animum
in proposito suae intentionis, non in effectu exterioris operis,
30 diiudicat. Opera quippe quae, ut prediximus,[l] eque reprobis ut
electis communia sunt, omnia in se indifferentia sunt[m] nec nisi pro
intentione agentis bona uel mala dicenda sunt, non uidelicet quia
bonum uel malum sit ea[n] fieri, sed quia bene uel male fiunt, hoc

---

[a] in peracta fornicatione A; peracta fornicacionum D; imperacta fornicacione E; incendium in peracta fornicacionum B; incentiua peracta fornicacione C
[b] habeantur BC        [c] minora BCD        [d] contingere incommoditas possit C; incommoditas contingere possit B; contingere incommodites posset D
[e] puniatur ABDE        [f] prosequamur nostra dispensacione C *corrected from*
nostro dispensacionem *as in* ABDE        [g] supplicio BCD        [h] fuerint BCD

than in the case of fornication, although before God the latter is
considered far graver than the former.

These proceedings are in accordance not so much with the
obligation of justice as with the practicalities of government, so as
to ensure, as we have said, the common utility by preventing
public injuries. Therefore we often punish the smallest sins with
the largest penalties, not so much considering with the fairness of
justice what fault went before, as thinking with the wisdom of
foresight how much trouble can arise if they are punished lightly.
So, in reserving faults of the mind for divine judgement, we pursue with our own the effects of these faults which we have to judge
and in such things we have less regard for pure equity than for
government, that is, the consideration of foresight which we mentioned. God, however, distributes everyone's punishment according to the amount of fault, and all who offer equal contempt to
him are later punished with an equal punishment whatever their
condition or profession. For if a monk and a layman alike come to
consent to fornication, and the mind of the layman is also so incited that if he were a monk he would not hold back in reverence
for God from that baseness, he earns the same punishment as the
monk. We should think similarly of two men of whom one sins
openly and scandalizes many and corrupts by his example, but
the other, sinning secretly, harms only himself. For if the one who
should sin secretly is in the same resolve and in an equal contempt
of God as the other, with the result that what does not corrupt
others turns out by chance to be something greater than he who
does not control himself for God's sake will forego for God's
sake, he is certainly bound before God in an equal guilt. God considers only the mind in rewarding good or evil, not the results of
deeds, and he thinks not of what comes forth from fault or from
our good will but judges the mind itself in the design of its intention, not in the outcome of an outward deed. Works in fact, which
as we have previously said are common to the damned and the
elect alike, are all indifferent in themselves and should be called
good or bad only on account of the intention of the agent, not, that
is, because it is good or bad for them to be done but because they
are done well or badly, that is, by that intention by which it is or

---

[i] enim: is *add.* CD, his *add.* B      [j] peccat CD; *om.* B      [k] persistit BCD
[l] supra dicimus BCD          [m] omnia . . . indifferentia sunt B; omnia . . . indifferentia C; omniaque . . . indifferentia ADE          [n] illa BCD

est, ea intentione qua conuenit fieri, aut minime.[1] Nam, ut beatus
meminit Augustinus,[2] ipsum malum esse est bonum, cum eo
quoque bene utatur Deus,[a] nec aliter ipsum esse permittat, cum
tamen ipsum nequaquam sit bonum. Cum itaque dicimus inten-
5 tionem hominis bonam et opus illius bonum, duo quidem distin-
guimus, intentionem scilicet ac[b] opus, unam tamen bonitatem
intentionis, ueluti si dicamus bonum hominem et filium boni
hominis, duos quidem homines, non duas bonitates, figuramus.[c]
Sicut ergo homo bonus ex propria bonitate dicitur, filius autem
10 boni hominis cum dicitur, nichil in se boni habere ex hoc mon-
stratur, ita cuiusque intentio bona in se uocatur, opus uero bonum
non ex[d] se appellatur sed quod ex bona procedit intentione. Vna
itaque est bonitas unde tam intentio quam operatio bona dicitur,
sicut una est bonitas ex qua bonus homo, et filius boni hominis
15 appellatur, uel una bonitas ex qua bonus homo et bona hominis
uoluntas dicitur.

Qui ergo solent obicere operationem quoque intentionis remuneratione dignam esse, uel ad aliquod remunerationis augmentum
proficere, adtendant quod[e] nugatoria eorum sit[f] obiectio. Duo,
20 inquiunt, bona sunt, intentio bona et bonae intentionis effectus,
et bonum bono adiunctum plus aliquid ualere quam singula debet.
Quibus respondeo, quod si ponamus plus illud totum ualere quam

---

[a] deus bene utitur B; bene deus utatur CD    [b] atque BCD    [c] signi-
ficamus BCD    [d] in BCD    [e] quam BCD    [f] sit eorum BCD

---

[1] Cf. Abelard, *Expositio* of Romans, i (*PL* 178. 810AB), *Dialogus* (1652B,
1676A–1678C), *Sic et non, cap.* 143 and 157 (1588–90, 1607–9). In the *Dialogus*
(1652B) virtues and vices are considered, unlike actions, to be good and evil *ex
se ipsis proprie et quasi substantialiter.* The author of the *Commentarius Cantabrigiensis* closely followed Abelard's ethical teaching (ed. A. M. Landgraf,
*Commentarius Cantabrigiensis in Epistolas Pauli e Schola P. Abaelardi*, Notre
Dame University Publications in Medieval Studies, ii, 4 parts (Notre Dame,
Indiana, 1937–45)). See the *Commentarius* on 1 Cor. (ii. 256–7), Gal. (ii. 359, 366),
1 Thess. (iii. 520–1), 1 Tim. (iii. 571–2). This writer reports that Abelard believed that a Judaical attitude of mind still persisted; just as Jews thought of
the touching of lepers or corpses as sins, some think of murder and adultery as
sins although they are deeds, Heb. (iv. 775). The author of the *Commentarius*
realized that Abelard's claim that murder and adultery are not sins needed
explanation if it was not to be scorned, Gal. (ii. 366). For criticism of Abelard
see the *Capitula Haeresum, cap.* 13 (*PL* 182. 1054B) and Bernard of Clairvaux,
*Epistola* 188 (*PL* 182. 353C). At the council of Sens Abelard was condemned for
teaching *quod neque opus . . . peccatum sit, Capitulum* 19, ed. J. Leclercq in
*Revue bénédictine*, lxxviii (1968), 104; he denied the charge in his *Confessio fidei*
(*PL* 178. 107–8). Abelard may not have been the first in the twelfth century to
propound that all actions are morally indifferent in themselves, for some writers
of the school of Anselm of Laon discussed the same view. See the so-called

is not fitting that they should be done.[1] For, as the blessed Augustine observed,[2] it is good for evil itself to be, since it too is used well by God, nor does he allow it to be otherwise, although it is itself in no way good. And so when we speak of a man's good intention and of his good work, we in fact distinguish two things, namely intention and work, but one goodness of the intention. For instance, if we speak of a good man and of the son of the good man, we conceive two men, not two goodnesses. So, just as the man is said to be good by his own goodness, but when we speak of the son of the good man by this nothing good is indicated in him, so anyone's intention is called good in itself, although the work is not called good by itself but because it proceeds from a good intention. And so there is one goodness whence the intention as much as the action is called good, just as there is one goodness by which are described the good man and the son of the good man, or one goodness by which we speak of a good man and of a man's good will.

Therefore, let those who usually object that the carrying out of an intention is also worthy of reward, or that it contributes to some increase of reward, consider that their objection is worthless. There are, they say, two goods, the good intention and the performance of the good intention, and good joined to good ought to be worth something more than single goods. To them I reply that, if we suppose that that total is worth more than single goods, surely we

---

*Sententie Anselmi*, ed. F. Bliemetzrieder, *Anselms von Laon systematische Sentenzen*, BGPTMA, xviii. 2–3 (1919), p. 71, and on this Lottin, *Psychologie et morale*, iv. 47 and ii. 421 n. 2; see also the collection entitled *Prima rerum origo*, ed. Lottin, 'Aux origines de l'école théologique d'Anselme de Laon', *Recherches de théologie ancienne et médiévale*, x (1938), 120, and Blomme, *La doctrine du péché*, pp. 14–20. The radical nature of the thesis may be gauged by referring to other writers. Augustine in *Contra Mendacium*, cap. 7, n. 18 (*PL* 40. 528) wrote that the goodness or badness of works varied according to their causes but some, such as blasphemy and theft, were always bad. Anselm of Canterbury in *De conceptu uirginali et de originali peccato* (ed. Schmitt, *Anselmi opera*, ii. 144–5) thought that killing or sexual relations may be just but perjury can only be unjust; he distinguished the action which is momentary from the sin which remains. The *Summa Sententiarum* of the school of Hugh of Saint-Victor presented adultery and perjury as actions which are always bad, *tract.* iii, *cap.* xv (*PL* 176. 113AC), and Peter Lombard followed Augustine in isolating some actions which cannot occur without prevarication and which are *per se mala*, *Sententiarum liber* ii, *dist.* xl, *cap.* 1 (2nd edn., Ad Claras Aquas, 1916), pp. 518–22. See Lottin, *Psychologie et morale*, ii. 421 et seq.

[2] Cf. Augustine, *Enchiridion*, *cap.* 11 and 27 (*PL* 40. 236 and 245), *De ciuitate dei*, xxii. 1, n. 2 (*CCL* 48, p. 806, or *PL* 41. 751), and *Opus imperfectum contra Iulianum*, v. 60 (*PL* 45. 1495), Cf. also Abelard, *Dialogus* (*PL* 178. 1679D–1680B).

singula, numquid ideo maiori remuneratione dignum cogimur concedere? Non utique. Multa quippe sunt tam animata quam inani-
mata, quorum multitudo ad plura utilis est quam unumquotque in
ea multitudine comprehensum, quibus tamen omnibus nulla pror-
5 sus remuneratio debetur. Ecce enim bos boui uel equo adiunctus,
siue lignum ligno uel ferro, res quidem bonae sunt, et plus eorum
multitudo quam singula ualet, cum tamen nichilomnino remunerationis amplius habeat. Reuera, inquies, ita est, quia non sunt talia
quae mereri possint[a] cum ratione careant. Sed numquid opus
10 nostrum rationem habet ut mereri possit?[b] Nequaquam, inquies,
sed tamen mereri opus[c] dicitur quia nos mereri facit, hoc est, dignos
remuneratione uel saltem maiore. Sed[d] hoc profecto supra negauimus, et cur negandum sit, extra ea quae diximus, accipe. Sunt duo
in eodem proposito edificandi domos pauperum, quorum alter
15 deuotionis suae effectum[e] inplet, alter uero pecunia quam pre-
parauerat[f] sibi uiolenter ablata, quod proposuit consummare non
permittitur, nulla sui culpa interueniente, sed sola eum uiolentia
prepediente.[1] Numquid eius meritum id quod exterius est actum
minuere potuit apud Deum aut malicia alterius eum minus accep-
20 tabilem Deo facere[g] potuit, qui quantumcumque potuit[h] pro Deo
fecit? Alioquin pecuniae magnitudo unumquemque meliorem ac
digniorem facere posset, si uidelicet ad meritum uel augmentum
meriti proficere ipsa posset, et quo ditiores homines essent meliores
fieri possent, cum ipsi ex copia diuitiarum deuotioni suae plus
25 possent in operibus addere. Quod quidem existimare, ut opes scilicet
ad ueram beatitudinem uel ad animae dignitatem quicquam ualeant
conferre, uel de meritis pauperum quicquam auferre, summa
est insania. Si autem animam meliorem efficere non potest posses-
sio rerum,[i] utique nec eam Deo[j] cariorem facere potest, nec in
30 beatitudine meriti quicquam[k] obtinere.

## De remuneratione operum exteriorum[l]

Nec tamen negamus in hac uita bonis istis operibus uel malis
aliquid tribui,[m] ut ex presenti retributione in premio uel pena

---

   [a] possunt C *and possibly* D        [b] posset D; aliquid possint B; possit aliquid C         [c] opus: quoque *add.* BC        [d] Sed . . . accipe AE; Sed profecto supra ea quae dicimus habe. negauimus supra et cur negandum sit B; Set
haec profecto iam supra negauimus . . . supra id quod dicimus habe C; Sed hoc
profecto iam supra . . . accipe D        [e] effectum: uel uotum *add.* B        [f] parauerat BCD        [g] deo effecere B; deo efficere D; efficere deo C        [h] ualuit
BCD        [i] diuiciarum BCD        [j] deo cariorem facere AE; deo facere
cariorem B; facere deo cariorem CD        [k] quicquam: de remuneracione
operum temporalium *add.* B        [l] ADE        [m] retribui BC

are not therefore compelled to grant that it is worth a greater reward? Not at all. There are indeed many things, animate as well as inanimate, of which a multitude is useful in more ways than each one contained in that multitude, yet certainly no reward is owing to them all. For consider, an ox joined to an ox or to a horse, or wood joined to wood or iron, are indeed good things and they are worth more together than separately, although none the less they do not by any means have any greater reward. That is indeed so, you will say, because they are not the kinds of things which can gain merit since they lack reason. But does our work have reason by which it may earn merit? In no way, you will say; but on the other hand a work is said to earn merit because it makes us earn merit, that is, be worthy of reward or even of a greater reward. But this we have actually denied above and, apart from what we have said, observe why it should be denied. Two men share the same design to build houses for the poor; one of them fulfils the desire of his devotion, but the other has the money which he had made ready taken away from him by violence and is not permitted to finish what he intended through the intervention of no fault of his own but because violence alone has obstructed him.[1] Could an outward event diminish his merit with God or could the wickedness of someone else make less acceptable to God him who did for God as much as he could do? Otherwise, a great amount of money would be able to make anyone better and more worthy if it could contribute to merit or the increase of merit, and the richer men were, the better they could become, since out of the abundance of their riches they could add in their works more to their devotion. To think this, that is, that wealth can contribute anything to true happiness or to worthiness of soul or can take away anything from the merits of the poor, is the height of madness. But if material possessions cannot make the soul better, neither certainly can they make it dearer to God nor can they obtain any merit in happiness.

### Of the reward of outward works

We do not, however, deny that in this life something is bestowed for those good or bad works, so that by a ready return in the form

---

[1] Cf. Abelard, *Theologia 'Scholarium'*, iii (ed. Cousin, *Opera P. Abaelardi*, ii. 147–8).

amplius ad bona incitemur uel a malis retrahamur, et de aliis alii exempla sumant in faciendis[a] quae conueniunt uel cauendis quae non conueniunt.

### *Quod Deus et homo in Christo uniti non sit melius aliquid quam solus Deus*[b]

Denique ut ad premissa redeamus ubi uidelicet dictum est quia bonum bono additum quiddam[c] melius efficit quam unumquodque eorum[d] per se sit, uide ne illuc usque ducaris ut Christum, id est, Deum et hominem[e] sibi inuicem in persona unitos, melius quiddam dicas quam ipsa Christi diuinitas uel humanitas sit, hoc est, ipse Deus homini unitus, uel ipse homo a Deo assumptus. Constat quippe in Christo tam assumptum hominem quam Deum assumentem esse bonum et utramque substantiam[f] non nisi bonam intelligi posse, sicut et in singulis hominibus tam corporea quam incorporea substantia bona est, licet ad dignitatem uel meritum animae bonitas corporis nichil referat. At uero quis totum id quod Christus dicitur, hoc est simul Deum[g] et hominem, uel quamcunque rerum multitudinem, Deo preferre audebit, tamquam eo melius aliquid[h] esse possit qui et summum bonum est, et ab ipso quicquid boni habent accipiunt omnia? Quamuis enim ad aliquid agendum nonnulla ita necessaria uideantur, ut non id facere Deus sine illis possit tamquam quibusdam amminiculis uel primordialibus causis, nichil tamen, quantacumque[i] sit rerum magnitudo, Deo melius dici potest. Etsi enim bonarum rerum numerus constat[j] ut bonitas in pluribus sit, non ideo bonitatem maiorem esse contingit, ueluti si scientia in pluribus habundet, aut scientiarum numerus crescat, non ideo scientiam cuiusque crescere necesse est ut maior scilicet scientia[k] fiat quam prius. Sic et cum in se Deus bonus sit et innumerabilia creet[l] quae nec esse nec bona esse nisi per illum habent, bonitas per eum in pluribus est ut maior sit numerus bonarum rerum, nulla tamen bonitas eius bonitati preferri uel equari[m] potest. Bonitas quidem in homine et bonitas in Deo est, et cum diuersae sint substantiae uel naturae quibus bonitas inest, nullius tamen rei bonitas diuinae preferri uel equari potest, ac

---

[a] faciendis ... conueniunt ... non conueniunt AE; faciendis que conuenit ... non conuenit BC; faciendis uel cauendis que non conuenit D    [b] ADE
[c] quoddam CD    [d] ipsorum BC    [e] hominem et deum BCD
[f] utramque naturam uel substantiam BCD    [g] deum simul BC    [h] aliquid melius BCD    [i] quantumcumque C; quantamcunque B    [j] crescat B    [k] scientia *om.* A    [l] creet: bona *add.* BCD    [m] adequari uel preferri BC

of profit or penalty we may be spurred on to good things or drawn away from evil, and so that some should follow the examples of others in doing what is fitting or in avoiding what is unfitting.

### That God and man united in Christ are not something better than God alone

To return, then, to earlier remarks, namely where it was said that good added to good produced something better than any one of them on its own, take care lest you are led as far as to say that Christ, that is, God and man joined to each other in a person, is something better than the divinity itself or the humanity of Christ —that is, God himself joined to man or the very man assumed by God. It is clear indeed that in Christ the man assumed, as much as the God who assumes him, is good and each substance can only be understood as good, just as in individual men too the corporeal as much as the incorporeal substance is good, although the goodness of the body is not related to the dignity or merit of the soul. But who truly will venture to put above God the whole that is said to be Christ, that is God and man together, or any aggregate of things whatsoever, as if something can be better than he who is the highest good and from whom all things receive whatever good they have? For although, to do something, there seem to be certain things which are so necessary that God cannot do it without them as supports or as primordial causes, yet, whatever the magnitude of things, nothing can be said to be better than God. For although it is evident that there is a number of good things so that goodness exists in plurality, it does not follow therefore that goodness is greater; for example, if learning is diffused among more people, or if the number of the sciences is increased, each man's learning does not necessarily increase to become greater than it was before. And so, since God is good in himself and creates innumerable things which do not have, except through him, either being or good being, goodness through him exists in plurality; so, the number of good things is greater, yet no goodness can be set above or equated with his goodness. There is in fact goodness in man and goodness in God, and although the substances or natures in which goodness is present are various, yet the goodness of nothing can be set above or equated with the divine; and therefore nothing

per hoc nichil melius, hoc est, maius bonum quam Deus uel eque bonum dicendum est.

## *Quod multitudo bonorum non est melius uno bonorum*[a]

In opere uero et[b] intentione nec bonitatum aut bonarum rerum
5 numerus consistere uidetur. Cum enim bona intentio et bona operatio dicitur, hoc est, ex bona intentione[c] procedens, sola bonitas intentionis designatur,[d] nec in eadem significatione nomen boni retinetur,[e] ut plura bona dicere possimus. Nam et cum dicimus simplicem hominem esse et simplicem dictionem,[f] non ideo
10 haec esse concedimus plura simplicia, cum hoc nomen 'simplex' aliter hic et aliter ibi sumatur.[g] Nemo ergo nos cogat, ut cum bonae intentioni bona operatio additur, bonum bono superaddi tamquam plura sint bona pro quibus remuneratio crescere debeat cum, ut dictum est, nec plura bona recte dicere possimus illa quibus boni
15 uocabulum nequaquam uno modo conuenit.

## *Quod intentione bona sit opus bonum*[h]

Bonam quippe intentionem, hoc est, rectam in se dicimus, operationem uero non quod boni aliquid in se suscipiat, sed quod ex bona intentione procedat.[1] Vnde et ab eodem homine cum in
20 diuersis temporibus idem fiat, pro diuersitate tamen intentionis eius operatio modo bona modo mala dicitur, et ita circa bonum et malum uariari uidetur, sicut haec propositio 'Socrates sedet' uel eius intellectus circa uerum et falsum uariatur, modo Socrate sedente modo stante. Quam quidem permutationem uarietatis[i] circa
25 uerum et falsum ita in his contingere Aristotiles dicit,[2] non quod ipsa quae circa uerum uel[j] falsum mutantur aliquid suscipiant sui mutatione, sed quod res subiecta, id est, Socrates in seipso moueatur, de sessione scilicet ad stationem, uel e conuerso.

---

[a] AE; Quod multitudo bonorum non prefertur uno D      [b] uero et: uero uel C; sibi uel B      [c] uoluntate B      [d] solam bonitatem intencionis designamus BC      [e] retinemus BC      [f] hominem esse et simplicem dictionem: dictionem et simplicem hominem esse BCD      [g] sumatur *om.* B; accipiatur C      [h] A; Quod in intencione bona sit opus bonum E; De opere bono et intentione D; *in B the scribe has left a space where a title could be inserted*      [i] ueritatis B; uariatis C      [j] et BD

---

[1] On the importance of intention in the thought of the rival school of Anselm of Laon see Blomme, *La doctrine du péché*, pp. 68–85.
[2] *A. M. S. Boetii In Categorias Aristotilis lib. IV, De oppositis (PL* 64. 278D–

should be said to be a better, that is, a greater, good than God or equally as good as he.

## That a multitude of good things is not better than one of the good things

Now, in a deed and in an intention there does not seem to exist a number either of goodnesses or of good things. For when one speaks of a good intention and of a good action, that is, one proceeding from the good intention, the goodness of the intention alone is indicated and the name 'good' does not keep the same meaning so as to enable us to say there are more good things. For example, when we say a man is simple and a saying is simple, we do not therefore grant that these are several simple things, since this name 'simple' is employed differently here and differently there. Let no one urge us, therefore, that when a good action is added to a good intention, good is added to good as if there are more good things for which the reward ought to be enlarged, since, as has been said, we cannot rightly say that they are several good things which the word 'good' does not fit in a single way.

## That a work is good by reason of a good intention

In fact we say that an intention is good, that is, right in itself, but that an action does not bear anything good in itself but proceeds from a good intention.[1] Whence when the same thing is done by the same man at different times, by the diversity of his intention, however, his action is now said to be good, now bad, and so it seems to fluctuate around the good and the bad, just as this proposition 'Socrates is seated' or the idea of it fluctuates around the true and the false, Socrates being at one time seated, at another standing. Aristotle says[2] that the way in which this change in fluctuating around the true and the false happens here is not that what changes between being true and being false undergoes anything by this change, but that the subject, that is Socrates, himself moves from sitting to standing or vice versa.

279A, 280AB, 281AB, 282D). Cf. Abelard's *Logica Ingredientibus, Glossae Super Praedicamenta Aristotelis*, ed. B. Geyer, *Peter Abaelards philosophische Schriften*, i BGPTMA, xxi (1919–27), pp. 281–4.

## Vnde bona intentio sit dicenda[a]

Sunt autem qui bonam uel rectam intentionem esse arbitrantur
quotiescumque se aliquis bene agere credit, et Deo[b] placere id quod
facit, sicut et[c] illi qui martires persequebantur, de quibus Veritas
5 in Euangelio,[1] 'Venit hora ut omnis qui interficit uos arbitretur
obsequium se prestare Deo.' Qualium ignorantiae Apostolus quidem[d] compatiens ait,[2] 'Testimonium illis perhibeo quod emulatio-
nem Dei habent, sed non secundum scientiam', hoc est, magnum
feruorem habent[e] ac desiderium in his faciendis quae Deo placere
10 credunt. Sed quia in hoc[f] animi sui zelo uel studio decipiuntur,
erronea est eorum intentio nec simplex est oculus cordis ut
clare uidere queat, hoc est, ab errore sibi prouidere. Diligenter
itaque Dominus, cum secundum intentionem rectam uel non
rectam opera distingueret, oculum mentis, hoc est, intentionem
15 'simplicem' et quasi a sorde purum[g] ut clare uidere possit, aut a
contrario 'tenebrosum' uocauit, cum[h] diceret,[3] 'Si oculus tuus[i]
simplex fuerit, totum corpus tuum lucidum erit', hoc est, si intentio recta fuerit, tota massa operum inde prouenientium, quae
more corporalium rerum uideri possit,[j] erit luce digna, hoc est,
20 bona. Sic e contrario. Non est itaque intentio bona dicenda quia
bona uidetur, sed insuper quia talis est, sicut existimatur,[k] cum
uidelicet illud ad quod tendit, si Deo placere credit, in hac insuper
existimatione sua nequaquam fallatur. Alioquin ipsi etiam infideles
sicut et nos bona opera haberent, cum ipsi etiam non minus quam
25 nos per opera sua se[l] saluari uel Deo placere credant.

## Quod peccatum non est nisi contra conscientiam[m]

Si quis tamen querat utrum illi martirum uel Christi per-
secutores in eo peccarent quod placere Deo credebant, aut illud
sine peccato dimittere possent quod nullatenus esse dimittendum
30 censebant, profecto secundum hoc quod superius peccatum esse
descripsimus,[n] contemptum Dei uel consentire in eo in quo credit
consentiendum non esse, non possumus dicere eos in hoc peccasse
nec ignorantiam cuiusquam uel ipsam etiam infidelitatem, cum qua

---

[a] AE; Vnde bona intencio dicatur D; *in* B *the scribe has left a space here*
[b] deo placere id AE; deo id placere BD; ideo id placere C     [c] et *om.* B;
etiam CD    [d] quoque BCD    [e] habent *om.* BC     [f] hoc in B;
nichil D    [g] puram AE    [h] cum diceret ADE; cum uidelicet dixit *or*
dixerit BC    [i] tuus *om.* BC    [j] possunt CD    [k] exstimatur B;
estimatur C    [l] se . . . deo AE; saluari uel se deo BCD      [m] ADE
[n] descripsimus esse BCD

---

[1] John 16: 2.            [2] Rom. 10: 2.

## *Whence an intention should be said to be good*

There are those who think that an intention is good or right whenever someone believes he is acting well and that what he does is pleasing to God, like the persecutors of the martyrs mentioned by Truth in the Gospel:[1] 'The hour cometh that whosoever killeth you will think that he doth a service to God.' The Apostle had compassion for the ignorance of such as these when he said:[2] 'I bear them witness that they have a zeal for God, but not according to knowledge', that is, they have great fervour and desire in doing what they believe to be pleasing to God. But because they are led astray in this by the zeal or the eagerness of their minds, their intention is in error and the eye of their heart is not simple, so it cannot see clearly, that is, guard itself against error. And so the Lord, in distinguishing works according to right or wrong intention, carefully called the mind's eye, that is, the intention, sound and, as it were, free of dirt so that it can see clearly; or, conversely, dark when he said:[3] 'If thy eye be sound thy whole body shall be full of light', that is, if the intention was right, the whole mass of works coming from it, which like physical things can be seen, will be worthy of the light, that is, good; conversely also. And so an intention should not be called good because it seems to be good but because in addition it is just as it is thought to be, that is, when, believing that one's objective is pleasing to God, one is in no way deceived in one's own estimation. Otherwise even the unbelievers themselves would have good works just like ourselves, since they too, no less than we, believe they will be saved or will please God through their works.

## *That there is no sin unless it is against conscience*

However, if one asks whether those persecutors of the martyrs or of Christ sinned in what they believed to be pleasing to God, or whether they could without sin have forsaken what they thought should definitely not be forsaken, assuredly, according to our earlier description of sin as contempt of God or consenting to what one believes should not be consented to, we cannot say that they have sinned in this, nor is anyone's ignorance a sin or even the

---

[3] Matt. 6: 22–3; Luke 11: 34. Cf. Augustine, *De sermone Domini in monte*, ii. 13, nn. 45–6 (*CCL* 35, pp. 136–8, or *PL* 34. 1289–90) and *Quaest. euangeliorum*, ii. 15 (*PL* 35. 1339).

nemo saluari potest, peccatum esse.[1] Qui enim Christum ignorant
et ob hoc fidem Christianam respuunt, quia eam Deo contrariam
credunt, quem in hoc contemptum Dei habent quod propter Deum
faciunt, et ob hoc bene se[a] facere arbitrantur, presertim cum
5 Apostolus dicat,[b2] 'Si cor nostrum non reprehenderit[c] nos fidu-
ciam habemus apud Deum'?[d] Tamquam si diceret, ubi contra
conscientiam nostram non presumimus, frustra nos apud Deum
de culpa reos statui formidamus, aut si talium ignorantia peccato
minime est ascribenda, quomodo ipse Dominus pro crucifigentibus
10 se orat dicens,[3] 'Pater[e] dimitte illis, non enim sciunt quid faciunt',
uel Stephanus hoc instructus exemplo pro lapidantibus suppli-
cans ait,[4] 'Domine, ne statuas illis hoc peccatum'? Non enim
ignoscendum uidetur ubi culpa non precessit, nec aliud solet dici
ignosci nisi penam condonari quam culpa meruit. Stephanus
15 insuper peccatum patenter appellat quod de ignorantia erat.

## *Quot modis peccatum dicatur?*[f]

Sed ut obiectis plenius respondeamus, sciendum est nomen
peccati diuersis modis accipi.[5] Proprie tamen[g] peccatum dicitur
ipse Dei contemptus uel consensus in malum, ut supra meminimus,
20 a quo paruuli sunt immunes et naturaliter[h] stulti, qui cum merita
non habeant tamquam ratione carentes nichil eis ad peccatum
inputatur, et solummodo per sacramenta[i] saluantur.[6] Dicitur
etiam peccatum hostia pro peccato, secundum quod Apostolus
Dominum Ihesum Christum[j] dicit factum esse peccatum.[7] Pena
25 etiam peccati dicitur peccatum siue maledictum, iuxta quod
dicimus peccatum dimitti, hoc est, penam condonari, et Dominum Ihesum Christum[k] portasse peccata nostra, hoc est, penas[l]
peccatorum nostrorum uel ex eis prouenientes sustinuisse. Sed
cum paruulos originale peccatum dicimus habere uel nos omnes,
30 secundum Apostolum,[8] in Adam peccasse, tale est ac[m] si diceretur
a peccato illius originem[n] nostrae penae uel dampnationis sententiam incurrisse. Opera quoque ipsa peccati, uel quicquid non

---

a se bene BD    b dicit CD    c reprehendit BCD    d apud deum
AE; ad deum C; in domino B; ad dominum D    e Pater . . . sciunt ADE;
Pater ignosce his quia nesciunt BCD    f ADE; *in* B *the scribe has here left
a space*    g namque BC    h naturales BCD    i sacramenta: ecclesie
*add.* BC    j Christum *om.* BC    k Christum *om.* BCD    l penam
ABE    m ac si diceretur *om.* BC    n originalis B; originis C

---

[1] Cf. Abelard, *Expositio* of Romans, v. 13, 14 (*PL* 178. 950C–951A, 959B–D),
where he twice reserves this discussion to the *Ethica*.
[2] 1 John 3: 21.

unbelief with which no one can be saved.[1] For those who do not
know Christ and therefore reject the Christian faith because they
believe it to be contrary to God, what contempt of God have they
in what they do for God's sake and therefore think they do well—
especially since the Apostle says:[2] 'If our heart do not reprehend
us, we have confidence towards God'? As if to say: where we do
not presume against our conscience our fear of being judged
guilty of fault before God is groundless; alternatively, if the ignorance of such men is not to be imputed to sin at all, how does the
Lord pray for his crucifiers, saying:[3] 'Father, forgive them, for
they know not what they do', or Stephen, taught by this example,
say in prayer for those stoning him:[4] 'Lord, lay not this sin to
their charge'? For there seems no need to pardon where there
was no prior fault; nor is pardon usually said to be anything other
than the remission of a punishment earned by a fault. Moreover,
Stephen manifestly calls sin that which came from ignorance.

### In how many ways may we speak of sin?

But in order to reply more fully to objections, it should be realized that the name 'sin' is understood in various ways.[5] Properly,
as we observed above, sin is said to be that contempt of God
or consent to evil from which little children and the naturally
foolish are immune; since they have no merits and, as it were, lack
reason, nothing is imputed to them as sin and they are saved
through the sacraments alone.[6] Sin is also said to be the sacrifice
for sin in the sense in which the Apostle says the Lord Jesus Christ
was made sin.[7] The penalty of sin is also said to be a sin or a curse;
in this sense we say that sin is forgiven, that is, the penalty is
pardoned, and that the Lord Jesus Christ bore our sins, that is,
the penalties of our sins or those arising from them. But when we
say that little ones have original sin or that all of us, as the Apostle
says,[8] have sinned in Adam, the effect is as if to say that by his
sin we have incurred the beginning of our punishment or the sentence of damnation. We sometimes also say that the very works of

---

[3] Luke 23: 34.                                    [4] Acts 7: 59.
[5] Cf. Abelard, *Expositio* of Romans, ii (*PL* 178. 866BC).
[6] Cf. Abelard, *Expositio* of Romans, i and ii (*PL* 178. 810C, 866D et seq.).
[7] 2 Cor. 5: 21; cf. Gal. 3: 13.
[8] Rom. 5: 12, 19; 1 Cor. 15: 22.

recte facimus[a] aut uolumus, non numquam peccata dicimus. Quid
est enim aliquem fecisse peccatum, nisi peccati implesse effectum?
Nec mirum cum e conuerso ipsa peccata uocemus facta, iuxta illud
Athanasii,[1] 'Et reddituri sunt', inquit,[b] 'de factis propriis rationem,
5 et qui bona egerunt ibunt in uitam aeternam, qui uero mala in
ignem aeternum.' Quid est enim 'de factis propriis'? An[c] tamquam
de his tantum quae opere impleuerunt faciendum sit iudicium, ut
plus accipiat in remuneratione qui plus habuerit in opere, uel a
dampnatione[d] sit immunis qui in eo quod intendit effectu caruit,
10 sicut ipse diabolus qui quod presumpsit affectu non obtinuit[e]
effectu? Absit. 'De factis' itaque 'propriis' dicit de consensu eorum
quae implere[f] decreuerunt, hoc est, de peccatis quae apud
Dominum[g] pro opere facti deputantur,[h] cum ille scilicet sic
puniat illa sicuti nos opera. Cum autem Stephanus peccatum
15 dicit[i] quod per ignorantiam in ipsum[j] committebant Iudei, penam
ipsam quam patiebatur ex peccato primorum[k] parentum, sicut et
ceteras prouenientes,[l] uel iniustam eorum actionem quam habe-
bant in lapidando peccatum dixit. Quod quidem rogabat eis non
statui, hoc est, propter hoc eos nec corporaliter puniri. Sepe etenim
20 Deus aliquos hic corporaliter punit nulla eorum culpa hoc exigente, nec tamen sine causa, ueluti cum iustis etiam afflictiones
immittit ad aliquam eorum purgationem uel probationem, uel
aliquos cum[m] affligi permittit ut postmodum hinc liberentur et[n]
ex collato beneficio glorificetur, sicut in illo ceco actum est[o] de
25 quo ipse ait,[2] 'Neque hic peccauit neque parentes eius, ut[p] cecus
nasceretur, sed ut manifestentur opera Dei in illo.' Quis etiam
neget quandoque cum malis parentibus pro culpa eorum innocentes filios[q] periclitari uel affligi, sicut in Sodomis factum[r] est[3]
uel in multis populis sepe contingit, ut quo pena magis extenditur
30 amplius mali terreantur?[s] Quod diligenter beatus[t] Stephanus adtendens, peccatum, hoc est, penam quam tolerabat[u] a Iudeis uel
id quod non recte agebant, orabat eis non statui, hoc est,[v] propter
hoc nec corporaliter puniri.
   In hac quoque sententia Dominus fuerat cum dicebat,[4] 'Pater,

[a] scimus AE    [b] inquit *om.* BC    [c] An *om.* BC    [d] ad dampna-
cionem BC    [e] obtinuit: in *add.* BCD    [f] complere BC    [g] deum
BCE    [h] computatur B    [i] dixit BCD    [j] se BC    [k] *?* propriorum B; priorum C    [l] prouenientem DE *and ?* C    [m] cum aliquos BCD    [n] liberentur et AE; liberetur et D; liberando B; liberanda
C    [o] actum est ceco B; actu est ceco D    [p] ut . . . nasceretur *om.* BC
[q] filios: cum illis pariter *add.* BC; pariter *add.* D    [r] sodomitis actum BC
[s] mali terreantur: mollit reatum B    [t] beatus *om.* BC    [u] tollerabat
BCD    [v] est ACE; eos B; est eos D

[1] Pseudo-Athanasius, *Symbolum 'Quicumque'*, ed. H. Denzinger, *Enchiridion
Symbolorum* (33rd edn., Freiburg, 1965), p. 42.

sin, or whatever we do not rightly do or will, are sins. For what
does it mean for someone to have committed a sin if not that he
as completed the execution of a sin? And this is not surprising,
since conversely we call sins themselves deeds, as does Athanasius
who says:[1] 'And they will render an account of their deeds and
those who have done good things will enter into eternal life, but
those who have done evil will enter into eternal fire.' What in fact
is meant by 'their deeds'? Is it as if judgement is only to be passed
on what they have performed in deed, so that one who has more
by way of deeds will receive more in reward, or that one whose
intentions have lacked an outcome is safe from damnation, such
as the devil himself, who did not obtain in fact what he ventured in
desire? God forbid. He says, then, 'their deeds' in respect of the
consent to what they decided to perform, that is, the sins which
with the Lord are counted as the doing of a deed, since he clearly
punishes those in the way we punish deeds. Furthermore, when
Stephen says that what the Jews committed in ignorance against
him is sin, he meant sin as that penalty which one bore by virtue
of the sin of the first parents, together with other penalties arising
from it, or that unjust action of theirs in stoning him. He asked
that this should not be laid to their charge, that is, that they should
not be physically punished for this. For God often punishes people
here physically although no fault of theirs requires this, but he does
not do this without cause, as, for example, when he sends afflictions even upon the just as a trial or a test for them, or lets some be
afflicted in order later to be freed and to glorify him for the benefit
which he has granted, as happened with the blind man of whom he
said:[2] 'Neither hath this man sinned, nor his parents, that he should
be born blind, but that the works of God should be made manifest in him.' Who, moreover, will deny that sometimes innocent
sons are put to the test or are afflicted along with their evil parents
on account of their fault, as was done in Sodom[3] or as often
happens in many peoples, so that the more widely the punishment is
spread, the more the wicked are affrighted? Blessed, Stephen, carefully considering this, prayed that the sin, that is, the punishment
which he took from the Jews or their wrong action, should not
be laid to their charge, that is, that they should not be physically
punished for this.

The Lord was also in this mind when he said:[4] 'Father, forgive

[2] John 9: 3.          [3] Cf. Gen. 19.          [4] Luke 23: 34.

dimitte illis',[a] id[b] est, ne uindices id quod agunt in me uel corporali pena. Quod quidem fieri rationabiliter posset, si nulla etiam
culpa eorum[c] precessisset, ut ceteri scilicet hoc uidentes uel ipsi
etiam recognoscerent ex pena se non recte in hoc egisse. At uero
5 Dominum decebat hoc suae orationis exemplo nos maxime ad
patientiae uirtutem et ad summae dilectionis exhibitionem ex-
hortari, ut quod ipse docuerat uerbis, nos uidelicet pro inimicis
quoque orare,[1] proprio exemplo nobis exhiberet in opere. Quod
ergo dixit, 'dimitte',[d] non ad culpam precedentem uel[e] contemptum
10 Dei quem hic haberent respexit, sed ad rationem inferendae penae
quae non[f] sine causa, ut diximus, subsequi posset, quamuis culpa
non precessisset, sicut in Propheta contigit qui contra Samariam
missus comedendo egit quod Dominus prohibuerat.[2] In quo
tamen, cum nichil per Dei contemptum presumeret sed per alium
15 Prophetam deceptus, non tam ex reatu culpae quam ex operis
perpetratione innocentia eius mortem incurrit. 'Deus quippe', ut
beatus meminit Gregorius, 'non numquam sententiam mutat,
consilium uero[g] numquam',[3] hoc est, quod precipere uel com-
minari aliqua de causa decreuit, sepe id non implere disponit.
20 Consilium uero eius fixum permanet, hoc est, quod in prescientia[h]
sua disponit ut faciat, numquam efficacia caret. Sicut ergo in
Abraham preceptum de immolatione filii,[4] uel comminationem
Niniuitis[i] factam[5] non tenuit, et sic, ut[j] diximus, sententiam
mutauit, ita predictus propheta, cui prohibuerat comedere in uia,
25 mutari eius sententiam credidit et se maxime delinquere si alium
prophetam non audiret, qui se ad hoc a Domino mitti asserebat ut
eius lassitudinem reficeret cibo.[k] Absque culpa igitur hoc fecit in
quo culpam uitare decreuit, nec ei mors repentina nocuit quem ab
erumpnis uitae presentis liberauit, et multis ad prouidentiam
30 profuit cum iustum sic uideant sine culpa puniri, et illud in eo
impleri[l] quod alibi Domino dicitur,[6] 'Tu Deus cum iustus sis
iuste omnia disponis, cum eum quoque qui non debet puniri
condempnes.'[m] 'Condempnas', inquit, ad mortem non aeternam
sed corporalem. Sicut enim sine meritis nonnulli saluantur, ut

|   |   |   |   |
|---|---|---|---|
| [a] ignosce his BC | [b] hoc BCD | [c] ipsorum BC | [d] ignosce BC |
| [e] uel *om.* E; sed C | | [f] non sine causa ADE; sine causa B; sine culpa C | |
| [g] uero *om.* BCD | [h] presencia BC *and* Cousin | | [i] Niniuitis: in nine- |

uitis B; *in* C in *is marked for erasure*        [j] dic ut A; sicut DE; ita ut BC
[k] cibo reficeret BC        [l] compleri BCD        [m] condempnas BCD

---

[1] Matt. 5: 44; Luke 6: 27–8, 35.
[2] 3 Kings, 13: 11–32.
[3] Gregory the Great, *Moralium in Job lib.* xvi. 10, n. 14 (*PL* 75. 1127B). John
of Salisbury made use of Gregory's view in his *Letter* 31, ed. W. J. Millor and
H. E. Butler, revised by C. N. L. Brooke, *The Letters of John of Salisbury*, i

them', that is, do not avenge what they do to me, even with physical punishment. This could in fact have been done reasonably
even if there had been no prior fault on their part, in order that
others seeing this, or even they themselves, should recognize
by punishment that they had not acted rightly in this. But it
suited the Lord by the example of his prayer to urge us above all to
the virtue of patience and to display the highest love, so that what
he had taught us verbally, namely to pray also for our enemies,[1]
he showed us in practice by his own example. So his saying 'forgive' refers not to an anterior fault or contempt of God which
they might have here, but to the reason for inflicting punishment,
which, as we have said, could have followed justifiably although
there had been no anterior fault, as happened with the Prophet
who, sent against Samaria, by eating did what the Lord had forbidden.[2] But since in this he ventured nothing through contempt
of God but was deceived by the other Prophet, his innocence incurred death not so much through the guilt of a fault as through
the perpetration of a deed. As the blessed Gregory has observed,
God certainly 'sometimes changes his decision but never his purpose',[3] that is, he often arranges not to go through with what he
has decided for some reason to command or to threaten. But his
purpose remains fixed, that is, what in his prescience he arranges
to do never lacks efficacy. So, just as he did not maintain the command to Abraham to sacrifice his son,[4] or the threat made to the
Ninevites,[5] and thus, as we have said, changed his decision, so the
above-mentioned Prophet, whom he forbade to eat on the way,
believed his decision to be changed, and that he would offend
exceedingly if he did not listen to the other Prophet who said he
was sent by the Lord in order to refresh his weariness with food.
So he acted without fault in a determination to avoid fault and
sudden death did not harm him whom the Lord freed from the
toils of the present life; this helped many as a precaution, since
they thus saw a just man punished without fault and a fulfilment
of what is said to the Lord elsewhere:[6] 'For so much as thou art
just, O God, thou orderest all things justly: since thou dost not
condemn him who deserveth not to be punished.' 'Condemn', he
says, not to eternal but to bodily death. For just as some, such as

---

(Nelson's Medieval Texts, 1955), 49, and in his *Policraticus*, ii. 26, ed. C. C. J.
Webb, i (Oxford, 1909), 139.

[4] Gen. 22.          [5] Jonah 3.          [6] Wisdom 12: 15.

paruuli, et sola gratia uitam assecuntur aeternam, ita non absurdum est non nullos penas corporales sustinere quas non meru-
erunt, sicut et de paruulis constat sine babtismi[a] gratia defunctis,
qui tam corporali quam aeterna morte dampnantur,[b] et multi[c]
5 etiam innocentes affliguntur. Quid itaque mirum si crucifigentes
Dominum ex illa iniusta actione, quamuis eos ignorantia excusat[d]
a culpa, penam, ut diximus, temporalem non irracionabiliter incurrere possent? Atque ideo dictum est, 'dimitte[e] illis', hoc est,
penam quam hinc, ut diximus, non irracionabiliter incurrere
10 possent,[f] ne inferas.

Sicut autem quod isti per ignorantiam egerunt uel ipsa etiam
ignorantia peccatum proprie, hoc est, contemptus Dei, non dicitur,[1] ita nec infidelitas, quamuis ipsa necessario aeternae uitae
aditum adultis ratione iam utentibus intercludat. Ad dampna-
15 tionem quippe sufficit[g] Euangelio non credere, Christum ignorare, sacramenta aecclesiae non suscipere, quamuis hoc non tam[h]
per maliciam quam per ignorantiam fiat. De qualibus[i] et Veritas
ait,[2] 'Qui non credit iam iudicatus est.' Et Apostolus,[3] 'Et qui
ignorat', inquit, 'ignorabitur.'

20 Cum autem dicimus ignoranter nos peccare, hoc est, tale quid
quod non conuenit facere, 'peccare' non in contemptu sed in
operatione sumimus. Nam et philosophi peccare dicunt incon-
uenienter aliquid facere[j] seu dicere,[k] quamuis illud nichil ad
offensam Dei uideatur pertinere. Vnde Aristotiles in *ad aliquid*,

---

[a] *This spelling is observed in* A *and* E    [b] puniuntur BCD    [c] multi
etiam (etiam *om.* E) innocentes affliguntur AE; multis passionibus innocentes
etiam (etiam Innocentes D) affliguntur BCD    [d] excuset BC    [e] ignosce
BC    [f] possunt C *and ?* B    [g] sufficit: eis *add.* BC    [h] tam *om.*
AE    [i] qualibus ACE; libet B; qualibet D    [j] facere *om.* ADE
[k] seu dicere *om.* BC

---

[1] Although the expression 'invincible ignorance' is familiar to Abelard (see
the *Problemata Heloissae*, no. 13 (*PL* 178. 695A, 696A), *Theologia 'Scholarium'*,
iii (ed. Cousin, *Opera P. Abaelardi*, ii. 148), and the *Ethica*, below, p. 66; cf.
also the *Monita ad Astralabium* (*PL* 178, 1761CD)) and although in the *Confessio
fidei* Abelard distinguishes between invincible ignorance and negligence (*PL* 178.
107–8 and see the *Ethica*, below, p. 66), it may be said that Abelard in the
*Ethica* does not sufficiently indicate that there are different kinds of ignorance,
some less excusable than others. See Blomme, *La doctrine du péché*, pp. 147–54,
and S. Kuttner, *Kanonistische Schuldlehre von Gratian bis auf die Dekretalen
Gregors IX*. Studi e testi, lxiv (Vatican City, 1935), 137–8. For the needed
distinction of kinds of ignorance see the *Sentences* of Roland Bandinelli, ed. A. M.
Gietl, *Die Sentenzen Rolands* (Freiburg i. B., 1891), pp. 125–6, and S. Kuttner,
*Kanonistische Schuldlehre*, pp. 145–7.

Abelard's application of the excuse of ignorance to the crucifiers of Christ
aroused criticism. Bernard of Clairvaux in the *De baptismo, cap.* 4 (*PL* 182.

little children, are saved without merits and by grace alone attain
to eternal life, so it is not absurd that some should undergo bodily
punishments which they have not deserved, as is evident with little
children who die without the grace of baptism and are condemned
to bodily as well as to eternal death; and even many innocents are
cast out. So what is surprising if those who crucified the Lord were
able by that unjust action, as we said, to incur temporal punishment with reason, even though ignorance excuses them from
fault? And that is why it was said 'forgive them', that is, do not
inflict the punishment which they could, as we said, have reasonably incurred.

Moreover, just as what they did through ignorance or even ignorance itself is not said to be properly sin, that is, contempt of God,[1]
neither is unbelief, even though this necessarily blocks the entry
to eternal life for adults now using reason. It is sufficient for
damnation not to believe in the Gospel, to be ignorant of Christ,
not to receive the sacraments of the Church, even though this
occurs not so much through wickedness as through ignorance. And
of such Truth says:[2] 'He that doth not believe is already judged.'
And the Apostle says:[3] 'And any man who knows not shall not be
known.'

However, when we say we sin ignorantly, that is, do something
which is unfitting, we use 'sin' not in the sense of contempt but of
action. For the philosophers also say that to sin is to do or say
something unsuitably, even though it does not seem to amount to
an affront to God. Hence Aristotle, at 'to something', when he

1041C–1042D)—a work which is generally thought to be concerned with the teaching of Abelard or of one of his disciples—had already stressed the sinfulness of
the crucifixion; see on this L. Ott, *Untersuchungen zur theologischen Briefliteratur
der Frühscholastik*, BGPTMA, xxxiv (1937), pp. 539–43, and Blomme, *La
doctrine du péché*, pp. 275–8. William of Saint-Thierry, *Disputatio, cap.* 13 (*PL*
180. 282BC; see too *Epistola* 326 in *PL* 182. 532B) and the anonymous compiler
of *Capitula Haeresum, cap.* 11 (*PL* 182. 1053B) both produced passages which are
not to be found in Abelard's extant writings and which assert that Christ's
crucifiers did not sin, whereas Abelard in the *Ethica* exempts them from *culpa*
without explicitly also exempting them from sin in the broader sense of the word.
At the council of Sens he was condemned for teaching *quod non peccauerunt
qui Christum ignorantes crucifixerunt, et quod non sit culpae adscribendum
quidquid fit per ignorantiam, Capitulum* 9, ed. J. Leclercq in *Revue bénédictine*,
lxxviii (1968), 104. In the *Confessio fidei* (*PL* 178. 107–8) Abelard affirmed that
Christ's crucifiers committed *grauissimum peccatum*. See Blomme, *La doctrine
du péché*, pp. 279–88, and, on the sin of ignorance after Abelard, see Lottin,
*Psychologie et morale*, III. i. 18 et seq.
    [2] John 3: 18.                                                    [3] 1 Cor. 14: 38.

cum de uiciosa relatiuorum assignatione loqueretur, ait,[1] 'At
uero aliquotiens non uidebitur conuerti[a] nisi conuenienter ad
quod dicitur assignetur. Si enim peccet is qui assignat, ut ala si[b]
assignetur aui,[c] non conuertitur ut sit auis alae.' Si ergo isto modo
5 peccatum dicamus omne quod uiciose agimus uel contra salutem
nostram habemus, utique et infidelitas et ignorantia eorum quae
ad salutem credi necesse est peccata dicemus, quamuis ibi nullus
Dei contemptus[d] uideatur.[e] Proprie tamen peccatum illud dici
arbitror quod nusquam sine culpa contingere potest. Ignorare
10 uero Deum uel non ei credere uel opera ipsa quae non recte fiunt,
multis sine culpa possunt accidere. Siquis enim Euangelio uel
Christo non credit,[f] quia predicatio ad ipsum non peruenerit,
iuxta[g] illud Apostoli,[2] 'Quomodo credent ei quem non audierunt?
Quomodo autem audient sine predicante?' Quae hinc ei culpa
15 potest assignari quod non credit? Non credebat Cornelius in
Christum donec Petrus ad eum missus de hoc ipsum instruxit.[3]
Qui quamuis antea lege naturali Deum recognosceret atque dilige-
ret, ex quo meruit de oratione sua exaudiri[h] et Deo acceptas elemo-
sinas habere, tamen si eum ante fidem Christi de hac luce migrasse
20 contingeret, nequaquam ei uitam promittere auderemus, quantum-
cunque bona opera eius[i] uiderentur, nec eum fidelibus sed magis
infidelibus connumeraremus, quantocunque studio[j] salutis esset
occupatus. 'Abyssus quippe multa Dei iudicia sunt',[4] qui non numquam reluctantes uel minus de salute sua sollicitos trahit et se offe-
25 rentes uel ad credendum paratiores profundissimo dispensationis
suae[k] consilio respuit. Sic[l] enim illum se offerentem et dicentem[5]
'Magister, sequar te quocumque ieris' reprobauit, et alterum
excusantem se per sollicitudinem quam habuit de patre[m] nec ad
horam in hac pietatis excusatione tolerauit.[6] Denique et quarum-
30 dam ciuitatum obstinationem increpans ait,[7] 'Ve tibi, Corozaim,
ue tibi, Bethsaida, quia si in Tyro et Sidone uirtutes factae fuissent[n]
quae factae sunt in uobis, iam olim in cilicio et cinere penitentiam

[a] conuerti ADE; conueniens asignacio B; conueniens assignacio C. *In C these
words are added over an erasure*      [b] si ... convertitur *om.* B      [c] auis
ADE; aui C, *though a letter after* i *has been erased*      [d] contemptus dei BCD
[e] uidebatur AE      [f] credat BCD      [g] Iuxta BCD      [h] audiri BC
[i] eius opera BC      [j] studio: inquirende BC      [k] sue dispensationis
BCD      [l] Sic ... dicentem ADE; Sic et offere⟨n⟩tem se illum et dicentem
B; Sic enim offerentem illum se et dicentem C      [m] de patre habebat BCD
[n] uirtutes facte fuissent AC; uirtutes facte B; facte fuissent uirtutes D; uirtutes
facte essent E

[1] A. M. S. *Boetii In Categorias Aristotilis lib.* ii, *De relatiuis* (PL 64. 223AB).

spoke of the wrongful correlation of relatives, said:[1] 'Sometimes, however, there appears to be no reciprocity unless there is a suitable correlation with what is said. For if one sins in making a correlation—for example, if wing is correlated with bird—the correlation is not reciprocal for bird is not correlative with wing.' So if in this way we call sin whatever we do wrongly, or whatever we have that conflicts with our salvation, we shall certainly say that both unbelief and ignorance of what it is necessary to believe for salvation are sins, even though no contempt of God appears there. However, I think that sin is properly said to be that which can nowhere happen without fault. But ignorance of God or unbelief in him, or those works which are not done rightly, can happen to many people without fault. For if someone does not believe in the Gospel or in Christ for the reason that no preaching has reached him—as the Apostle says:[2] 'How shall they believe him of whom they have not heard? And how shall they hear without a preacher?' —what fault can be ascribed to him on account of his unbelief? Cornelius did not believe in Christ until Peter, when sent to him, taught him about Christ.[3] Although previously by the natural law he recognized and loved God, and through this deserved to be heard in his prayer and to have his alms accepted by God, yet if he had happened to depart from this light before he believed in Christ, we should by no means dare to promise him life however good his works seemed, nor should we number him with the faithful but rather with the unfaithful, however eagerly he had worked for his salvation. 'The judgements of God are a great deep';[4] he sometimes brings to himself the reluctant or those less solicitous for their salvation and rejects in the deepest design of his dispensation those who offer themselves or are more ready to believe. So indeed he reproved the man who offered himself and said:[5] 'Master, I will follow thee whithersoever thou shalt go' and did not tolerate even for an hour the filial excuse of the other man who excused himself on account of the anxiety he had over his father.[6] And finally he said rebuking the obstinacy of certain cities:[7] 'Woe to thee Corozain! Woe to thee Bethsaida! For if in Tyre and Sidon had been wrought the miracles that have been wrought in you, they had long ago done penance in sackcloth and ashes.' Consider, he

---

[2] Rom. 10: 14.　　　　　[3] Cf. Acts 10.　　　　　[4] Ps. 35: 7.
[5] Matt. 8: 19; cf. Luke 9: 57–60.
[6] Matt. 8: 21–2.　　　　　　　　　　　[7] Matt. 11: 21.

egissent.' Ecce illis obtulit non solum predicationem suam uerum etiam miraculorum exhibitionem, quas tamen prius nouerat non esse credituras. Has uero gentilium alias ciuitates quas ad fidem suscipiendam faciles esse non ignorabat, sua tunc uisitatione non
5 censuit dignas. In quibus quidem cum aliqui, subtracto sibi predicationis uerbo, tamen ad suscipiendum ipsum parati, perierunt, quis hoc eorum imputet culpae quod nulla[a] negligentia uidemus accidere? Et tamen hanc eorum infidelitatem in qua defuncti sunt ad dampnationem[b] sufficere dicimus, quamuis huius cecitatis, in qua
10 Dominus eos dimiserit, causa minus nobis appareat. Quam profecto siquis peccato eorum sine culpa asscribat, fortassis licebit, cum absurdum ei uideatur tales sine peccato dampnari.

Nos tamen proprie peccatum, ut sepe iam meminimus, illud solum dici arbitramur quod in culpa negligentiae consistit, nec in
15 aliquibus esse potest, cuiuscumque sint aetatis, quin ex hoc dampnari mereantur. Non credere uero Christum, quod infidelitatis est, quomodo paruulis uel his quibus non est annuntiatum culpae debeat asscribi non uideo, uel quicquid per ignorantiam inuincibilem fit, cui uel[c] preuidere[d] non ualuimus, ueluti siquis forte
20 hominem quem non uidet in silua sagitta interficiat dum feris uel auibus sagittandis intendit.[1] Quem tamen dum peccare per ignorantiam dicimus, sicut nos quandoque fatemur non solum in consensu uerum etiam in cogitatione, locutione, operatione peccare, hoc loco non proprie pro culpa ponimus, sed large accipimus
25 pro eo scilicet quod nos facere minime conuenit, siue id per errorem siue per negligentiam uel quocumque modo inconuenienti fiat. Tale est ergo per ignorantiam peccare, non culpam in hoc habere, sed quod nobis non conuenit facere, uel peccare in cogitatione, hoc est, uoluntate, quod nos uelle minime conuenit, uel in locu-
30 tione aut in operatione loqui nos uel agere quod non oportet, etsi per ignorantiam nobis inuitis illud eueniat. Sic et illos qui persequebantur Christum uel suos quos persequendos credebant per operationem peccasse[e] dicimus, qui tamen grauius per[f] culpam peccassent si contra conscientiam eis parcerent.

---

[a] nulla: eorum *add.* BCD      [b] dampnationem: eis *add.* BD, eorum *add.*
C      [c] scilicet BCD      [d] prouidere BC      [e] peccasse per operacionem
BCD      [f] per *om.* A

offered them not only his preaching but also a show of miracles, both of which he knew in advance would not be believed. But these other cities of the Gentiles, which he knew would be disposed to receive faith, he did not then consider to be worth a visit by him. In these cities, when some perished who had the word of preaching kept away from them yet were ready to receive it, who will impute this to their fault? We see that it happened without negligence. And yet we say that this unbelief of theirs in which they died sufficed for damnation, even though the reason for this blindness in which the Lord may have left them is less apparent to us. If anyone actually ascribes this to a sin of theirs which had no fault, he may perhaps do so, since it may seem absurd to him that such should be damned without sin.

We, however, think, as we have now often mentioned, that sin should properly be said to be only that which consists in the fault of negligence and it cannot be present in any, whatever their age, without their deserving to be damned for it. But I do not see how, in the case of small children or of those to whom this was un-announced, not to believe in Christ, which is unbelief, should be ascribed to fault, or anything which is done through invincible ignorance or which we could not foresee, as, for instance, if some-one with an arrow happens to kill a man whom he does not see in a wood while endeavouring to shoot wild animals or birds.[1] How-ever, while we say he sins in ignorance, just as we sometimes say we sin not only in consent but also in thought, word, deed, in this case we do not use it in the proper sense as fault but understand it broadly, that is, as what is not at all fitting for us to do, whether it be done through error or negligence or any unsuitable way. This therefore is sinning in ignorance, not having here a fault but doing what is not fitting for us; or sinning in thought, that is, willing, what is by no means fitting for us to will, or for us to say or to do in speech or in deed what is not proper, even though it comes to us unwillingly through ignorance. And so we say that those who persecuted Christ or his disciples, who they thought should be persecuted, sinned in deed, yet they would have sinned more gravely in fault if they had spared them against their own con-science.

---

[1] Cf. Abelard, *Theologia christiana*, iii. 7 (*PL* 178. 1109BD). Hunting accidents were common enough: Miles, earl of Hereford, died in this way in 1143 and so perhaps did William Rufus in 1100.

### Vtrum omne peccatum sit interdictum[a]

Queritur autem utrum omne peccatum nobis Deus interdicat.
Quod si recipiamus, uidetur hoc irrationabiliter agere cum nequaquam uita ista sine peccatis saltim uenialibus transigi possit.
5 Si enim omnia nos cauere peccata[b] precepit,[c] nos autem omnia
cauere non possumus, utique nequaquam, sicut ipse promisit,
iugum suaue nobis uel onus leue imponit,[1] sed quod longe uires
transcendens[d] nostras minime portare ualemus, sicut et de iugo
legis Petrus Apostolus profitetur.[2] Quis enim a uerbo saltim
10 ocioso semper sibi preuidere[e] potest ut in eo numquam excedens
perfectionem illam teneat de qua Jacobus ait,[3] 'Siquis in uerbo
non offendit, hic perfectus est uir'? Qui etiam cum premisisset,[f3]
'In multis offendimus omnes',[g] et alius magnae dicat[h] perfectionis
Apostolus,[4] 'Si dixerimus quia[i] peccatum non habemus nos ipsos
15 seducimus et ueritas in nobis non est', quam difficile, immo impossibile, nostrae infirmitati[j] uideatur immunes omnino a peccato
manere neminem latere reor,[k] ita, inquam, si peccati uocabulum
large, ut diximus, accipientes illa etiam uocemus peccata quaecumque non conuenienter facimus. Si[l] autem proprie peccatum
20 intelligentes solum Dei contemptum dicamus peccatum, potest
reuera sine hoc uita ista transigi, quamuis cum maxima difficultate.
Nec profecto illud,[m] ut supra meminimus, nobis a Deo prohibitum
est nisi consensus mali quo[n] Deum contempnimus, etiam cum
de opere preceptio fieri uidetur, sicut superius exposuimus, ubi[o]
25 etiam ostendimus aliter[p] nequaquam a nobis precepta posse sua
custodiri.

Peccatorum[q] autem alia uenialia dicuntur et quasi leuia, alia
dampnabilia sive grauia.[5] Rursus dampnabilium quaedam criminalia dicuntur quae in illis[r] personam infamem uel criminosam
30 facere habent si in audientiam[s] ueniant, quaedam uero minime.[6]
Venialia quidem uel leuia peccata sunt, quando in eo consentimus
cui non consentiendum esse scimus, sed tunc tamen non[t] occurrit

---

[a] AE; Vtrum omne peccatum sit prohibitum D; *in B the scribe has left a
vacant space*    [b] peccata . . . cauere *om.* B    [c] precipit CD    [d] nostras
transcendens (transcendens nostras D) portare minime BCD    [e] prouidere
BCD    [f] premiserit C *and* ? B    [g] offendimus omnes *add. over an
erasure in* C; omnes *om.* D    [h] perfectionis dicat BC    [i] quoniam BC
[j] immortalitati B    [k] arbitror B    [l] Sin BC    [m] aliud BCD
[n] mali quo AE; mali in quo BC; m aliquo D    [o] Vbi ABE    [p] aliter
. . . custodiri AE; nequaquam aliter . . . (sua *om.*) custodiri BD; nequaquam
a nobis precepta aliter posse custodiri C    [q] D *provides a heading here*:
Distinccio peccatorum    [r] in illis AE; uidelicet BCD    [s] audientiam AE;
noticiam BCD    [t] memorie non occurrit BC

## *Whether every sin is forbidden*

It is furthermore asked whether God forbids every sin in us. If we admit this, he seems to do it unreasonably, since this life can by no means be spent without at least venial sins. If in fact he has commanded us to guard against all sins, we nevertheless cannot guard against them all; at any rate he does not lay on us, as he himself promised, a sweet yoke and a light burden[1] but one which far exceeds our strength and which we cannot bear at all, just as the Apostle Peter professed in respect of the yoke of the Law.[2] For who can always be on his guard against even an idle word, so that never exceeding in this he maintains that perfection of which James says:[3] 'If any man offend not in word, the same is a perfect man'? Since he had also said:[3] 'in many things we all offend' and since another Apostle of great perfection says:[4] 'If we say that we have no sin we deceive ourselves and the truth is not in us', how difficult, nay impossible, it seems for our weakness to stay wholly free from sin is, I imagine, hidden from no one. So I say, if we take the word 'sin' broadly, as we said, we shall also call sins whatever we do unfittingly. If, however, understanding sin properly we say that sin is only contempt of God, this life can truly be passed without it, although with very great difficulty. Nor, as we have mentioned above, is anything prohibited to us by God except the consent to evil by which we offer contempt to God, even when a command seems to be made about a deed, as we showed above, where we also showed that otherwise his commands could not be kept by us at all.

Some sins are said to be venial and, as it were, light, others damnable or grave.[5] Again, some damnable sins are said to be criminal and are capable of making a person infamous or criminous if they come to the hearing of other people, but some are not in the least.[6] Sins are venial or light when we consent to what we know should not be consented to, but when, however, what we

---

[1] Matt. 11: 30.          [2] Acts 15: 10.          [3] James 3: 2.
[4] 1 John 1: 8.
[5] This distinction owed much to Augustine, *Enchiridion*, cap. 69–71 (*PL* 40. 265); see too *Contra duas epistolas Pelagianorum*, i. 14, n. 28 (*PL* 44. 563–4).
[6] On the distinction between *peccatum* and *crimen* (as moral and juridical notions) see Gregory the Great, *Moralia*, xxi. 12, n. 19 (*PL* 76. 201). See also S. Kuttner, *Kanonistische Schuldlehre von Gratian bis auf die Dekretalen Gregors IX.*, Studi e testi, lxiv (Vatican City, 1935), pp. 4–6.

memoriae illud quod scimus.[1] Multa quippe scimus etiam[a] dor-
mientes uel quando eorum non[b] recordamur. Non enim dormiendo
nostras amittimus scientias uel stulti efficimur aut, cum uigilamus,[c]
sapientes efficimur. Quandoque itaque uel in uaniloquium uel in
5 superfluum esum uel potum[d] consentimus, quod tamen nequaquam
esse faciendum scimus, sed tunc minime recordamur[e] quod non
sit faciendum. Tales itaque consensus quos per obliuionem incurrimus uenialia aut leuia dicuntur peccata, hoc est, non magnae
satisfactionis pena[f] corrigenda, ut uel extra aecclesiam positi uel
10 graui abstinentia pressi ob[g] talia plectamur. Pro quibus quidem
negligentiis penitentibus dimittendis uerba cottidianae confessionis
frequentamus, in qua minime commemoratio grauiorum[h] culparum
facienda est, sed tantum leuiorum. Neque enim ibi dicere[i] debemus:[j]
peccaui in periurio, in homicidio, in adulterio, et consimilibus[k]
15 quae dampnabilia et grauiora dicuntur peccata.[2] Haec quippe
non per obliuionem sicut illa incurrimus, sed tamquam ex studio et
deliberatione committimus, abhominabiles etiam Deo effecti iuxta
illud Psalmistae,[3] 'Abhominabiles facti sunt in studiis suis', quasi
execrabiles et ualde odibiles[l] ex his in quibus scienter presump-
20 serunt. Horum autem alia criminalia dicuntur, quae per effectum
cognita neuo[m] magnae culpae hominem maculant et eius famae
plurimum detrahunt, ut consensus periurii, homicidii, adulterii,
quae plurimum aecclesiam scandalizant. Cum uero supra quam
necesse est cibo indulgemus, uel non mediocri cultu ex uana gloria
25 nos adornamus, et si hoc[n] scienter presumimus, non haec crimini as-
scribuntur, et apud multos plus laudis habent quam uituperationis.

[a] etiam scimus BC      [b] minime BC      [c] euigilamus BD; euigilamur C
[d] uel potum *om.* B      [e] recordabamur . . . esset ADE      [f] satisfactione
pene BC      [g] ob *om.* BC      [h] grauiorum . . . leuiorum AE; grauiarum
. . . leuiarum D; de grauioribus culpis . . . est (*om.* B) . . . de leuioribus BC
[i] ibi dicere ADE; indicere B; dicere C      [j] debemus: confiteor deo et uobis
fratres quia *add.* BC      [k] et consimilibus: in consensu B      [l] ociosi
BD; odiosi C      [m] neuo AE *and add.* C *over an erasure*; *om.* B; neruo D
[n] hoc ACDE

[1] On the question whether Abelard understood venial sin to be sin proper

know does not occur to our memory.[1] We know many things even when asleep or when we do not remember them. For we do not lay aside our knowledge or become foolish when sleeping or become wise when awake. And so sometimes we consent either to boasting or to excessive eating or drinking, yet we know this should by no means be done, but we do not remember then that it should not be done. So such consents as we fall into through forgetfulness are said to be venial or light sins, that is, not to be corrected with a penalty of great satisfaction such as being punished on account of them by being put outside the church or being burdened with a heavy abstinence. Indeed to have such carelessness forgiven by repenting, we frequently resort to the words of the daily confession in which mention should by no means be made of graver faults, but only of lighter ones. For we should not say there: I have sinned in perjury, in murder, in adultery, and such like, which are said to be damnable and weightier sins.[2] We do not incur these like the others through forgetfulness, but commit them with assiduity, as it were, and with deliberation, and are made abominable to God also, according to the Psalmist:[3] 'They are become abominable in their ways', as if execrable and exceedingly hateful for what they have knowingly presumed. Others of these sins are called criminal which, known through their effect, blot a man with the mole of a great fault and greatly detract from his reputation; such are consent to perjury, murder, adultery which greatly scandalize the church. But when we indulge in food beyond what is necessary or in vanity adorn ourselves with immoderate dress, even if we presume this knowingly, these are not classed as crime and among many receive more praise than blame.

according to his definition of the latter see Blomme, *La doctrine du péché*, pp. 122–8, who answers affirmatively.

[2] The ninth-century Sacramentary of Amiens contained a form of *Confiteor* according to which the priest on approaching the altar confesses to God that he had sinned, *inter alia*, in fornication and perjury and all their attendant vices, but according to J. A. Jungmann, *Missarum Solemnia*, i (3rd ed., Vienna, 1952), 386–402, the eleventh and twelfth centuries witnessed the establishment of dialogue forms of confession according to which those present at Mass or at the Office collectively and daily confessed to each other as well as to God and did so in a less particularized way. None the less, some twelfth-century writers felt obliged to stress that the confession of specific sins, such as murder or adultery, should not occur openly during the confession made at Mass. See, for example, John Beleth, *Rationale diuinorum officiorum*, cap. 33 (*PL* 202. 43C), Sicard of Cremona, *Mitrale*, iii. 2 (*PL* 213. 95A), Pope Innocent III, *De sacro altaris mysterio*, ii. 13 (*PL* 217. 306A).　　　　　　[3] Ps. 13: 1.

*Vtrum melius sit a leuioribus culpis quam grauioribus abstinere*[a]

Sunt qui perfectius et[b] ideo melius dicunt prouidere a uenialibus peccatis quam a criminalibus, eo quod difficilius id uideatur et maioris studii sollicitudine indigeat. Quibus primum illud re-
5 spondeo Tullianum, 'Quod si laboriosum non ideo gloriosum.'[1] Alioquin maioris meriti apud Dominum[c] essent qui graue iugum legis portauerunt quam qui euangelica libertate deseruiunt, quia timor penam habet quem[d] perfecta karitas foras mittit,[2] et quae- cumque timore aguntur plus in opere laborant quam quos karitas
10 spontaneos facit. Vnde laborantes et oneratos ad suaue iugum et onus leue sumendum Dominus exhortatur[3] ut uidelicet de serui- tute legis, qua premebantur, ad libertatem transeant Euangelii, et qui a timore inceperant karitate[e] consummentur[f] quae sine difficultate omnia suffert, omnia sustinet.[4] Nichil quippe amanti
15 difficile,[g] maxime cum non carnalis sed spiritualis amor Dei tanto est fortior quanto uerior. Quis etiam nesciat difficilius nobis prouideri[h] a pulice quam ab hoste, uel ab offendiculo parui lapidis quam magni? Sed numquid ideo id cauere quod difficilius est melius aut salubrius iudicamus? Non utique. Quare? Quia quod
20 difficilius est cauere, minus potest nocere. Sic ergo, etsi ponamus difficilius a uenialibus peccatis quam a criminalibus prouidere,[i] plus tamen haec[j] uitari[k] quae periculosiora sunt conuenit, et quae maiorem merentur penam, et quibus amplius[l] offendi credi- mus Deum, et magis ei ea displicere. Quo enim amplius ipsi per
25 amorem inheremus, ea sollicitius cauere debemus quibus magis offenditur et quae ipse magis improbat. Qui enim uere aliquem diligit non tam dampnum suum quam offensam amici uel con- temptum cauere satagit, iuxta illud Apostoli,[5] 'Karitas non querit quae sua sunt.' Et rursum,[6] 'Nemo quod suum est querat sed quod
30 alterius.' Si ergo non tam pro nostro dampno quam pro Dei offensa debemus cauere peccata, profecto plus ea cauenda sunt in quibus magis offenditur. Quod si illam quoque poeticam adtendamus sententiam de morum scilicet honestate, 'oderunt peccare boni uirtutis amore',[7] tanto maiori odio quaelibet sunt habenda quanto

---

[a] ADE; D *and* E *read*: quam a grauioribus *and* D *offers* An *in place of* Utrum
[b] atque BC       [c] deum BCDE       [d] quam BD; et perfecta caritas foris mittit timorem C       [e] karitate: in caritate BCD       [f] consummantur CD *and ?* B       [g] difficile: est *add.* BCD       [h] prouidere BCD       [i] quam . . . prouidere: prouidere quam a criminalibus BCD       [j] hoc ABE [k] uitari: quam *omisi*       [l] amplius . . . deum (*om.* D) ADE; amplius deum offendi credimus BC

---

[1] *Rhetorica ad C. Herennium*, iv. 4.       [2] Cf. 1 John 4: 18.
[3] Matt. 11: 28–30.       [4] Cf. 1 Cor. 13: 7.       [5] 1 Cor. 13: 5.
[6] 1 Cor. 10: 24.       [7] Horace, *Epistles*, i. 16. 52.

## Whether it is better to abstain from lighter faults than from graver

There are people who say it is more perfect and therefore better to beware of venial than of criminal sins because it seems more difficult and requires the solicitude of greater endeavour. To them I reply first with Tully: 'If it is laborious, it is not therefore glorious.'[1] Otherwise they who bore the heavy yoke of the Law would be of greater merit before the Lord than they who serve with evangelical freedom, because fear, which perfect charity casts out,[2] has pain and they toil more in their work when all things are done in fear than those whom charity makes spontaneous. Whence the Lord exhorts those who labour and are burdened to take up a sweet yoke and a light burden,[3] in order, that is, to pass from subjection to the Law by which they are oppressed to the freedom of the Gospel; and they who had started from fear may be perfected in charity, which without difficulty beareth all things, endureth all things.[4] Nothing indeed is difficult to a lover, especially since the spiritual and not carnal love of God is so much stronger for being more true. Moreover, who can fail to know that it is more difficult for us to guard against a flea than a foe or a small stone than a large one? But do we therefore judge it better or more beneficial to guard against what is more difficult? Certainly not. Why? Because what is more difficult to guard against can hurt us less. So, although we consider it more difficult to beware of venial than of criminal sins, nevertheless it is more important to avoid these which are more dangerous and which earn a greater punishment and by which we believe God is more offended and which displease him more. For the more we cleave to him by love, the more carefully we ought to guard against what offends him more and what he himself condemns more. For he who truly loves someone has enough to do to beware less of injuring himself than of hurting or showing contempt for a friend, according to the Apostle:[5] 'Charity seeketh not her own' and again:[6] 'Let no man seek his own, but that which is another's.' So if we should guard against sins less for the sake of avoiding injury to ourselves than for the sake of avoiding hurt to God, surely what should be more guarded against are those in which more hurt is given. If we also consider that poetic opinion on moral honour: 'good men hate to sin out of love of virtue',[7] all things should be held in so much greater

turpiora in se[a] censentur et ab honestate uirtutis amplius recedunt, et naturaliter quoslibet magis offendunt.

Denique ut singula sibi conferendo diligentius peccata diiudicemus, comparemus uenialia criminalibus,[b] utpote superfluam
5 comestionem periurio et[c] adulterio, et queramus in transgressione cuius magis peccetur, uel amplius Deus contempnatur atque offendatur. Nescio, fortassis respondebis, cum non nulli philosophorum omnia peccata paria censuerunt.[1] At si hanc philosophiam, immo manifestam stulticiam, sequi uelis, eque bonum est[d] a
10 criminalibus et uenialibus abstinere peccatis, quia eque malum est haec et illa committere. Cur ergo abstinere a uenialibus preferre quis audeat abstinentiae criminalium? Quod siquis forte requirat unde conicere possimus Deo magis displicere transgressionem adulterii quam superfluitatem[e] cibi, lex diuina, ut arbitror,
15 docere nos potest quae ad aliud[f] puniendum nullam penae satisfactionem instituit, hoc uero non qualibet pena, sed summa mortis afflictione dampnari decreuit.[2] Quo enim karitas proximi quam Apostolus 'plenitudinem legis' dicit[3] amplius leditur, magis contra eam agitur et amplius peccatur.

20 Quod si ad hunc modum singulis uenialibus pariter et criminalibus peccatis inuicem collatis, simul etiam tam ista omnia quam illa conferre uelimus ut omnino scilicet satisfacere ualeamus, nequaquam refugio. Ponamus ergo ut aliquis magno studio ab omnibus uenialibus caueat peccatis et nulla criminalia curet uitare,[g] et cum
25 illa omnia caueat haec praesumat, quis eum in hoc leuius peccare iudicabit aut meliorem esse si haec precauens illa incurrat? Collatione itaque facta tam singulorum, ut diximus, quam omnium simul inuicem peccatorum, liquere arbitror non melius uel maioris perfectionis esse uenialia peccata cauere quam criminalia.

---

[a] in se turpiora BCD    [b] uenalia criminibus B    [c] uel BCD
[d] est *om.* AE    [e] superflui BC    [f] illud BCD    [g] euitare BCD

---

[1] Cf. Abelard, *Dialogus* (*PL* 178. 1647C et seq.). The Stoics taught that there are no degrees of virtue and that an intention or an action must be either good or bad. Hence the paradox: all good actions are equally good, all bad ones equally bad. The standard of moral judgement is absolute. See E. Zeller, *Die Philosophie der Griechen in ihrer geschichtlichen Entwicklung*, III. i (5th edn., Leipzig, 1923), 253. Among Roman writers who discussed this doctrine cf. Cicero, *Lucullus*, cap. 43, §133; *Paradoxa*, iii; *De finibus bonorum et malorum*, iv. 27–8; *Pro Murena*, cap. 29, §61. Also cf. Seneca, *Ad Lucilium epistulae morales*, 66 and 71, ed. L. D. Reynolds, *tom.* i, Scriptorum Classicorum Bibliotheca Oxoniensis (Oxford, 1965), 181–94, 210–17. Isidore of Seville referred to it in his *Etymologies*, viii. 6, ed. W. M. Lindsay, i, Scriptorum Classicorum Bibliotheca Oxoniensis (Oxford, 1911). Both Augustine of Hippo and Jerome dissented from the

hatred the baser they are considered to be in themselves, and the
more fully they are removed from the honourableness of virtue
and the more they naturally harm everyone.

To distinguish more carefully between sins by collating them
with each other, let us finally compare venial to criminal, such as
overeating to perjury and adultery, and let us inquire in which
transgression there is more sin or greater contempt and offence
against God. Perhaps you will reply: I do not know, since some
philosophers have thought that all sins are equal.[1] But if you wish
to follow this philosophy, nay, manifest silliness, it is equally
wrong to commit both. So why should one be so bold as to put
abstinence from venial before abstinence from criminal sins? If
perhaps someone asks whence we can infer that the transgression
of adultery displeases God more than overeating, I think divine law
can teach us, which has not instituted any satisfaction of punishment to penalize the latter, but it has decreed that the former be
damned not with any penalty but with the supreme affliction of
death.[2] For where the love of our neighbour, which the Apostle
says is 'the fulfilling of the Law',[3] is more fully damaged, more is
done against it and sin is greater.

I am by no means hiding the fact that if in this way particular
venial and criminal sins are equally compared to each other, we
shall also want at the same time to compare all the venial sins, as
well as all the criminal sins, in order to be able to be completely
convincing. So let us suppose that someone guards with great care
against all venial sins and takes no care to avoid criminal sins and
ventures upon these while guarding against all the others. Who will
judge him in this to sin more lightly or to be better, if, avoiding
the former, he incurs the latter? And so, when particular sins, as
we have said, as well as all sins are compared at the same time with
each other, I think it is clear that it is not better or more perfect
to avoid venial rather than criminal sins. But if anyone, having

---

Stoics. See Jerome, *Commentaria in Ezechielem*, iii. ix, at Ezekiel 9: 9 (*PL* 25.
91A), and *Aduersus Iouinianum*, ii. 21–34 (*PL* 23. 315–33); Augustine, *Epist.*
clxvii, *cap.* ii–vi, nos. 4–21, to Jerome (*CSEL*, xliv, pp. 591–609, or *PL* 33. 735–
41), *Epist.* civ, *cap.* iv, nos. 13–17, to Nectarius (*CSEL*, xxxiv, pp. 591–5,
or *PL* 33. 394–5), and *Ad Consentium contra Mendacium*, xv. 31 (*CSEL*, xli,
p. 511, or *PL* 40. 539).

[2] Abelard has momentarily abstracted the gravity of offences from the quality
of intentions which itself determined the wrongness of actions. See Blomme,
*La doctrine du péché*, pp. 125–6.

[3] Rom. 13: 10.

Siquis tamen cum illa primum uitauerit haec postmodum, ut
oportet, uitare ualuerit, in hoc quidem fateor uirtutem eius ad
perfectionem peruenisse, nec tamen ideo posteriora, in quibus
consummatio uirtutis consistit, sunt prioribus preferenda, nec
5 tanta retributione sunt digna. Sepe namque in operatione alicuius
edificii minus agunt qui perficiunt ipsum quam qui antea operati
sunt et qui extremo assere in consummatione operis[a] posito ipsum[b]
perficiunt ut sic domus perfecta fiat, quae, dum imperfecta fuit,
domus opus non erat.
10  Sufficere huc usque arbitror nos ad cognitionem peccati, quantum memoriae occurrit, laborasse, ut eo melius caueri possit quo
diligentius cognitum fuerit. Mali quippe noticia iusto deesse non
potest, nec cauere quis uicium nisi cognitum ualet.[c]

## De peccatorum reconciliatione[d]

15  Et quoniam plagam animae monstrauimus,[e] curationis reme-
dium studeamus ostendere.[f] Vnde[g] illud[h] Hieronimi, 'O medice,
si peritus es, sicut posuisti causam morbi ita indica sanitatis.'[1]
Cum igitur peccando Deum offendimus, superest quibus ei modis
reconciliari possimus. Tria itaque sunt in reconciliatione pecca-
20 toris ad Deum,[i] penitentia scilicet, confessio, satisfactio.

## Quid proprie dicatur penitentia[j]

Penitentia autem proprie dicitur dolor animi super eo in quo
deliquit cum aliquem scilicet piget in aliquo excessisse.[2] Haec
autem penitentia tum[k] ex amore Dei accidit et fructuosa est, tum[l]
25 dampno aliquo quo nollemus grauari, qualis est illa dampnato-
rum penitentia de quibus scriptum est,[m3] 'Videntes turbabuntur
terrore horribili et mirabuntur in subitatione insperatae salutis

---

[a] domus BCD    [b] eam BC    [c] ualet: potest C; malet D    [d] ADE
[e] ostendimus BC    [f] ostendere: monstrare C, *om.* B    [g] unde: et *add.*
BC    [h] illud: est *add.* BCD    [i] ad deum *om.* B; necessaria *add.* C
[j] ADE    [k] animi C; cum D    [l] tum (cum D) ... quo (*om.* E) ... grauari
ADE; tum ex damno aliquo nostri quo ... grauari B; C *is heavily corrected from*
cum (*or* tum) ex dampno aliquo nostri quo ... grauari *to* In fructuosa penitencia cum (?) tamen accidit ex dampno aliquo nostri quo ... grauari    [m] est:
Quid sit infructuosa penitentia *add.* D *as a rubricated heading*

---

[1] I have not been able to find the source of this phrase—perhaps one of the
many medical allusions in the writings of Jerome; see A. S. Pease, 'Medical
Allusions in the Works of St. Jerome', *Harvard Studies in Classical Philology*,
xxv (1914), 73–86.

first avoided all the former, has been able next, as one should, to avoid all the latter, I say indeed his virtue in this has reached perfection; yet the latter, in which completion of virtue lies, are not therefore to be put before the former nor are they worthy of so great a retribution. For often in the erection of a building those who have worked earlier on it do more than those who finish and complete it by putting in the last beam to end the job, so that thereby a house is finished which, while it was unfinished, was not a house.

I think it sufficient for us to have striven thus far to acquire knowledge of sin as far as it occurs to our memory, so that the more carefully it is known, the better it can be guarded against. Certainly a knowledge of evil cannot be lacking in the just man, nor can anyone guard against vice unless it can be known.

## Of the reconciliation of sins

And since we have displayed the soul's wound, let us strive to show the medicine which heals. Whence Jerome says: 'Doctor, if you are skilful, just as you have stated the cause of the disease, so also show that of health!'[1] Although therefore we offend God by sinning, there remain ways by which we can be reconciled to him. And so there are three things in the reconciliation of the sinner to God, namely repentance, confession, satisfaction.

## What may be said properly to be repentance

Now, repentance is properly called the sorrow of the mind over what it has done wrong, when, namely, someone is ashamed at having gone too far in something.[2] However, this repentance at one time happens out of love of God and is fruitful, at another because of some penalty with which we do not want to be burdened; such is that repentance of the damned of whom it has been written:[3] 'These seeing it shall be troubled with terrible fright, and shall be amazed at the suddenness of their unexpected salvation,

[2] By the mid twelfth century penance came to be counted as one of the seven sacraments, but Abelard, unlike most of his contemporaries, does not consider it in its sacramental aspect. See Anciaux, *La théologie du sacrement de pénitence*, pp. 140–1.

[3] Wisdom 5: 2–3.

dicentes intra se, penitentiam agentes et pre angustia spiritus
gementes, Hi sunt quos aliquando habuimus in derisu', etc.[1] Legimus[a] et penitentiam Iudae super hoc quod Dominum tradiderat.[b2]
Quod non[c] tam pro culpa peccati quam pro uilitate sui, qui se
5 omnium iudicio dapnatum sentiebat, credimus accidisse. Cum
enim quis alium pecunia uel quomodo[d] corruptum ad perditionem
traxerit, nemini uilior quam ei proditor habetur, et nemo ei minus
se credit quam is qui infidelitatem eius amplius expertus est.[e]
Multos quippe[f] cottidie de hac uita recessuros de flagiciis perpetra-
10 tis peniteri uidemus, et graui compunctione ingemiscere, non tam
amore Dei quem offenderunt uel odio peccati quod commiserunt
quam timore penae in[g] quam se precipitari uerentur.[3] Qui in eo
quoque iniqui permanent, quod non tam eis iniquitas[h] displicet
culpae quam quae iusta est grauitas penae, nec tam[i] habent odio
15 id quod commiserunt quia malum fuit, quam iustum Dei iudicium
quod in pena formidant, equitatem potius quam iniquitatem
odientes. Quos diu obcecatos[j] atque uocatos ut a malitia sua
conuerterentur, ita tandem in reprobum sensum diuina iusticia
tradit,[4] et cecitate percussos a facie sua prorsus abicit, ut ne
20 salubris penitentiae noticiam habeant, nec qualiter satisfaciendum
sit aduertere queant.

Quam plurimos quippe cottidie cernimus morientes grauiter
ingemiscere, multum se accusare super usuris, rapinis, oppres-
sionibus pauperum uel in[k] quibuscumque iniuriis quas com-
25 miserunt, et pro emendatione istorum sacerdotem consulere.
Quibus si hoc, ut oportet, primum consilium detur, ut uenditis
omnibus quae habent restituant aliis quae abstulerunt, iuxta illud
Augustini, 'Si res aliena cum reddi possit non redditur, non agitur

---

[a] ⟨ ⟩emimus B, *where the capital awaits its rubricator*    [b] tradidit BD
[c] non tam pro culpa; quod tamen non procul pena C *where the corrector has
attempted above the line and illegibly to restore meaning to the phrase*    [d] quoquomodo CD    [e] est expertus BC; expertus es E    [f] quoque BC
[g] in quam se precipitari uerentur (uidentur D) ADE; quam se meruisse co-
gnoscunt BC    [h] iniquitas . . . est (*om.* E) . . . pene ADE; iniquitas culpe
quam pene que iusta est grauitas displicet BC    [i] tam C *and possibly* D;
*om.* B; tantum AE    [j] expectatos BCD    [k] in *om.* BC

---

[1] Cf. Abelard, *Sermo VIII in Ramis Palmorum* (*PL* 178. 441B–442A). For an

saying within themselves, repenting and groaning for anguish of spirit: These are they whom we had some time in derision', etc.[1] And we read the repentance of Judas for having betrayed the Lord.[2] We believe this happened not so much on account of the fault of a sin as on account of the vileness of him who felt himself damned in everyone's judgement. For when a man who is corrupted by money or by some other means has betrayed another man into perdition, he is considered a traitor who is vile to no one more than to this man, and no one trusts him less than he who has a specially full experience of his faithlessness. Daily indeed we see many about to depart from this life repenting of their shameful accomplishments and groaning with great compunction, not so much out of love of God whom they have offended or out of hatred of the sin which they have committed as out of fear of the punishment into which they are afraid of being hurled.[3] Moreover, they remain wicked because the wickedness of their fault does not displease them as much as the just severity of the punishment and they do not hate what they have done because it was wrong so much as the just judgement of God which they fear in the form of punishment, hating equity rather than iniquity. Having long been blinded and called upon to turn away from their wickedness, divine justice at last delivers them up to a base mind,[4] and having struck them with blindness absolutely casts them away from his face, so that they should not have knowledge of wholesome repentance nor be able to observe how satisfaction should be made.

How very many indeed do we daily see dying, groaning deeply, reproaching themselves greatly for usuries, plunderings, oppressions of the poor, and all kinds of injuries which they have committed, and consulting a priest to free them from these faults. If, as is proper, the first advice given to them is this, that selling all they have, they restore to others what they have taken—in accordance with Augustine: 'If something which belongs to another is not returned when it can be returned, repentance is not done but is

analysis of the motives for penance by a disciple of Anselm of Laon see *Sententia*, no. 383 (ed. Lottin, *Psychologie et morale*, v. 280–1). On the influence of Abelard's analysis see Anciaux, *La théologie du sacrement de pénitence*, pp. 155 et seq.

[2] Cf. Matt. 27: 3.

[3] The antithesis *amor justitiae | timor poenae* was a favourite of Augustine; see *Sermo* 159, *cap.* 5, n. 6; 252, *cap.* 7, n. 6; 270, n. 4 (*PL* 38. 870, 1171, 1241); and *De fide et operibus*, *cap.* 21, n. 39 (*PL* 40. 222).      [4] Rom. 1: 28.

penitentia sed fingitur',[1] statim quam inanis eorum sit penitentia,
responsione sua profitentur. Vnde ergo, inquiunt, domus mea
uiueret? Quid filiis meis, quid uxori relinquerem? Vnde se
sustentare[a] possent? Quibus illa primum dominica occurrit[b] in-
5 crepatio, 'Stulte, hac nocte animam tuam repetunt a te, quae
autem parasti cuius erunt?'[2] O miser quicumque talis es, immo
miserorum omnium miserrime et stultorum stultissime, non
prouides quid tibi conserues, sed quid aliis thesaurizes? Qua pre-
sumptione Deum offendis ad cuius horrendum iudicium raperis,
10 ut tuos habeas propitios quos ditas de pauperum ra pinis?Quis
super te non rideat, si audierit te sperare alios magis tibi propi-
cios fore quam te ipsum? Confidis in elemosinis tuorum quos,
quia successores habere te credis, iniquitatis pariter heredes con-
stituis, quibus aliena per rapinam possidenda relinquis. Vitam
15 pauperibus eripis, sua illis auferendo unde sunt sustentandi, et in
eis rursum occidere Christum machinaris, iuxta illud quod ipsemet
ait,[3] 'Quod uni ex minimis meis fecistis mihi fecistis.' Quid ergo
tu male pius in tuos et crudelis in te pariter atque Deum a iudice
iusto[c] expectas, ad quem uelis nolis iudicandus properas, qui[d] non
20 solum de rapinis sed[e] etiam de ocioso uerbo rationem exigit? Qui
quam districtus sit in uindicta priorum hominum statim exhi-
buit pena. Semel Adam peccauit, et comparatione nostrorum,
sicut beatus meminit Hieronimus,[4] leuissimum eius peccatum
fuit. Non quemquam per uiolentiam oppressit nec quicquam ali-
25 cui abstulit, de fructu qui reparabilis erat semel gustauit. In qua
quidem tam leui transgressione, in posteritatem quoque totam
per penam redundante, premonstrare Dominus decreuit quid de
maioribus facturus sit culpis. Diues quem ad inferos Dominus
descendisse dicit, non quod aliena rapuerit, sed quia propria[f]

[a] sustentare se BCD        [b] incurrit BD        [c] isto BCD        [d] Qui
BCD        [e] uerum BC        [f] propria . . . uescebatur (et *add* B) indigenti: propriis tanquam licitis uescebatur et indigenti C

---

[1] Augustine, *Epistola* 153 (*ad Macedonium*), *cap.* 6, n. 20 (*CSEL* xliv, p. 419,
or *PL* 33. 662). According to Peter the Chanter, Abelard once told Count Theo-
bald of Blois and Champagne (d. 1152) that he would accept gifts from him
only if they were taken from his revenues and that he would give away those
coming from elsewhere to dogs, beasts, and birds, *Verbum abbreuiatum*, c. 46
(*PL* 205. 146BC). Abelard wrote in his poem to Astralabe:

> Multa Theobaldus largitur relligiosis;
> Sed, si plura rapit, sunt data rapta magis . . .
> Conuenit hoc magis ut rapiat nihil atque nihil det
> Quam perdat grates et sua dona simul,

ed. B. Hauréau in *Notices et extraits de la Bibliothèque nationale*, xxxiv. 2 (1895),
155. The problem of violent misappropriations by the nobility was serious in
Abelard's day, as may be judged from Guibert of Nogent in his description of

feigned'[1]—instantly by their reply they declare how hollow is their repentance for these things. How then, they say, could my household live? What might I leave to my sons, what to my wife? How could they support themselves? That rebuke of the Lord for the first time occurs to them: 'Thou fool, this night do they require thy soul of thee; and whose shall those things be which thou hast provided?'[2] Such a wretch, whoever you are, nay, most wretched of all wretches and most foolish of fools, you are not attending to what you will keep for yourself but to what you will hoard for others. With what presumption do you offend God, to whose dreaded judgement you will be snatched, in order to propitiate your relatives, whom you enrich with plunder from the poor? Who would not laugh at you if he heard you hoped to make others more kindly to you than you were yourself? You trust in the alms of your relatives whom, because you believe you have successors, you make alike heirs to your wickedness, and you leave to them the property of other people to hold through plunder. You snatch life away from the poor, by taking from them their sustenance, and in them you contrive to kill Christ again, in accordance with what he himself said:[3] 'What you did to one of the least of mine, you did it to me.' So what do you, who are wrongly loyal to your relatives and cruel to yourself as much as to God, expect from the just judge to whom, whether you want to or not, you are hastening to be judged and who demands a reason not only for plunder but even for an idle word? He has steadfastly shown in the punishment of earlier men how severe is his vengeance. Adam sinned but once and by comparison with our own, as the blessed Jerome has observed,[4] his sin was very slight. He oppressed none with violence and he took nothing away from anyone; he partook but once of the fruit which could have been restored. In this very slight transgression, which also recoiled through its punishment upon all posterity, the Lord decided to point out what would be done with greater faults. The rich man, who the Lord says descended into hell, not because he had seized the possessions of others but because he did not

Thomas of Marle and from Suger of Saint-Denis in his description of Hugh of Le Puiset. In 1219 the dying William Marshall, earl of Pembroke, was to declare that he could not return his booty and that the clerical teaching that no man would be saved who had not returned all he had ever taken was false. See the *Histoire de Guillaume le Maréchal*, ed. P. Meyer, Société de l'histoire de France (Paris, 1891–1901), ii, ll. 18476–501.

[2] Luke 12: 20.           [3] Matt. 25: 40.           [4] Where?

quibus tamquam licitis uescebatur indigenti Lazaro non inperti-
uit,[1] patenter edocet qua pena feriendi sunt qui rapiunt aliena si sic
ille dampnatus est atque in inferno sepultus qui non tribuerit bona[a]
sua. Tecum[b] memoria tui sepulta et cito siccatis lacrimis eorum[c]
5 quas in exequiis habuisti, iuxta illud[d] rethoris Apollonii, 'Lacrima
citius nichil arescit',[2] tua coniux in proximo ad nouas nuptias se
preparauit,[e] ut noui mariti uoluptatibus deseruiret de his quas ei
dimisisti rapinis, et presente[f] adhuc corpore tuo lectulum calefaciet alieno, te misero in flammis gehennae uoluptates istas
10 plexuro. Idem et a filiis tuis expectandum est. Quod siquis forte
interroget cur non tui recordantes elemosinis suis tibi propicientur,
multis se de causis excusare posse[g] uidentur. Quia enim sic[h] respon-
deant, 'cum ille sibi propitius esse noluerit, quanta stulticia fuit
sibi[i] alios sperare propitios, et animae suae salutem aliis com-
15 mittere de qua ipse debuit plurimum[j] prouidere. Quem sibi propi-
tium magis credidit quam seipsum? Qui sibi crudelis erat, de
cuius misericordia confidebat?' Possunt denique et in excusatio-
nem auariciae suae pretendere ac dicere, 'Scimus insuper ea quae
ipse[k] nobis dereliquit non huiusmodi esse ut de ipsis nobis[l] sint
20 elemosinae faciendae.' Ridebunt omnes, et ridere debent[m] qui haec
audient. Ille uero miser qui exspoliatos pauperes[n] ad horam flere
coegit, in perpetuum ibi flebit. Sunt qui suam negligentiam hominibus non Deo uolentes occultare ad excusandas excusationes in
peccatis[3] dicunt tot eos esse quos exspoliauerunt ut[o] omnino
25 cognoscere uel reperire nequeant. De quo cum nullam sollicitudinem assumant, illud apostolicae sententiae iudicium incurrunt,[4]
'et qui ignorat ignorabitur'. Non inueniunt illos quia non querunt,
inueniet illos dextera Dei quem contempserunt. De qua etiam
scriptum est,[5] 'Dextera tua inueniet omnes qui te oderunt.' Quam
30 idem Propheta qui hoc dixit uehementer expauescens, et locum
nullum[p] euadendi considerans, alibi ait,[6] 'Quo ibo a spiritu tuo,
et quo a facie tua fugiam? Si ascendero in caelum tu illic es, si

---

[a] bona *om.* BCD        [b] Tecum . . . lacrimis: tecum pariter et cito tui
memoria sepulta scitatis lacrimis B        [c] tuorum BCD        [d] illud *om.* AE
[e] preparauit ut . . . deseruiret: preparabit (preparati B) et (in *add.* B) . . . de-
seruiet BCD        [f] presente adhuc corpore tuo lectulum calefaciet alieno AE;
repentem adhuc lectulum (*om.* D) corpore tuo lectulum calefaciet alieno CD;
tepentem adhuc lectulum corpore tuo. lectulum calefaciet alieno B        [g] posse
*om.* CD        [h] si ABCDE        [i] alios sibi BC        [j] plurimum debuit BC
[k] ipse *om.* BC        [l] nobis *om.* BC        [m] debebunt BC        [n] pauperes:
hic BCD        [o] ut omnino . . . nequeant: ut non eos (uel *add.* C) cognoscere . . .
queant BC        [p] nullum locum BCD

---

[1] Cf. Luke 16: 19 et seq.
[2] Cicero in *De inuentione*, i. 109 ascribes this saying to the rhetorican Apollonius of Rhodes On its history in antiquity see G. D. Kelly, 'Study of a Proverb

share his own with the needy Lazarus and ate them as if this were lawful,[1] plainly shows what punishment will strike those who seize other people's goods, if he, who did not give away his own goods, was thus damned and buried in hell. Once your memory was buried with you and their tears which you had at your funeral had quickly dried—according to the rhetor Apollonius, 'nothing dries quicker than a tear'[2]—your wife next prepared herself for a new wedding to devote herself to the pleasures of a new husband with the aid of the plunder which you bequeathed to her, and she will warm with another body the bed in which your body has been hitherto, while you will smart wretchedly in the flames of hell at those pleasures. And the same should be expected from your children. If perhaps someone asks why in remembering you they are not propitious to you with their alms, they seem able to excuse themselves on many grounds. For they would reply thus: 'Since he refused to be kind to himself, how foolish was it for him to hope others would be kind to him and to commit to others the salvation of his soul for which he definitely should himself have provided! Who did he believe would be kinder to him than he himself? He was cruel to himself: in whose mercy did he trust?' And then they can bring forward his avarice as an excuse and say: 'We know moreover that what he left to us is not meant to be used by us as alms.' All will laugh and ought to laugh who hear these things. But the wretch who in his time reduced to weeping the poor whom he plundered shall weep there for ever. Some who wish to hide their negligence from men, not from God, say, to make excuses in sins,[3] that they have plundered so many that they are quite unable to identify or trace them. Since they assume no concern for this they incur that judgement of apostolic opinion:[4] 'And if any man know not, he shall not be known.' They do not find them because they do not look; the right hand of God to whom they showed contempt will find them. It has also been written of this:[5] 'Thy right hand will find out all them that hate thee.' The same Prophet who said this feared it exceedingly and, thinking there was no place of escape, said elsewhere:[6] 'Whither shall I go from thy spirit? And whither shall I flee from thy face? If I ascend into heaven, thou art there: if I descend into hell, thou art present.'

---

attributed to the Rhetor Apollonius', *American Journal of Philosophy*, xxviii (1907), 301–10.                                   [3] Ps. 140: 4.
    [4] 1 Cor. 14: 38.          [5] Ps. 20: 9.          [6] Ps. 138: 7–8.

descendero ad infernum ades.' Et quia plerumque non[a] minor est
auaricia sacerdotis quam populi, iuxta illud Prophetae,[1] 'et erit
sicut sacerdotes sic[b] populus', multos morientium seducit cupiditas sacerdotum uanam eis securitatem promittentium, si quae
5 habent[c] sacrificiis obtulerint, et missas emant quas nequaquam
gratis haberent. In quo quidem mercimonio prefixum apud eos
precium constat esse,[d] pro una scilicet missa unum denarium, et
pro uno tricenali de missis et omnibus horis quinque solidos et pro
uno annuali, sexaginta. Non consulunt morientibus ut rapinas
10 restituant, sed ut in sacrificio ipsas[e] offerant, cum e contrario
scriptum sit,[2] 'qui offert sacrificium de substantia pauperis, quasi
qui uictimet filium in conspectu patris.' Plus enim grauat patrem
occisio filii coram se facta quam si non uideret eam.[f] Et quasi
filius[g] immolatione occiditur, dum substantia pauperis in qua uita
15 eius consistebat in sacrificio ponitur. Et Veritas sacrificio misericordiam[h] preferens, 'euntes', inquit,[3] 'discite quid est, misericordiam uolo et non sacrificium.' Peius autem est rapinas retinere
quam misericordiam non impendere, hoc est, pauperibus auferre
sua quam non impendere nostra, sicut et supra in dampnatione
20 diuitis meminimus.

## De fructuosa penitentia[i]

Et quia de infructuosa diximus penitentia, tanto diligentius
quanto salubrius fructuosam consideremus. Ad quam Apostolus
quemlibet inuitans obstinatum,[j] nec horrendum Dei iudicium
25 adtendentem ait,[4] 'An diuitias bonitatis eius et patientiae et
longanimitatis contempnis? Ignoras[k] quoniam benignitas Dei ad
penitentiam te adducit?' Quibus uidelicet uerbis quae sit penitentia salubris et ex amore Dei potius quam ex timore proueniens,
manifeste declarat ut uidelicet doleamus Deum offendisse uel
30 contempsisse quia est bonus magis quam quia iustus est.[l] Quo
enim diutius eum contempnimus, quia statim eum contemptum
suum iudicare non credimus, sicut e contrario principes seculi
faciunt qui cum offenduntur nesciunt parcere nec suarum iniuri-
arum ultionem differre, eo iustius grauiorem infert sui contemptus

---

[a] si ADE    [b] sicut sacerdotes sic; sacerdos (?) sicut BC; sicut sacerdos
sic D    [c] habent: in *add.* BD    [d] esse constat BCD    [e] ipsas *om.*
B; ea C    [f] eam non uideret (uiderit B) BC    [g] filius: in *add.* BCD
[h] misericordiam sacrificio BC    [i] ADE    [j] obstinatum inuitans BC
[k] ignorans BCD    [l] iustus est A; est iustus BD; iustus CE

---

[1] Hos. 4: 9. On his death-bed in 1219 William Marshall rejected a cleric's
suggestion that he should sell his furs for money with which to secure his salva-

And because often the greed of the priest is no less than that of the people—according to the Prophet:[1] 'And as the people so shall the priests be'—the cupidity of priests seduces many of the dying by promising them a false security if they offer their property in sacrifices and buy Masses which they would certainly not get free. In this trade they clearly have a fixed price, namely one denarius for a Mass and five solidi for Masses and all the hours for thirty years and sixty for once a year. They do not advise the dying to restore their plunderings but to offer them in sacrifice, although it is written against this:[2] 'He that offereth sacrifice of the goods of the poor is as one that sacrificeth the son in the presence of his father.' For the killing of a son hurts a father more when done in his own presence than if he did not see it. And it is as if a son were killed by immolation when the goods of the poor, in which their livelihood consists, are put into a sacrifice. And Truth, preferring mercy to sacrifice, says:[3] 'Go, learn what this meaneth: I will have mercy and not sacrifice.' Furthermore, it is worse to retain plunder than not to give mercy, that is, to take from the poor what belongs to them rather than not to give our own, as we mentioned above in the damnation of the rich man.

## Of fruitful repentance

Because we have spoken of unfruitful repentance, let us consider fruitful repentance all the more carefully because it is more beneficial. The Apostle invites to it all who are stubborn and do not take thought for the dreadful judgement of God, saying:[4] 'Or despisest thou the riches of his goodness and patience and longsuffering? Knowest thou not that the benignity of God leadeth thee to penance?' With these words he plainly declares what is wholesome repentance, proceeding from the love of God rather than from fear, with the result that we are sorry to have offended or to have shown contempt of God because he is good rather than because he is just. For the longer we show contempt of him because we do not believe that he immediately judges contempt of himself (just as conversely secular princes do who, when they are offended, do not know how to spare or how to postpone the avenging of injuries to themselves), the more justly therefore he inflicts a heavier

---

tion. See the *Histoire de Guillaume le Maréchal*, ed. P. Meyer, Société de l'histoire de France (Paris, 1891–1901), ii, ll. 18679–735.

[2] Ecclus. 34: 24.          [3] Matt. 9: 13.          [4] Rom. 2: 4.

penam, et tanto districtior est in ultione, quanto patientior fuit in
expectatione. Quod subsequenter predictus Apostolus ostendit
dicens,[1] 'Secundum duriciam autem tuam et cor impenitens the-
saurizas tibi iram in die irae.' Tunc quidem irae, modo mansue-
5 tudinis, quia tunc uindictae, modo patientiae. Ibi iusticia exigente,
tanto grauius sui contemptum ulciscetur quanto minus contempni
debuit, et diutius tolerauit. Timemus homines offendere, et quorum offensam timore non effugimus, uerecundia uitamus. Latebras
querimus cum fornicamur, ne ab hominibus uideamur, nec[a] unius
10 hominis aspectum tunc sustinere[b] possumus. Scimus Deum
presentem esse quem nichil potest latere. Videri ab ipso et[c] tota
curia caeli in huius actione turpitudinis non erubescimus, qui ad
unius homunculi aspectum confunderemur. Ante[d] iudicem terre-
num presumere aliquid maxime timemus a quo nos iudicandos
15 scimus temporali tantum[e] pena, non aeterna. Multa nos facere uel
tolerare carnalis affectus cogit, pauca spiritualis. Vtinam tanta
propter Deum cui omnia debemus, quanta propter uxorem uel
filios,uel quamcunque meretricem facimus, uel toleramus.

Qua obsecro pena haec iniuria est iudicanda ut meretricem quo-
20 que ipsi preponamus?[f] Conqueritur ipse per Prophetam quod nec
ei amor tamquam patri nec timor exhibeatur tamquam domino.
'Filius', inquit,[2] 'honorat patrem, et seruus dominum suum timet.
Si ego pater, ubi honor meus? Et si ego dominus, ubi timor meus?'
Conqueritur[g] sibi patrem uel dominum preferri. Adtende igitur
25 quantum indignetur meretricem quoque sibi anteferri, et de summa
suae bonitatis patientia, unde plus debuit amari, magis contempni.
Quam quidem bonitatem et patientiae longanimitatem hi qui
salubriter penitent adtendentes, non tam timore penarum quam
ipsius amore ad compunctionem mouentur, iuxta predictam Apo-
30 stoli exhortationem,[h] ubi salubrem penitentiam diligenter de-
scripsit, cum e contrario dixit,[3] 'An diuitias bonitatis eius',[i] hoc
est, diuitem et copiosam bonitatem[j] siue habundantem benignitatem longanimis patientiae, qua[k] tamdiu te tolerat, 'contempnis',
quia uidelicet non cito punit, 'ignorans', hoc est, non adtendens,
35 'quoniam tanta eius benignitas ad penitentiam' quantum in se est

---

a ne AE        b sustinere tunc BCD        c et: a *add.* BCD        d aut
AE; *in* C *the corrector has added the letter* e *to* aut (aute)        e temporali (*om.*
B) tamen BC        f preponimus BD        g Conqueritur . . . contempni *om.*
B        h exhortacionem apostoli BC        i eius *om.* BCD        j bonitatem
*om.* BC        k qua . . . tolerat AE; quantam dici te tollerat B; qua tam diu
tollefte C; qua tam dure tolerat D

---

1 Rom. 2: 5.
2 Mal. 1: 6.                                                  3 Rom. 2: 4.

punishment for contempt of himself and is more severe in vengeance according as he was more patient in waiting. The same
Apostle later showed this saying:[1] 'But according to thy hardness
and impenitent heart thou treasurest up to thyself wrath, against
the day of wrath.' Then indeed wrath, now mildness, because
vengeance then, patience now. Demanding justice there he will
avenge contempt of himself all the more heavily the less he should
have been held in contempt and the longer he endured it. We are
afraid to offend men, and when we do not flee in fear from those
we offend we avoid them in shame. We seek a hiding-place when
we fornicate lest we be seen by men and we cannot then endure
to be seen even by one man. We know that God is present, from
whom nothing can be concealed. We would be thrown into confusion at the sight of one little man, but we do not blush to be seen
in this act of shame by him and by the whole court of heaven. We
are very greatly afraid to presume anything in front of an earthly
judge by whom we know we shall be sentenced with only a temporal, not an eternal, penalty. Carnal desire makes us do or endure
many things, spiritual desire few. Would that we would do or
endure as much for God to whom we owe all as for our wife or
children or any mistress!

With what penalty, I pray, should this wrong be condemned
whereby we put a mistress before him? He himself complains
through the Prophet that love is not shown to him as a father nor
fear as to a master. 'The son', he says,[2] 'honoureth the father and
the servant fears his master. If I be a father, where is my honour?
And if I be a master, where is my fear?' He complains that a father
or a master is preferred to him. Consider, therefore, how indignant
he is that a mistress too is put before him and that he is held in
greater contempt for the supreme patience of his goodness for
which he ought to be loved the more. These who repent healthily,
gonsidering this goodness and the forbearance of his patience, are
moved to compunction less by fear of penalties than by love of him,
in accordance with the exhortation of the Apostle mentioned above.
Here he carefully described healthy repentance by saying conversely:[3] 'Or the riches of his goodness', that is, the rich and copious
goodness or the overflowing benignity of his forbearing patience
with which he endures you for so long, 'despisest thou', because,
that is, he does not punish quickly, 'not knowing', that is, not
considering, 'that his benignity is such' that in itself 'it leads thee

'te adducit', hoc est, facit cur eam[a] adtendendo ad penitentiam deberes conuerti quod tam benignum[b] contempsisti? Et haec quidem reuera fructuosa est penitentia peccati, cum hic dolor atque contritio animi ex amore Dei, quem tam benignum ad-
5 tendimus, potius quam ex timore penarum procedit. Cum hoc autem gemitu et contritione cordis, quam ueram penitentiam dicimus, peccatum non permanet, hoc est, contemptus Dei siue consensus in malum, quia karitas Dei hunc gemitum inspirans non patitur culpam. In hoc statim gemitu Deo reconcilia-
10 mur et precedentis peccati ueniam assequimur, iuxta illud Prophetae,[1] 'Quacumque hora peccator ingemuerit, saluus erit', hoc est, salute animae suae dignus efficietur.[2] Non ait, quo anno, uel quo mense, siue qua ebdomada, uel quo die, sed qua hora, ut sine dilatione uenia dignum ostendat nec[c] ei penam aeternam deberi,
15 in qua consistit condempnatio peccati.[3] Et si enim articulo necessitatis preuentus non habeat locum ueniendi ad confessionem uel peragendi satisfactionem, nequaquam in hoc gemitu de hac uita recedens gehennam incurrit,[d] quod est condonari a Deo peccatum, hoc est, eum talem fieri quem iam non sit dignum sicut
20 antea[e] propter illud quod precessit peccatum aeternaliter a Deo puniri. Non enim Deus cum peccatum penitentibus condonat omnem penam eis ignoscit, sed solummodo aeternam. Multi namque penitentes qui preuenti morte satisfactionem penitentiae in hac uita non egerunt, penis purgatoriis, non dampna-
25 toriis, in futura[f] reseruantur. Vnde[g] suprema iudicii dies qua repente multi fidelium puniendi sunt, quanto spatio temporis extendatur incertum est, quamuis resurrectio 'in momento, in ictu oculi'[4] fiat, ut uidelicet ibi de culpis satisfaciant quantum Deus decreuerit, de quibus[h] satisfacere distulerint[i] aut permissi non sunt.

---

[a] eum B; eum C *where* u *is erased but not replaced*; ei D      [b] benignum: scilicet *add.* BC      [c] nec: iam *add.* BC      [d] incurret BCD      [e] anima AE; *in* C *the first two letters of* anima *are marked for erasure and* antea *is added in the margin*      [f] futura: uita *add.* BCD      [g] Vnde: et *add.* BCD
[h] quibus: hic *add.* BCD      [i] distulerunt BCD

---

[1] Ezek. 33: 12: 'impietas impii non nocebit ei, in quacunque die conuersus fuerit ab impietate sua.'
[2] Cf. Abelard, *Sermo VIII in Ramis Palmarum* (*PL* 178. 440B, 444CD) and *Expositio* of Romans, ii (840C). For the same doctrine see *Sententia*, no. 383 of the school of Anselm of Laon (ed. Lottin, *Psychologie et morale*, v. 281) and the so-called *Sententie Anselmi*, ed. F. Bliemetzrieder, *Anselms von Laon systematische Sentenzen*, BGPTMA, xviii. 2–3 (1919), p. 121. Cf. H. Weisweiler, *Das Schrifttum der Schule Anselms von Laon und Wilhelms von Champeaux in deutschen Bibliotheken*, BGPTMA, xxxiii. 1–2 (1936), p. 217, and Anciaux, *La théologie du sacrement de pénitence*, p. 183.
[3] Hugh of Saint-Victor taught that the fault of a sinner was remitted in con-

to penance', that is, brings it about that through considering it you ought to be converted to repentance because you showed contempt for one who is so kind? And this indeed is truly fruitful repentance for sin, since this sorrow and contrition of mind proceeds from love of God, whom we consider to be so kind, rather than from fear of punishments.

Moreover, with this sigh and contrition of heart which we call true repentance sin does not remain, that is, the contempt of God or consent to evil, because the charity of God which inspires this sigh does not put up with fault. In this sigh we are instantly reconciled to God and we gain pardon for the preceding sin, according to the Prophet:[1] 'In what hour soever the sinner shall sigh, he shall be saved', that is, he will be made worthy of the salvation of his soul.[2] He did not say: in what year or in what month or in what week or on what day, but in what hour, so as to show that he is worthy of pardon without delay, and that eternal punishment, in which the condemnation of sin consists, is not owing to him.[3] For although he may be prevented by some necessity from having an opportunity of coming to confession or of performing satisfaction, he by no means meets with hell on leaving this life sighing thus. This is God's pardon for sin, namely, making him what he is not yet worthy of being, just as previously because of the preceding sin he could be eternally punished by God. For when God pardons penitents their sin, he does not forgive them every penalty but only the eternal one. For many penitents who, prevented by death, have not performed the satisfaction of penance in this life are detained for purgatory, not damnatory, punishments in the future. Whence it is uncertain how long a time the supreme day of judgement will last, on which many of the faithful are to be suddenly punished, although the resurrection will occur 'in a moment, in the twinkling of an eye',[4] with the result, that is, that there, as far as God shall determine, they will render satisfaction for faults for which they have deferred, or have not been permitted to make, satisfaction.

trition but the eternal penalty owed for the sin remained, unless death intervened, to be remitted by a priest, *De Sacramentis*, ii. xiv, c. 8 (*PL* 176. 564–5). Cf. *Summa Sententiarum*, vi. x (*PL* 176. 148–9). Peter Lombard, *Sententiarum liber* iv. xvii, c. 1, and xviii, c. 4 (2nd edn., Ad Claras Aquas, 1916), pp. 848, 859, agreed with Abelard that contrition secured the remission both of faults and of the eternal penalty owed for sin, provided that the will to confess was present in the penitent.                                        [4] 1 Cor. 15: 52.

*Vtrum quis de uno peccato sine alio penitere possit*[a]

Sunt qui querunt utrum quis de uno peccato penitere possit et
non de alio ut pote de homicidio et non de fornicatione quam adhuc
perpetrare non desistit.[1] Sed si fructuosam illam penitentiam intel-
5 ligamus quam Dei amor inmittit, et quam Gregorius describens
ait, 'penitentia est commissa deflere et flenda non committere',[2]
nequaquam penitentia dici potest ad quam nos amor Dei com-
pellit, quotiens unus[b] contemptus retinetur. Si enim amor Dei, sicut
oportet, ad hoc me inducit atque animum trahit ut de hoc consensu
10 doleam propter hoc tantum quia in eo Deum offendi, non video[c]
qualiter idem amor de alio contemptu eadem de causa penitere
non cogat, hoc est, in eo proposito mentem meam[d] statuat ut
quisquis excessus meus[e] memoriae occurrerit,[f] de ipso similiter
doleam,[g] et ad satisfaciendum paratus sim.[h] Vbicumque igitur
15 uera est penitentia, ex amore scilicet Dei solo proueniens, nullus
Dei contemptus remanet maxime cum Veritas dicat,[3] 'Siquis
diligit me sermonem meum seruabit, et Pater meus diliget eum
et ad eum ueniemus et mansionem apud eum faciemus.' Quicumque ergo in amore Dei persistunt saluari necesse est. Quae
20 saluatio nequaquam contingeret uno peccato, id est, uno Dei contemptu retento. Cum autem in penitente iam nullum Deus re-
perit peccatum, nullam ibi inuenit dampnationis causam, et ideo
necesse est ut, peccato cessante, non restet dampnatio, hoc est,
perennis penae afflictio. Et hoc est peccatum quod precessit a
25 Deo condonari, a pena aeterna quam inde meruerat ei, ut diximus, a Deo prouideri. Quamuis enim Deus iam non inueniat in
penitente quod perenniter debeat punire, penam tamen precedentis peccati dicitur condonare, cum per hoc quod gemitum ei
penitentiae inspirauerit, eum indulgentia dignum fecit, hoc est,
30 talem cui nulla tunc[i] debeatur pena aeterna et quem in hoc statu
de hac uita recedentem saluare[j] necesse est.[k] Quod si forte et in
eundem recidat contemptum, sicut redit ad peccatum, ita etiam
relabitur ad penae debitum, ut rursum puniri debeat qui prius
penitendo non puniri meruerat.

[a] A (*which reads* peniteri) *and* E; An quis posset penitere de uno peccato dum
remanet in alio D      [b] unus: dei *add.* BCD      [c] uidero AE      [d] nostram BC      [e] nostre C; noster *or* nostre B      [f] occurreret C *and* ? B
[g] dolerem C; doleo ? B      [h] essem BC      [i] tunc nulla BC      [j] saluari
BC      [k] esset necesse BCD

---

[1] On this question see further the Victorine *Summa Sententiarum*, VI. xiii (*PL*
176. 151D), Roland Bandinelli, *Sententiae*, ed. A. M. Gietl, *Die Sentenzen
Rolands* (Freiburg i. B., 1891), pp. 240–3, and Peter Lombard, *Sententiarum
liber* iv. xv. 1–7 (2nd edn., Ad Claras Aquas, 1916), pp. 828–38.

*Whether one can repent of one sin without repenting of another*

There are those who ask whether one can repent of one sin and not of another, for example, of murder and not of the fornication which one has not yet stopped committing.[1] But if we understand fruitful repentance to be that which is sent by God's love and which Gregory describes, saying: 'Repentance is weeping for what one has done and not doing what one weeps for',[2] as long as one contempt remains there can by no means be said to be a repentance to which the love of God is urging us. For if God's love, as is proper, leads me to this and brings my mind to be sorry for this consent purely because I have thereby offended God, I do not see how the same love does not for the same reason cause us to repent of the other contempt, that is, does not put me in that frame of mind that whatever excess of mine occurs to my memory I should similarly be sorry for it and be ready to make satisfaction. Therefore, wherever there is true repentance coming only from God's love, no contempt of God remains, especially since Truth says:[3] 'If anyone love me, he will keep my word. And my Father will love him; and we will come to him and will make our abode with him.' So whoever persist in the love of God must be saved. This salvation would by no means happen if one sin, that is, one contempt of God remains. Moreover, since in the penitent God now finds no sin, he finds there no cause for damnation and therefore it is necessary that, when sin ceases, damnation does not remain, that is, the affliction of everlasting punishment. By God's pardoning a preceding sin we mean, as we said, that God takes care of the eternal punishment which one had thereby earned. For although God may not now find in the penitent any reason for punishing him for ever, none the less he is said to pardon the punishment of a preceding sin when, by inspiring in him the sigh of repentance, he made him worthy of indulgence, that is, such a man to whom no eternal penalty is then owing and whom it is necessary to save if he departs this life in this state. And if perhaps he falls back into the same contempt, just as he returns to sin, so he also relapses to the debt of punishment, with the result that he, who earlier by repenting had not deserved to be punished, must be punished again.

---

[2] Gregory the Great, *Homiliarum in Evangelia lib.* ii. xxxiv. 15: 'Poenitentiam quippe agere est et perpetrata mala plangere, et plangenda non perpetrare' (*PL* 76. 1256B). Cf. Ps.-Ambrose, *Sermo* xxv. 1 (*PL* 17. 655A).

[3] John 14: 23.

Siquis forte dicat peccatum a Deo condonari tale esse tamquam
si diceretur Deum propter illud quod commissum est nequaquam
hominem esse dampnaturum, uel hoc Deum apud se statuisse ut
eum propter hoc non dampnaret, profecto et antequam penitens
5 peccasset concedendum uidetur Deum condonasse illud peccatum,
hoc est, apud se statuisse quod propter illud non esset eum dam-
pnaturus. Nichil quippe recenter apud se Deus statuit uel disponit,
sed ab aeterno quaecumque facturus est in eius predestinatione[a]
consistunt, et in eius prouidentia prefixa sunt, tam de condonatione
10 cuiuscumque peccati quam de ceteris quae fiunt. Melius itaque
nobis esse uidetur ita intelligendum Deum condonare peccatum
quemlibet ut diximus per inspiratum ei penitentiae gemitum dignum indulgentia efficere, hoc est, talem cui tunc dampnatio non
debeatur nec umquam ulterius si in tali proposito perseueret.
15 Peccatum itaque Deus condonat cum ipse a quo pena fieri[b] debuit,
faciat penitentiam inspirando cur iam non debeat inferri.

### *Iniustum non esse dignum premio non donari*[c]

Sed fortassis requiris si is qui penitet iam dignus sit uita aeterna
qui dampnatione dignus non est. Quod si concedamus, obicitur
20 nobis eum quoque qui post penitentiam lapsus periit, dum peni-
teret dignum uita aeterna fuisse et Deum arguendum iniuriae[d]
esse uideri, qui premium quo ille tunc dignus erat ei tunc saltem
non reddidit, ut sic eius dampnationem preueniret. Sicut enim si
tunc moreretur ex illo in quo erat proposito dignus uita aeterna
25 saluaretur, ita et si postea lapsus sit ex eodem animo quem prius
habuit dignus saluari fuit. Sed dico quia sicut multi sepe dampnatione digni sunt nec tamen in hac sua nequicia moriuntur ut
dampnatio quam meruerant eis a Deo reddatur, nec tamen ideo
Deus iniusticiae est arguendus quia non reddidit eis penam quam
30 meruerant, ita nec in premiis reddendis quae perseuerantibus
tantum promittuntur, Veritate adtestante,[1] 'qui perseuerauerit
usque in finem, hic saluus erit'. Non ergo concedere cogimur ut
quia quandoque premio uel pena quis dignus fuerit,[e] ideo dignum
uel iustum sit Deum illud ei conferre, cum alio modo melius

---

[a] proposito BCD      [b] inferri BCD      [c] ADE      [d] iniurie arguendum BCD      [e] fuerit dignus BC

---

[1] Matt. 24: 13 and 10: 22.

Perhaps if someone says that to say 'sin is pardoned by God' is the equivalent of saying 'God will by no means damn a man for what has been committed' or 'God has decided with himself not to damn him for this', surely even before the penitent sinned it seems it ought to be granted that God had pardoned that sin, that is, had decided with himself that he would not damn him for it. God certainly decides with himself or arranges nothing anew, but whatever he is to do exist from eternity in his predestination and are fixed in his providence, as much as regards the pardoning of every sin as the other things which happen. And so it seems to us better to understand God's pardoning sin in this way, making anyone worthy of pardon, as we said, through the sigh of repentance which he inspires in him, that is, making him such to whom damnation is not owing then, nor ever again if he perseveres in such a resolve. And so God pardons sin when he by, whom punishment should be rendered, now by inspiring repentance makes it unnecessary for it to be inflicted.

### *It is not unjust for a worthy man not to be given a reward*

But perhaps you ask if he who repents and is not worthy of damnation is now worthy of eternal life. If we allow this we face the objection that he too who perished, having lapsed after repenting, was worthy of eternal life while he was repentant, and it seems that God should be accused of a wrong for not at least granting then the reward of which he was then worthy in order thereby to prevent his damnation. For just as, were he to have died then, being worthy of eternal life by the frame of mind he was in, he would be saved, so too, if later he lapsed, by the same mind which he had earlier he was worthy of being saved. But I say that, just as many are often worthy of damnation and yet do not die in this wickedness of theirs, to be given by God the damnation which they had earned, nevertheless God should not therefore be accused of injustice for not giving them the punishment which they had earned; neither should he be accused of this in respect of giving rewards which are only promised to the persevering, as Truth attests:[1] 'He that shall persevere to the end, he shall be saved.' We are not bound therefore to allow, because someone sometime has been worthy of reward or punishment, that it is therefore proper or just that God should grant that to him, since

utendum eo esse prouiderit, qui etiam malis[a] bene utitur, et
quaeque pessima optime disponit. Quod si forte quis dicat eum
qui ad horam Deum amando uere penituit, sed tamen in hac
penitentia uel amore non perseuerauerit, non ideo fuisse premio
5 dignum[b] uitae, profecto cum nec tunc dampnatione[c] dignus fuisse
conceditur,[d] nec iustus nec peccator tunc exstitisse uidebitur.

## *De peccato inremissibili*[e]

Cum autem, ut diximus, omne peccatum per penitentiam statim
remissionem accipiat, queritur cur Veritas quoddam peccatum
10 inremissibile dixerit uel nunquam ipsum remissionem, hoc est,
condonationem, habiturum, quale est illud peccatum blasphemiae
in Spiritum Sanctum, de quo eum dixisse Matheus sic[f] refert,
'Omne peccatum et blasphemia remittetur hominibus, Spiritus
autem blasphemia non remittetur. Et quicumque dixerit uerbum
15 contra Filium hominis remittetur ei, qui autem dixerit[g] contra
Spiritum Sanctum, non remittetur ei neque in hoc seculo neque
in futuro.'[1] Quod quare diceret Marcus aperuit dicens,[2] 'quoniam dicebant, Spiritum immundum habet.' Hoc autem peccatum quidam desperationem ueniae dicunt, cum quis uidelicet ob
20 magnitudinem peccatorum diffidit penitus a bonitate Dei,[3] quae
per Spiritum Sanctum intelligitur, ut nec penitendo uel aliqua
satisfactione ueniam possit inpetrare. Sed si hoc dicimus peccare
uel blasphemare in Spiritum, quid dicemus peccare in Filium
hominis?[4] Quantum uero mihi uidetur, peccare siue blasphemare
25 in Filium hominis hoc loco dicitur excellentiae humanitatis Christi
derogare, tamquam eam negaremus sine peccato conceptam uel a
Deo assumptam propter uisibilem carnis infirmitatem. Id quippe
nulla humana racione comperi[h] poterat, sed Deo tantum reue-
lante credi. Tale est ergo quod ait,[5] 'Omne peccatum et blasphemia
30 remittetur hominibus, Spiritus autem blasphemia[i] non remittetur.' Tamquam si diceretur, De nulla alia blasphemia diffinitum
est apud Deum quod nullis hominibus dimittatur nisi de ista. 'Et
quicumque dixerit uerbum contra Filium hominis, remittetur ei',

---

[a] malis etiam BCD      [b] dignum premio BCD      [c] tunc dampnatione
A; dampnacione E; tam dampnacione D; dampnacione tunc BC      [d] sequitur de peccato inremissibili *add.* D      [e] ADE      [f] sic *om.* BC
[g] dixerit: uerbum *add.* BCD      [h] comperiri BC      [i] blasphemia non
remittetur: etc. BCD

---

[1] Matt. 12: 31–2. Cf. Abelard, *Problemata Heloissae*, no. 13 (*PL* 178. 694A–
696B).                                          [2] Mark 3: 30.
[3] Cf. *Glossa ordinaria* at Rom. 2: 5 (e.g. in the Strasbourg edn. printed by
A. Rusch, 1480).

he who uses even evils well, and arranges all the worst things in the best way, has foreseen that he would use him better in another way. If someone says, perhaps, that he who truly repented by loving God at the time, but yet did not persevere in this penance or love, was therefore unworthy of the reward of life, surely, since it is not conceded that he was then worthy of damnation, he will seem to have been then neither a just man nor a sinner.

## *Of irremissible sin*

Since, as we have said, every sin receives remission instantly through repentance, it is a question why Truth has said that a certain sin is irremissible or that it will never have remission, that is, pardon. Such is that sin of blasphemy against the Holy Spirit, of which Matthew reports him to have said this: 'Every sin and blasphemy shall be forgiven men, but the blasphemy of the Spirit shall not be forgiven. And, whosoever shall speak a word against the Son of man, it shall be forgiven him; but he that shall speak against the Holy Ghost, it shall not be forgiven him, neither in this world nor in the world to come.'[1] Mark revealed why he said this, saying:[2] 'Because they said: He hath an unclean spirit.' Now, some say this sin is despair of pardon, when someone, that is, because of the magnitude of his sins utterly distrusts the goodness of God[3] which is comprehended through the Holy Spirit, so that neither by repentance nor by some satisfaction is he able to obtain pardon. But if we call this sinning or blaspheming against the Spirit, what shall we call sinning against the Son of man?[4] Now, as far as it seems to me, to sin or blaspheme against the Son of man means in this passage to detract from the excellence of the humanity of Christ, as if we denied its conception without sin or its assumption by God on account of the visible weakness of flesh. Certainly human reason could not have discovered that; it is believed only because God reveals it. So what he said:[5] 'Every sin and blasphemy shall be forgiven men, but the blasphemy of the Spirit shall not be forgiven', is the equivalent of saying: with no other blasphemy has God determined that it shall not be forgiven to any men except with this one. 'And whosoever shall speak a word against the Son of man, it shall be forgiven him', that is, no one who detracts, as

[4] Cf. Ambrose of Milan, *De spiritu sancto*, i, c. 3, n. 54 (*PL* 16. 717).
[5] Matt. 12: 31.

hoc est, nullus qui assumpti hominis dignitati, ut diximus, deroget
propter hoc dampnabitur, si aliae non interueniant dampnationis
causae. Non enim in hoc aliquis contemptus Dei notari potest si
ueritatem per errorem contradicet nec contra conscientiam agat,
5 maxime cum id tale sit quod humana ratione inuestigari non
possit, sed magis rationi uideatur contrarium. Blasphemare autem
in Spiritum est ita opera manifestae gratiae Dei[a] calumpniari, ut
illa quae credebant per Spiritum Sanctum, hoc est, diuina bonitate
misericorditer fieri, per diabolum tamen assererent agi, tamquam si
10 dicerent illum quem Spiritum Dei credebant esse spiritum nequam
et sic Deum esse[b] diabolum. Quicumque igitur sic in Christum
peccauerunt, dicendo scilicet contra conscientiam eum in Beelzebub principe demoniorum eicere demonia,[1] ita prorsus a regno Dei
sunt proscripti et ab eius gratia penitus exclusi, ut nullus illorum
15 deinceps per penitentiam mereretur[c] indulgentiam. Nec quidem
negamus eos saluari posse[d] si peniterent, sed solummodo eos
dicimus[e] nec penitentiae actus assecuturos[f] esse.

*Vtrum penitentes gemitum sui doloris hinc secum deferant*[g]

Querit fortassis aliquis utrum hi qui de hac uita penitentes
20 recedunt in hoc gemitu cordis et contritione doloris ubi uerum Deo
sacrificium offertur, iuxta illud,[2] 'sacrificium Deo spiritus contri-
bulatus', utrum, inquam, tales de hac luce migrantes hunc gemitum et dolorem secum deferant ut in uita quoque illa[h] caelesti haec
se commisisse doleant, quo, ut scriptum est,[3] 'aufugit dolor et
25 gemitus atque tristicia'. Sed profecto sicut Deo uel angelis peccata
nostra sine aliqua pena doloris displicent, eo uidelicet quod illa
non approbant quae mala[i] considerant, ita et tunc nobis illa dis-
plicebunt in quibus deliquimus. Sed utrum nos illa fecisse uelimus quae bene ordinata esse a Deo scimus, et nobis quoque in
30 bonum cooperata iuxta illud Apostoli,[4] 'scimus quoniam diligen-
tibus Deum omnia cooperantur in bonum',[j] questio est alia quam
pro uiribus nostris tercio *Theologiae* nostrae libro absoluimus.[5]

---

[a] dei: per inuidiam *add.* BC    [b] deum esse: ipsum deum BC    [c] meretur BCE    [d] posse *om.* BC    [e] dicimus eos BC    [f] assecutos BC
[g] AE; An peccantes saluandi gemitum doloris hinc deferant D    [h] uita
quoque illa ADE; hac uita B; uita quoque C    [i] mala: esse *add.* BCD
[j] bonum: etc. *add.* BCD

---

[1] Cf. Luke 11: 15.    [2] Ps. 50: 19.
[3] Isa. 35: 10.    [4] Rom. 8: 28.
[5] Cf. Abelard, *Theologia 'Scholarium'*, iii (ed. Cousin, *Opera P. Abaelardi*,

we have said, from the dignity of the assumed man, will be damned
for this unless other reasons for damnation are present. For no contempt of God can be noted in this, if in error he contradicts truth
and does not act against his conscience, especially since it is something which cannot be investigated by human reason but seems
rather to be contrary to reason. On the other hand, to blaspheme
against the Spirit is so to slander the works of God's evident
grace, that what is believed to be done mercifully through the
Holy Spirit, that is, by divine goodness, is claimed none the less
to be done through the devil, as if to say that he who is believed
to be the spirit of God is a wicked spirit and thus that God is
a devil. Therefore, whoever have thus sinned against Christ, that
is, by saying against their conscience that he casts out devils by
Beelzebub, the prince of devils,[1] are thus proscribed absolutely
from the kingdom of God and excluded wholly from his grace,
so that none of them subsequently deserves his indulgence through
repentance. We do not deny that they can be saved if they repent,
but we say only that they will not pursue acts of repentance.

### *Whether penitents take away with them from here the sigh of their sorrow*

Perhaps someone is asking whether these who withdraw from
this life repenting, in this sighing of heart and contrition of sorrow,
where true sacrifice is offered to God according to this:[2] 'A sacrifice to God is an afflicted spirit', whether, I say, such, departing
from this life, take away with them this sigh and sorrow, so that
in the heavenly life also they grieve for having committed these
things, where, as has been written,[3] 'sorrow and mourning and
sadness flee away'. But surely, just as without any of the pain of
sorrow our sins displease God or the angels through the fact that
they do not approve what they consider to be evil, in the same way
also what we have done wrong will then displease us. But whether
we will want to have done what we know to have been well
ordained by God and also to have worked with us unto good—
according to the Apostle:[4] 'We know that to them that love God
all things work together unto good'—is another question which we,
to the best of our ability, resolve in the third book of our *Theology*.[5]

ii. 148–9). Cf. Peter Lombard, *Sententiarum liber* iv, *dist.* xliii, *cap.* 5 (2nd edn.,
Ad Claras Aquas, 1916), pp. 997–8.

## De confessione[a]

Nunc de confessione peccatorum nobis agere incumbit. Ad
hanc nos Apostolus Iacobus adhortans ait,[1] 'Confitemini alterutrum peccata uestra et orate pro inuicem ut saluemini. Multum
5 enim ualet deprecatio iusti assidua.' Sunt qui soli Deo confitendum
arbitrantur, quod non nulli Grecis imponunt.[2] Sed quid apud
Deum confessio ualeat qui omnia nouit, aut quam indulgentiam
lingua nobis inpetret non uideo, licet Propheta dicat,[3] 'delictum
meum cognitum tibi feci et iniusticiam meam non abscondi.'
10 Multis[b] de causis fideles inuicem peccata confitentur iuxta illud
Apostoli quod premissum est, tum uidelicet propter supradictam[c]
causam ut orationibus eorum magis adiuuemur quibus confitemur,
tum etiam quia in humilitate confessionis magna pars[d] agitur
satisfactionis, et in relaxatione penitentiae maiorem assequimur
15 indulgentiam, sicut de Dauid scriptum est. Qui cum accusatus a
Nathan propheta responderit,[4] 'Peccaui', statim ab eodem Propheta
responsum[e] audiuit, 'Dominus quoque transtulit peccatum tuum.'
Quo enim maior erat regis sublimitas, acceptior Deo fuit con-
fitens[f] humilitas. Denique sacerdotes quibus animae confitentium
20 sunt commissae, satisfactiones penitentiae illis habent iniungere,
ut qui male arbitrio suo et superbe usi sunt Deum contempnendo
alienae potestatis arbitrio corrigantur, et tanto securius id agant,
quanto melius[g] prelatis suis obediendo non tam suam quam illorum uoluntatem secuntur. Qui si fortassis non recte preceperint,[h]
25 cum ille ad obediendum paratus sit, illis magis quam isti[i] impu-
tandum est. 'Non ignoramus', inquit Apostolus,[5] astutias Sathanae,
nec eius nequicia hoc loco pretereunda est qua nos ad peccatum
impellit, et a confessione retrahit. Ad peccatum quippe nos in-
citans, timore pariter ac uerecundia nos exuit ut nichil iam re-
30 stet quod nos a peccato reuocet. Multa namque timore penae
committere non audemus, multa pro detrimento nostrae famae

---

<sup>a</sup> ADE    <sup>b</sup> Multis: uero *add.* BCD    <sup>c</sup> subpositam ABDE    <sup>d</sup> pars:
iam *add.* BCD        <sup>e</sup> responsum: sibi BCD        <sup>f</sup> confitentis BCD
<sup>g</sup> humilius BC    <sup>h</sup> ceperint B; perceperint D    <sup>i</sup> istis ADE

<sup>1</sup> James 5: 16.
<sup>2</sup> Abelard may have had in mind a version of canon 33 of the second council
of Chalon (813), ed. J. D. Mansi, *Sacrorum Conciliorum noua et amplissima
collectio*, t. xiv (Venice, 1769), col. 100. The relevant part of this canon, with the
addition of two concluding words, appears in Burchard of Worms, *Decretum*,
xix. 145 (*PL* 140. 1011A) and in Ivo of Chartres, *Decretum, pars* xv, *cap.* 155
(*PL* 161. 892B): 'Quidam Deo solummodo confiteri debere peccata dicunt, ut
Greci.' On the obligation to confess see Abelard, *Sic et non, cap.* 151: 'Quod
sine confessione non dimittantur peccata et contra' (*PL* 178. 1599–1600) and
*Sermo VIII in Ramis Palmarum* (440B, 441B–444D). The obligation to confess
was generally agreed by twelfth-century writers, but their theoretical justifica-

## Of confession

It is incumbent upon us to deal now with confession of sins. The Apostle James urged us to this, saying:[1] 'Confess your sins one to another; and pray one for another, that you may be saved. For the continual prayer of a just man availeth much.' There are people who think that confession should be made to God alone— a view which some attribute to the Greeks.[2] But I do not see what confession avails with God who knows all, or what indulgence our tongue obtains for us, although the Prophet says:[3] 'I have acknowledged my sin to thee: and my injustice I have not concealed.' For many reasons the faithful confess their sins to one another, in accordance with the above quotation from the Apostle, both, that is, for the reason mentioned, that we may be more helped by the prayers of those to whom we confess, and also because in the humility of confession a large part of satisfaction is performed and we obtain a greater indulgence in the relaxation of our penance, as was written of David, who replied, when accused by the Prophet Nathan:[4] 'I have sinned'; immediately he heard a reply from the same Prophet: 'The Lord also hath taken away thy sin.' For the greater the sublimity of the king, the more acceptable was his humility in confessing to God. Lastly, priests, to whom have been committed the souls of those who confess, have to impose satisfactions of penance upon them, so that those who have used their judgement wrongly and proudly by showing contempt of God may be corrected by the judgement of another power, and that they may attend more safely to this the better they follow, by obeying their prelates, the will of these rather than their own. If perhaps these have not instructed rightly when he was ready to obey, that should be imputed to them rather than to him. 'For we are not ignorant', says the Apostle,[5] 'of Satan's devices', and we must not here pass over his wickedness by which he impels us to sin and draws us back from confession. In fact, in inciting us to sin he divests us of fear as well as of shame, so that now nothing remains which may call us back from sin. For there are many things we dare not do for fear of punishment; we are ashamed to undertake many things because of damage to our reputation, even though

---

tion of this obligation varied according to their view of the extent of the remission secured by inner contrition. See above, p. 88 n. 3, and, for a full survey of the literature, Anciaux, *La théologie du sacrement de pénitence*, part iii, chap. 2.

[3] Ps. 31: 5.          [4] 2 Kings 12: 13.          [5] 2 Cor. 2: 11.

aggredi erubescimus, etsi hoc inpune possemus.[a] His ergo duobus quasi retinaculis male quilibet[b] expeditus, preceps ad quoduis perpetrandum peccatum efficietur.[c] Quo quidem pacto eadem quae prius ei[d] abstulit ut peccatum perficeret, postmodum reddit 5 ut a confessione reuocet. Tunc[e] confiteri timet uel erubescit quod, cum oportuerit[f] primum, non timuit nec erubuit. Timet ne forte per confessionem cognitus[g] puniatur ab hominibus qui puniri non timuit a Deo. Erubescit ab hominibus sciri quod non erubuit coram Deo committi, sed qui plagae querit medicamentum, quantum-
10 cumque ipsa sordeat, quantumcumque oleat, medico reuelanda est ut conpetens adhibeatur curatio. Medici uero locum sacerdos tenet a quo, ut diximus, instituenda est satisfactio.

*Quod non numquam confessio dimitti potest*[h]

Sciendum tamen[i] non numquam salubri dispensatione confes-
15 sionem uitari posse, sicut de Petro credimus, cuius lacrimas de negatione sua nouimus, satisfactionem uero aliam uel confessionem[j] non legimus. Vnde et Ambrosius super Lucam[1] de hac ipsa Petri negatione ac fletu eius, 'Non inuenio', inquit,[k] 'quid dixerit, inuenio quod fleuerit.[1] Lacrimas eius lego, satisfactionem non
20 lego. Lauant lacrimae delictum quod uoce pudor est confiteri, et ueniae fletus consulunt et uerecundiae. Lacrimae sine horrore culpam locuntur, sine offensione[m] uerecundiae confitentur. Lacrimae ueniam non postulant sed[n] merentur. Inuenio cur tacuerit Petrus, ne scilicet[o] tam cito ueniae petitio plus offenderet.' Quae uero
25 ista sit uerecundia uel reuerentia confessionis, ut flendo magis quam confitendo Petrus satisfecerit, uidendum est. Si enim propter hoc unum confiteri uerecundabatur ne cognito peccato suo uilior haberetur, profecto superbus erat, et honoris sui gloriae[p] magis quam animae suae saluti consulens, sin autem uerecundia non
30 tam sua quam aecclesiae retinebatur, non est hoc inprobandum.

[a] possimus BC; possumus D     [b] quislibet BC     [c] efertur B; effertur D; offertur C     [d] ei *om.* B; *add.* diabolus BCD     [e] Tunc: enim *add.* BCD     [f] oportuit BCD     [g] cognitum ACE; cognitam D; *om.* B     [h] AE; Cur confessio quandoque dimitti potest D     [i] tamen: est etiam B; est *add.* E     [j] confessionem: eius CD; fuisse B     [k] inquit *om.* BC     [1] quid fleuerit B; quod (*bis*) deleuerit C     [m] cofessione B; ostensione C     [n] et BCD     [o] scilicet *om.* BCD     [p] glorie (gloria D) . . . saluti consulens ADE; gloriam (gloria C) . . . salutem querens BC

[1] Luke 22: 62; Ambrose of Milan, *Expositio Euangelii secundum Lucam*, x. 88 (*CCL* 45, p. 371, or *PL* 15. 1825B–1826A). Cf. Maximus, *Homilia LIII* (*PL* 57. 351–2) or *Homilia LXXVI* in the edn. of A. Mutzenbecher (*CCL* 23, p. 318). This and other texts are presented by Abelard in the *Sic et non*, cap. 151, 'Quod sine

we could do it with impunity. So anyone unimpeded by these two tethers, as it were, will become strongly inclined to commit any kind of sin. By this means the same things which he earlier took away from him so that he should commit sin, he later restores to him to call him away from confession. Then he is afraid or is ashamed to confess; when first he should have done so, he was not afraid nor was he ashamed. He fears lest by perhaps becoming known through confession he, who did not fear to be punished by God, be punished by men. He is ashamed that men should know what he was not ashamed to commit before God. But he who seeks medicine for a wound, however foul it is, however smelly, must show it to a doctor so that an effective cure may be applied. The priest in fact occupies the place of a doctor and he, as we have said, must establish the satisfaction.

## That sometimes confession may be dispensed with

However, it should be known that sometimes by a wholesome dispensation confession can be avoided, as we believe was true of Peter, whose tears over his denial we know, although we do not read of other satisfaction or of confession. Whence Ambrose on Luke[1] says of this very denial by Peter and of his weeping: 'I do not find what he said; I find that he wept. I read of his tears; I do not read of his satisfaction. Tears wipe away a wrong which it is disgraceful to confess with one's voice and weeping guarantees pardon and shame. Tears declare the fault without dread, they confess without prejudicing shame. Tears do not request pardon but deserve it. I find why Peter was silent, namely lest by asking for pardon so soon he should offend more.' We must ascertain what in fact is this shame or awe of confession whereby Peter satisfied by weeping rather than by confessing. For if he felt ashamed to confess for this single reason lest, if his sin became known, he be thought of as viler, surely he was proud and was providing for the renown of his honour rather than for the salvation

confessione non dimittantur peccata, et contra' (*PL* 178. 1599–1600). On the use of the quotation from Ambrose in the school of Anselm of Laon see L. Hödl, *Die Geschichte der scholastischen Literatur und der Theologie der Schlüsselgewalt*, i, BGPTMA, xxxviii. 4 (1960), pp. 35–8. Hugh of Saint-Victor refused to see in this passage any ground for qualifying the necessity to confess sin, *De Sacramentis*, II. xiv, c. 1 (*PL* 176. 553A–554D). Cf. *Summa Sententiarum*, VI. x (*PL* 176. 147AB).

Prouidebat se fortassis super dominicam plebem a Domino con-
stituendum[a] esse principem, et uerebatur ne si haec eius trina[b]
negatio per confessionem eius[c] cito in publicum prodiret, super
hoc aecclesia grauiter[d] scandalizaretur et erubescentia uehementi
5 confunderetur, quod tam facilem ad negandum et tam pusil-
lanimum Dominus ei prefecisset. Si ergo non[e] tam pro honore
sibi conseruando quam pro hac communi[f] erubescentia aecclesiae
confiteri distulit, prouide hoc non superbe fecit. Timor quoque in
causa rationabilis fuit de dampno aecclesiae magis quam de propriae
10 detrimento famae. Sciebat quippe sibi specialiter a Domino aecclesiam esse commissam cum ei diceret,[1] 'et tu aliquando conuersus
confirma fratres tuos.' Si ergo eo propria confessione conuicto ad
aures aecclesiae perueniret hic eius tam abhorrendus[g] lapsus, quis
non leuiter diceret, 'nolumus hunc regnare super nos',[2] et non
15 facile dominicum improbaret consilium, quod ad confirmandos
fratres eum elegit qui primus defecit? Hac quoque prouidentia
multi confessionem differre uel omnino dimittere possent sine
peccato, si uidelicet plus illam nocere quam prodesse crederent,
quia nullam Dei offensam ex culpa incurrimus, in quo eum ne-
20 quaquam contempnimus. Distulit Petrus confiteri peccatum cum
adhuc tenera in fide atque infirma esset aecclesia, donec uirtus Petri
predicatione ipsius uel miraculis esset probata. Postea uero cum
de hoc iam constaret, ipsemet Petrus sine ullo aecclesiae scandalo
contra desperationem lapsorum confiteri hoc potuit ut scriptum
25 etiam relinqueretur ab Euangelistis.

Sunt fortassis quibus uideatur Petrum,[h] qui ceteris omnibus
preerat, nec superiorem habebat cui anima eius esset commissa,
nequaquam habere[i] necessarium homini confiteri peccatum,
tamquam ab illo instituenda[j] esset ei satisfactio ac si precepto eius
30 quasi superioris obediret. Sed si non pro satisfactione iniungenda
confiteri alicui debuerit,[k] propter orationis suffragium non incon-
grue fieri potuit. De quo quidem cum diceretur,[3] 'confitemini
alterutrum peccata vestra', subiunctum est, 'et orate pro inuicem
ut saluemini.' Nichil etiam inpedit ne prelati eligant subiectos[l] ad
35 confessionem faciendam uel ad satisfactionem suscipiendam, ut

---

[a] constitutum BC      [b] tercia BD       [c] ipsius BC       [d] grauiter ecclesia BCD       [e] non *om.* AE       [f] animi ACDE       [g] horrendus BC
[h] petrus B; *om.* C       [i] haberet AE       [j] constituenda BC       [k] debuit
BC       [l] subiectos eligant BC

---

[1] Luke 22: 32.      [2] Luke 19: 14.      [3] James 5: 16.

of his soul. But if what was being protected was the shame of the Church rather than his own, this should not be derided. He perhaps foresaw that the Lord would establish him as leader over the Lord's people, and he feared lest, if this triple denial of his quickly became public knowledge through his confession, the Church would be gravely scandalized by it and shaken in mighty embarrassment that the Lord had placed over it one so ready to deny and so pusillanimous. So if he put off confessing less to safeguard his own position than on account of this general embarrassment of the Church, he did it with foresight, not from pride. His fear of damage to the Church rather than of loss of his own reputation was also reasonably caused. He knew indeed that the Church had been specially committed to him by the Lord, when he said to him:[1] 'And thou, being once converted, confirm thy brethren.' So if, convicted by his own confession, this very dreadful lapse of his were to reach the ears of the Church, who would not swiftly say: 'We will not have this man to reign over us',[2] and would not readily censure the Lord's judgement which chose to strengthen the brethren the one who was first to fail? And by this forethought many could put off confession, or completely dispense with it, without sin, if they believed confession would do them more harm than good, because we incur no offence against God by fault where we in no way offer contempt of him. Since Peter was still tender in faith and the Church was weak, he put off confessing his sin until his virtue had been proved by his preaching or miracles. Later, however, when this was at last evident, the same Peter, without any commotion in the Church against the desperation of those who lapse, was able to confess this, with the result, moreover, that a written account was left by the Evangelists.

There are perhaps people to whom it may seem that Peter, who was set over all the others and did not have a superior to whom his soul had been committed, had no necessity at all to confess his sin to a man, as if satisfaction should be arranged by him and he should obey his command as that of a superior. But if he need not have had to confess to someone in order that satisfaction should be imposed, he could have done so without incongruity for the sake of obtaining the help of prayer. Indeed, when it was said:[3] 'Confess your sins one to another', there followed: 'and pray one for another that you may be saved.' Moreover, nothing prevents prelates from choosing subjects in order to make confession or to

quod agitur tanto Deo fiat acceptius quanto ab illis geritur humilius. Quis etiam uetet quemlibet in talibus personam religiosiorem uel magis discretam eligere, cuius arbitrio satisfactionem suam committat, et orationibus eius plurimum adiuuetur? Vnde et cum
5 premissum sit: 'et orate pro inuicem ut saluemini', statim adiunctum est, 'Multum enim ualet deprecatio iusti assidua.' Sicut enim multi fiunt[a] imperiti medici, quibus infirmos committi periculosum est aut inutile, ita et in prelatis aecclesiae multi reperiuntur nec religiosi nec discreti, atque insuper ad detegendum confitentium
10 peccata leues, ut confiteri eis[b] non solum inutile uerum etiam perniciosum uideatur. Tales quippe nec orare intendunt nec in orationibus suis exaudiri merentur,[c] et cum instituta canonum ignorent, nec in statuendis satisfactionibus[d] moderari sciant, frequenter in talibus uanam securitatem promittunt, et spe cassa
15 ipsos confitentes[e] decipiunt iuxta illud Veritatis,[1] 'Ceci sunt duces cecorum'[f] et rursum, 'Si cecus ceco ducatum prestet, ambo in foueam cadunt.'[2] Qui cum etiam, ut diximus, leuiter confessiones quas suscipiunt reuelant, penitentes ad indignationem commouent, et qui curare peccata debuerant nouas peccatorum plagas
20 inferunt, et a confessione audientes deterrent.

Non numquam etiam peccata uel ex ira uel ex leuitate reuelando grauiter aecclesiam scandalizant, et eos qui confessi sunt in pericula magna constituunt. Vnde qui pro his incommoditatibus prelatos suos uitare decreuerunt et alios in talibus eligere quos ad
25 ista[g] commodiores credunt,[h] nequaquam sunt inprobandi,[i] sed potius comprobandi quod ad sollertiorem medicum declinant. In quo tamen faciendo si assensum prelatorum inpetrare possunt ut ab eis ad alios[j] dirigantur, tanto id conuenientius agunt quanto humilius per obedientiam hoc faciunt. Sin autem prelati superbi
30 hoc eis interdicunt, tamquam se uiliores estimando si meliores medici requirantur, egrotus tamen de salute sua sollicitus, quod melius credit medicamentum maiori sollicitudine requirat et meliori consilio cedat plurimum. Nemo enim ducem sibi ab aliquo

---

[a] sunt BCD          [b] eis confiteri BC          [c] merentur exaudiri BCD
[d] in statuendis satisfactionibus AE; in statuendas satisfactiones B; instituendas satisfactiones C; in statuendis satisfacciones D          [e] confitentes BC
[f] sunt duces cecorum AE; cecorum duces effecti BCD          [g] istas B; istam
C          [h] credant A          [i] inprobandi sunt BC; sunt improbanda D
[j] illos BC

---

[1] Matt. 15: 14.
[2] One writer of a manual of confession (*c.* 1155–65) also stressed the need for judges to be learned and to undergo training, but offered Peter Abelard himself as an illustration of one quality which a judge should not have: 'Sed confidet

receive satisfaction, so that what is done may be made more acceptable to God the more humbly they carry it out. And who will forbid anyone to choose in such matters a more religious or more discreet person, to whose judgement he may entrust his satisfaction and by whose prayers he may be very greatly helped? Whence, although it was first said: 'and pray one for another that you may be saved', there was added immediately: 'for the continual prayer of a just man availeth much.' For just as many become unskilful doctors to whom it is dangerous or useless for the sick to be entrusted, so too many are found among the prelates of the Church who are neither religious nor discreet, and are moreover liable to disclose the sins of those who confess, so that to confess to them seems not only useless but also ruinous. Such indeed neither intend to pray nor deserve to be heard in their prayers, and since they do not know the canonical rules nor know how to arrange the fixing of satisfactions, frequently they promise in such things false security and with a worthless hope deceive those who confess, according to the Truth:[1] 'They are blind and leaders of the blind', and again: 'If the blind lead the blind, both fall into the pit.'[2] And since, as we have said, they lightly reveal confessions which they receive, they rouse penitents to indignation, and they, who should have healed sins, inflict new wounds of sin and frighten those who hear them away from confession.

Sometimes also by revealing sins either in anger or in levity, they gravely scandalize the Church and place those who have confessed in great dangers. Whence they, who have decided on account of these disadvantages to avoid their prelates and to choose in such matters others whom they believe to be more suitable for them, should by no means be condemned but rather approved of for turning to a more expert doctor. However, if in doing so they can obtain the assent of their prelates to direct them to others, they act so much more suitably the more humbly they do this in obedience. But if proud prelates forbid this to them, as if considering that, if better doctors are required, they must themselves be rather vile, none the less the sick man anxious for his health may seek with greater anxiety what he believes is better medicine and may give greatest preference to better advice. For no one should follow into

aliquis de ingenio suo et dicit se intelligere quidquid ei proponatur, sicut magister Petrus Abailardus', ed. P. Michaud-Quantin, 'Un manuel de confession archaïque dans le manuscrit Avranches 136', *Sacris Erudiri*, xvii (1966), 31.

commissum, si eum cecum deprehenderit, in foueam sequi debet, et melius est eligere eum uidentem ut quo tendit[a] perueniat, quam male sibi traditum male sequi ad precipitium. Quippe qui ei talem ducem tradidit tamquam uiam ostensurum, aut scienter
5 hoc fecit per maliciam aut innocenter per ignorantiam. Si per maliciam, cauendum fuit ne malicia eius inpleretur, si per ignorantiam, nequaquam contra eius uoluntatem agitur si illum non sequimur ad periculum quem ipse dederat nobis ad ducatum. Vtile tamen est ut eos primum consulamus quibus animas
10 nostras committi scimus, et eorum consilio audito, salubrius, si quod speramus medicamentum non deserere, maxime cum eos legem ignorare credamus, et[b] non solum quid agant curent, sed[c] quid doleant ignorent, deteriores[d] habendi his de quibus Veritas ait,[1] 'Super cathedram Moysi sederunt Scribae et Pharisei. Quae-
15 cumque ergo dixerint uobis seruate et facite, secundum autem opera eorum nolite facere.' Tamquam si diceret, Magisterium legis tales obtinent quorum opera cum sint mala et ob hoc respuenda, uerba tamen Dei quae de cathedra Moysi, hoc est, de magisterio legis, proferunt, suscipienda sunt ut simul quae ipso-
20 rum sunt opera reiciamus, et quae Dei sunt uerba retineamus.

Non est ergo talium doctrina contempnenda qui bene predicant licet male uiuant, et qui erudiunt uerbo licet non edificent exemplo, et uiam ostendunt quam sequi nolunt, non tam de cecitate ignorantiae quam de culpa negligentiae iudicandi.[e] Qui uero nec
25 uiam subiectis ostendere ualent, qui ducatui eorum committere se debent et ab eis requirere documentum qui docere nesciunt? Nec tamen desperandum est subiectis a misericordia Dei, cum ad satisfactionem omnino parati prelatorum suorum, quamuis cecorum, arbitrio se tradunt, et quod illi per errorem minus
30 instituunt, isti per obedientiam diligenter exsecuntur. Non enim error prelatorum subiectos dampnat, nec illorum uicium istos accusat, nec iam in subiectis culpa remanet qua moriantur quos iam antea penitentia Deo, ut diximus,[f] reconciliauerat priusquam

---

[a] tendit *om.* B; tendat C     [b] ut BCDE     [c] sed: et *add.* BC
[d] deteriores: in hoc *add.* BCD     [e] iudicando AE     [f] ut diximus deo
BCD

---

[1] Matt. 23: 2–3.

the ditch a leader whom someone has granted to him if he discovers he is blind; and it is better to choose him who sees, so that
one arrives where one is going, than to follow wrongly to the
precipice a leader who has been wrongly assigned to one. Indeed, the man who has assigned to him such a leader, so as to
show him the way, has either done this knowingly through malice
or innocently through ignorance. If through malice, one should
have been on one's guard lest his malice be implemented; if through
ignorance, by no means is it to go against his will if we do not
follow into danger him who had been given to us as a leader. However, it is useful first to consult those to whom we know our souls
are committed and, having heard their advice, not to forsake
their wholesome medicine if it is what we hope for, especially
when we believe that they are ignorant of the law and are not just
unconcerned about what they should do, but unaware of what
they should deplore; they should be considered worse than they
of whom Truth says:[1] 'The Scribes and the Pharisees have sitten
on the chair of Moses. All things therefore whatsoever they shall
say to you, observe and do; but according to their works do ye not.'
As if to say: such obtain a mastership of the law whose deeds,
since they are bad, are for this reason to be rejected, yet the words
of God which they utter from the chair of Moses, that is, from
the mastership of the law, are to be accepted, so that we should
simultaneously reject the actions which are their own and retain
the words which are of God.

So the teaching of such men is not to be held in contempt; they
preach well although they live badly, and they instruct in the word
although they do not edify in example, and they show the way which
they refuse to follow; they should be condemned less for the blindness of ignorance than for the fault of negligence. But in the case
of those who are not capable of showing the way to their subjects,
who should commit themselves to their leadership and seek a
lesson from them who know not how to teach? Yet subjects should
not despair of the mercy of God when, wholly ready for satisfaction, they deliver themselves to the judgement of their prelates,
although they are blind, and in obedience diligently perform what
they in error inadequately determine. For the error of prelates does
not damn their subjects, nor does their vice reproach them, nor
does there now remain in their subjects any fault in which they
may die; repentance had already beforehand, as we have said,

scilicet ad confessionem uenirent uel satisfactionis[a] institutio-
nem susciperent. Siquid tamen de pena satisfactionis minus est
institutum quam oporteat, Deus qui nullum peccatum inpuni-
tum dimittit, et singula quantum debet punit, pro quantitate
5 peccati satisfactionis equitatem seruabit, ipsos uidelicet penitentes
non aeternis suppliciis reseruando,[b] sed in hac uita uel in futura
penis purgatoriis affligendo, si nos, inquam, in nostra satisfactione negligentes fuerimus. Vnde Apostolus,[1] 'Si nos', inquit,
'diiudicaremus, non utique diiudicaremur.'[c] Quod est dicere, Si
10 nos ipsi nostra puniremus uel corrigeremus peccata, nequaquam
ab ipso grauius essent punienda. Magna profecto misericordia
Dei cum nos nostro iudicio dimittit, ne ipse puniat grauiori.
Has autem penas uitae presentis quibus de peccatis satisfacimus,
ieiunando uel[d] orando, uigilando uel quibuscumque modis car-
15 nem macerando uel quae nobis subtrahimus egenis inpendendo,
satisfactionem uocamus, quas alio nomine in Euangelio 'fructus
penitentiae' nouimus appellari, ubi uidelicet ait,[e2] 'facite fructus
dignos penitentiae'. Ac si aperte diceretur, Digna[f] satisfactione
quod deliquistis emendando, ita hic reconciliamini Deo, ut dein-
20 ceps quod ipse puniat nequaquam inueniat et grauiores penas
mitioribus preuenite. Vt enim beatus asserit Augustinus,[3] 'Penae
uitae futurae etsi purgatoriae sint, grauiores sunt istis omnibus
uitae presentis.' Magna itaque cautela est eis adhibenda, et magna
opera danda ut secundum instituta sanctorum patrum talis hic[g]
25 satisfactio suscipiatur, ut nichil ibi purgandum restet. Cum ergo
indiscreti fuerint sacerdotes qui haec instituta canonum ignorant,[h]
ut minus de satisfactione quam oportet iniungant, magnum hinc
incommodum penitentes incurrunt, cum male de ipsis confisi
grauioribus penis postmodum plectentur, unde hic per leuiores
30 satisfacere potuerunt.

Sunt[i] nonnulli sacerdotum, non tam per errorem quam[j]
cupiditatem subiectos decipientes, ut pro nummorum oblatione
satisfactionis iniuncte penas condonent uel relaxent, non tam adtendentes quid uelit Dominus, quam quid ualeat nummus. De
35 quibus[k] ipse Dominus per Prophetam conquirens ait,[4] 'Sacerdotes

---

ᵃ satisfactionem BDE      ᵇ seruando B; reseruandos AE      ᶜ iudica-
remur BC      ᵈ scilicet BCD      ᵉ dicitur BCD      ᶠ dignos BD
ᵍ haec AE      ʰ ignorent BC      ⁱ sunt: et *add.* B; tamen et C      ʲ quam:
per *add.* BCD      ᵏ qualibus BCD

---

[1] 1 Cor. 11: 31.                                                  [2] Matt. 3: 8.
[3] Cf. Pseudo-Augustine, *Liber de uera et falsa poenitentia, cap.* 18: 'Hic autem
ignis (purgationis) etsi aeternus non fuerit . . . excellit omnem poenam quam
umquam passus est aliquis in hac uita' (*PL* 40. 1128).
[4] Jer. 2: 8.

reconciled them to God, that is, before they came to confession or got their satisfaction determined. However, if any part of the penalty of satisfaction is determined as less than it should be, God, who forgives no sin without punishment and punishes each as much as he should, upholds the fairness of satisfaction according to the amount of the sin, not, that is, by reserving those penitents for eternal torture, but by afflicting them in this life or in the future with purgatorial punishments, if we, I say, have been negligent in our satisfaction. Whence the Apostle says:[1] 'If we would judge ourselves, we should not be judged.' Which is to say: if we would ourselves punish or correct our own sins, they would not be punished by him more severely at all. Surely God's mercy is great when he forgives us on the basis of our own sentencing in order not to punish us more severely. Now these penalties of our present life with which we make satisfaction for sins, by fasting or praying, by keeping vigil, or by whatever means macerating the flesh, or by distributing to the needy what we forgo ourselves, these we call satisfaction. We know they are called by another name in the Gospel, 'the fruits of penance', that is, where it is said:[2] 'Bring forth fruits worthy of penance', as if to say openly: by correcting what you have done wrong with a fitting satisfaction, be thus reconciled to God here, so that in turn he may by no means find what he himself would punish, and prevent severer penalties by means of milder ones. For as the blessed Augustine states:[3] 'The penalties of the future life, although they are purgatorial, are graver than all these of the present life.' And so great caution should be shown concerning them and great care should be taken, so that, according to the rules of the holy Fathers, such satisfaction should be undertaken here that nothing remains to be purged there. So when priests who do not know these canonical rules have been unwise, with the result that they impose less satisfaction than they should, penitents thereby incur a great disadvantage since, having wrongly trusted in them, they are later punished with heavier penalties for that for which they could have made satisfaction here by means of lighter penalties.

There are some priests who deceive their subjects less through error than through greed, so that for an offering of denarii they pardon or relax the penalties of an imposed satisfaction, not considering so much the will of the Lord as the power of money. Of these the Lord himself complained through the Prophet, saying:[4]

mei non dixerunt, ubi est Dominus?' tamquam si diceret, sed ubi
est nummus? Nec solum sacerdotes uerum etiam ipsos principes
sacerdotum, hoc est, episcopos, ita inpudenter in hanc cupiditatem
exardescere nouimus ut cum in dedicationibus aecclesiarum uel in
5 consecrationibus altarium uel benedictionibus cymiteriorum uel
in aliquibus sollempnitatibus populares habent conuentus unde
copiosam oblationem expectant, in relaxandis penitentiis prodigi
sint,[a] modo terciam modo quartam penitentiae partem omnibus[b]
communiter indulgentes, sub quadam scilicet[c] specie karitatis,
10 sed in ueritate summae cupiditatis.[1] Qui de sua se iactantes potestate quam, ut aiunt, in Petro uel apostolis susceperunt cum eis
a Domino diceretur,[2] 'quorum remiseritis peccata remittentur eis',
uel,[3] 'quaecumque solueritis super terram erunt soluta et in
caelis', tunc maxime quod suum est agere gloriantur, cum hanc
15 benignitatem subiectis inpendunt, atque utinam id saltem pro
ipsis non pro nummis facerent, ut qualiscumque benignitas
potius quam cupiditas uideretur. Sed profecto si hoc in laude
benignitatis habendum est quod terciam uel quartam penitentiae
partem relaxant, multo amplius eorum pietas predicanda erit si
20 dimidiam uel totam ex integro penitentiam dimitterent,[d] sicut
licere sibi profitentur, et a Domino concessum esse, et quasi in
manibus eorum caelos esse positos, secundum remissionis uel
absolutionis peccatorum supra posita testimonia. Magnae denique
inpietatis econtrario arguendi uidentur cur non omnes subiectos
25 ab omnibus absoluant peccatis, ut uidelicet neminem illorum
dampnari permittant, si ita, inquam, in eorum potestate constitutum est quae uoluerint peccata dimittere[e] uel retinere, uel caelos
his quibus decreuerint aperire uel claudere. Quod utique beatis-
simi predicandi essent, si hos sibi, cum uellent, aperire possent.
30 Quod quidem si non possunt uel nesciunt, certe illud poeticum, in
quantum arbitror, incurrunt, 'Nec prosunt domino quae prosunt
omnibus artes.'[4] Appetat quislibet, non ego, potestatem illam[f] qua
potius aliis quam sibi proficere possit, tamquam in potestate sua
habeat alienas animas saluare magis quam propriam, cum econ-
35 trario quislibet discretus sentiat.

a sunt B; fiunt C      b omnibus *om.* C; hominibus B      c quidem BC
d relaxarent BC      e remittere BC      f hanc B; istam CD

1 According to Anciaux, *La théologie du sacrement de pénitence*, p. 502,
Abelard was alone in the first half of the twelfth century in criticizing the value
of general absolutions accorded by bishops; see also ibid., pp. 50–1.

'My priests did not say: Where is the Lord?' as if to say: where, then, is the money? And not only priests but even the very leaders of priests, the bishops that is, are, we know, so shamelessly ablaze with this greed that when, at dedications of churches or consecrations of altars or blessings of cemeteries or at any solemnities, they have gatherings of people from which they expect a plentiful offering, they are prodigal in relaxing penances, remitting to all in common now a third, now a fourth, part of their penance under some pretext of charity of course, but really of the highest cupidity.[1] They extol themselves for their power which they received, they say, in Peter or the apostles when the Lord said to them:[2] 'Whose sins you shall forgive, they will be forgiven them' or:[3] 'Whatsoever you shall loose upon earth shall be loosed also in heaven'; then especially do they boast what they can do when they impart this kindness to their subjects. And would that they at least did it for them, not for money, so that it seemed a sort of kindness rather than greed. But surely if this is to be taken as commendation of their kindness that they relax a third or fourth part of a penance, their piety will be much more amply proclaimed if they remit a half or a whole penance altogether, just as they avow that it is lawful and has been granted to them by the Lord and that the heavens, as it were, had been put in their hands in accordance with the testimonies given above concerning the forgiveness or absolution of sins. Finally, and on the other hand, it seems they should be accused of great impiety, for the reason that they do not absolve all their subjects from all their sins and allow none of them to be damned, if, I say, it has thus been placed in their power to forgive or to retain what sins they will, or to open or shut the heavens to those whom they choose. At any rate they would be proclaimed most blessed if they could, when they wanted to, open these for themselves. But if in fact they cannot or do not know how to, certainly to my thinking they fall under that poetic saying: 'The arts which benefit all do not benefit the lord.'[4] Anyone, not I, may seek that power by which he can benefit others rather than himself, as if he had it in his own power to save other souls rather than his own; on the other hand, anyone who is discerning may think the opposite.

[2] John 20: 23.      [3] Matt. 18: 18.      [4] Ovid, *Metamorphoses*, i. 524.

*Vtrum generaliter ad omnes pertineat prelatos soluere et ligare*[a]

Cum ergo queritur quae sit illa potestas, uel claues regni caelorum quas apostolis Dominus tradidit ac similiter eorum uicariis, scilicet episcopis, concessisse legitur,[b] non parua questio
5 uidetur. Cum enim multi sint[c] episcopi nec religionem nec dis-
cretionem habentes, quamuis episcopalem habeant potestatem,
quomodo eis eque ut apostolis conuenire dicemus, 'quorum remiseritis peccata remittentur eis, et quorum retinueritis retenta
sunt'? Numquid si indiscrete uel supramodum uelit episcopus
10 penam peccati augere uel relaxare, hoc in eius est potestate ut
uidelicet secundum eius arbitrium penas Deus disponat, ut quod
minus puniendum est ipse magis puniat, uel[d] e converso, cum
equitatem rei magis quam hominum uoluntatem Deus adtendere
debeat? Numquid si episcopus per iram uel odium quod habeat in
15 aliquem tantundem eum penitere[e] decreuerit de leuioribus peccatis[f] quantum de grauioribus, uel penam eius in perpetuum
extendere, uel numquam ei relaxare statuerit, quantumcumque
ille peniteat? Numquid hanc eius sententiam Dominus confirmabit? Quod itaque Dominus apostolis ait, 'quorum remiseritis pec-
20 cata remittuntur eis' etc., ad personas eorum, non generaliter
ad omnes episcopos, referendum uidetur, sicut et quod eis alibi
ait,[1] 'Vos estis lux mundi', et,[g] 'uos estis sal terrae', uel pleraque
alia de personis eorum specialiter accipienda. Non enim hanc dis-
cretionem[2] uel sanctitatem quam apostolis Dominus dedit suc-
25 cessoribus eorum equaliter concessit, nec omnibus eque dixit,[3]
'beati oculi qui uident quae uos uidetis', et rursum,[4] 'uos autem dixi
amicos, quia omnia quaecumque audiui a Patre meo nota feci
uobis.' Et iterum,[5] 'Cum autem uenerit ille Spiritus ueritatis,
docebit uos omnem ueritatem.'
30 Quod si forte quis de Juda obiciat, qui etiam cum haec dicerentur
unus ex apostolis erat, sciat Dominum non ignorasse[h] ad quos id

---

[a] AE; D *reads* An *for* Vtrum.      [b] dicitur BCD      [c] sunt BC      [d] uel
*om.* AE      [e] punire BCD      [f] culpis BCD      [g] et *om.* BCD      [h] ignorare BCD

---

[1] Matt. 5: 14, 13.
[2] When Abelard wrote, the view was current that the two keys of the kingdom
of heaven were the power of binding and loosing and the power of discerning who
should be bound and loosed. In the *Ethica* Abelard does not explicitly advance
his view that *discretio* is not a key, although he refers to the lack of discretion
among many successors of the Apostles. The opinion that priests do not acquire
discretion at their ordination and that there is only one key, namely the power
of binding and loosing, is attributed to Abelard in a sentence of the school of
Anselm of Laon printed by H. Weisweiler in *Das Schrifttum der Schule Anselms
von Laon und Wilhelms von Champeaux in deutschen Bibliotheken*, BGPTMA,
xxxiii (1936), p. 169, and it is also found in the *Sentences* of Abelard's disciples,

*Whether it pertains generally to all prelates to loose and to bind*

When therefore it is asked what is that power or what are the keys of the kingdom of heaven which the Lord handed to the apostles and has likewise, one reads, granted to their vicars, namely the bishops, it seems no small question. For since there are many bishops who have neither religion nor discretion although they have episcopal power, how shall we say that 'Whose sins you shall forgive, they will be forgiven them; and whose sins you shall retain, they are retained' fits them just like the apostles? If a bishop wishes to increase or relax the punishment of sin unwisely or beyond measure, is this in his power, so that God disposes punishments according to his judgement, and consequently himself punishes more what ought to be punished less, or conversely, even though God should consider the fairness of the case rather than the will of men? If a bishop, through the anger or hatred which he may have against someone, has determined that he will do penance for his lighter sins as much as for the weightier, or has resolved to extend his punishment for ever, or never to relax it for him however long he does penance, will God confirm this sentence of his? It seems that what the Lord said to the apostles: 'Whose sins you shall forgive, they are forgiven them' etc. should be applied to them personally, not generally to every bishop, just as what he said to them elsewhere:[1] 'You are the light of the world', and 'You are the salt of the earth', or many other things, should be understood chiefly of them personally. For this discretion[2] or holiness which the Lord gave to the apostles he did not equally grant to their successors, nor did he say to all alike:[3] 'Blessed are the eyes that see the things which you see', and another time:[4] 'But I have called you friends; because all things, whatsoever I have heard of my Father, I have made known to you', and again:[5] 'But when he, the Spirit of truth, is come, he will teach you all truth.'

But if anyone perhaps objects concerning Judas, who was also one of the apostles when these were being said, he should know

Hermann (cod. Carpentras, Bibliothèque Inguimbertine, 110, f. 65ᵛ) and Omnebene (cited by A. M. Gietl, *Die Sentenzen Rolands* (Freiburg i. B., 1891), p. 265, l. 26 n.). According to these sources, Abelard taught that the use of the plural—'keys'—indicated the two effects of a single power—namely, of binding and loosing. To say that discretion is a key would simply signify that priests ought to use discretion when binding and loosing.

[3] Luke 10: 23.          [4] John 15: 15.          [5] John 16: 13.

quod dicebat deberet intendere, sicut et cum ait,[1] 'Pater, ignosce
his quia nesciunt quid faciunt', non de omnibus persequentibus
eum haec eius oratio accipienda censetur. Cum enim dicitur, 'his',
uel 'uos', quae demonstratiua pronomina sunt,[a] pro intentione
5 loquentis sermo dirigitur uel ad omnes pariter qui assunt, uel ad
aliquos ex illis[b] quos decreuerit, sicut et haec quae predicta sunt
non ad omnes generaliter apostolos, sed ad solos electos referenda
sunt. Sic et fortassis sentiendum uidetur de illo quod ait,[2] 'quaecumque ligaueris[c] super terram, erunt[d] ligata et in caelis', in quo
10 consimilis esse[e] putatur sententia.

Quod diligenter beatus adtendens Hieronimus, cum ad haec
uerba[f] in Matheo exponenda uenisset, ubi Dominus Petro ait,
'quodcumque ligaueris super terram,[3] istum', inquit, 'locum episcopi et presbyteri non intelligentes aliquid sibi de Phariseorum
15 assumunt supercilio, ut uel dampnent innocentes, uel soluere se
noxios arbitrentur, cum apud Deum non sententia sacerdotum,
sed reorum uita queratur. Legimus in Leuitico[4] de leprosis, ubi
iubentur ut ostendant se sacerdotibus et si lepram habuerint tunc
a sacerdote inmundi fiant, non quod sacerdotes mundos faciant
20 uel immundos, sed quod habeant noticiam de leprosis et non
leprosis, et possint discernere quis[g] inmundus uel mundus[h] sit.
Quomodo ergo ibi leprosum sacerdos immundum facit, sic et hic
alligat uel soluit episcopus uel presbyter, non eos qui sontes sunt
uel innoxii, sed pro officio suo cum peccatorum audierit uari-
25 etates, scit qui[i] ligandus uel qui soluendus sit.' Ex his, ni fal-
lor, uerbis Hieronimi liquidum est illud quod Petro uel ceteris
similiter apostolis dictum est de ligandis uel soluendis peccatorum uinculis, magis de personis eorum quam generaliter de omnibus episcopis accipiendum esse, nisi forte, iuxta hoc quod ipse
30 ait Hieronimus, hanc ligationem uel absolutionem[j] intelligamus
predictum iudicium omnibus generaliter concessum, ut uidelicet

---

[a] sunt demonstratiua pronomina BC      [b] ex ipsis B; de ipsis C      [c] ligaueritis BD          [d] erunt . . . celis *om.* BD; erunt . . . quo *om.* C          [e] sententia esse putatur (uidetur C) BC          [f] uerba mathei C; uerba in mathei
B          [g] qui BC          [h] mundus uel inmundus (non mundus C) BCD
[i] qui . . . sit: qui sit ligandus uel solvendus B; quid ligandum sit uel soluen-
dum sit C          [j] solutionem BCD

---

[1] Luke 23 : 34.
[2] Matt. 18 : 18. Cf. Matt. 16 : 19.
[3] Matt. 16 : 19. St. Jerome, *Commentariorum in Euangelium Matthaei lib.* iii,
*cap.* xvi, *v.* 19 (*PL* 26. 118AB). *Sententia,* no. 400 of the school of Anselm of Laon

that the Lord had not overlooked to whom he had to direct what he was saying, just as when he said:[1] 'Father, forgive them, for they know not what they do', it is not thought that this prayer of his should be understood of all his persecutors. For when one says 'them' or 'you' (these being demonstrative pronouns) the speech is aimed, according to the intention of the speaker, either equally to all present or to some of them whom he has selected, just as these quotations should be referred not to all the apostles in general but only to those who were chosen. And it seems that we should perhaps think likewise of his statement:[2] 'Whatsoever thou shalt bind upon earth shall be bound also in heaven', in which it is thought the opinion is entirely similar.

The blessed Jerome, carefully considering this, when he had come to expounding these words in Matthew where the Lord says to Peter: 'Whatsoever thou shalt bind upon earth',[3] says: 'Bishops and priests, not understanding that passage, assume something of the arrogance of the Pharisees, so that they either damn the innocent or think that they can loose the guilty, although what is examined with God is not the opinion of priests but the way of life of the guilty. We read in Leviticus[4] of lepers, where they are commanded to show themselves to priests and, if they have leprosy, then they are made unclean by the priest, not because priests make them clean or unclean but because they have knowledge of lepers and non-lepers and can distinguish who is unclean or clean. In the same way therefore as the priest there makes the leper unclean, so too here the bishop or priest does not bind or loose those who are guilty or blameless, but when he has heard in accordance with his duty the varieties of sins, he knows who is to be bound or loosed.' From these words of Jerome, unless I am mistaken, it is clear that what was said to Peter, or similarly to the other apostles, about binding or loosing the bonds of sins should be understood of them personally rather than of all bishops in general, unless perhaps, according to what Jerome himself said, we understand this binding or absolution in the sense of that examination which has been granted to all in general, whereby

(ed. Lottin, *Psychologie et morale*, v. 285–6) consists in reality of this passage from St. Jerome. On the use of the passage before Abelard see Anciaux, *La théologie du sacrement de pénitence*, pp. 38–9, 41, 60, and Hödl, *Die Geschichte der scholastischen Literatur und der Theologie der Schlüsselgewalt*, i, BGPTMA, xxxviii. 4 (1960), p. 17.
  [4] Levit. 13.

qui ligandi uel absoluendi sint a Deo, ipsi habeant iudicare et
inter mundum et immundum discernere.¹ Hinc et illud ᵃ Origenis
super ᵇ eundem locum in Matheo electos episcopos qui hanc gratiam
meruerint quae Petro concessa est, a ceteris ita distinguentis,²
5 '"Quaecumque ligaueris super terram". Quoniam', inquit, 'qui
episcopatus uendicant locum utuntur hoc textu quemadmodum
Petrus, et claues regni caelorum acceptas a Christo docent,ᶜ
qui ab eis ligati fuerint in caelo ligatos esse et qui ab eis soluti
fuerint, id est, remissionem acceperint esse et in caelo solutos,
10 dicendum est quiaᵈ bene dicunt si opera habent illa propter
quae dictum est illud Petro, tu es Petrus,³ et tales sunt ut
super eos edificetur aecclesia Christi, si portae inferorum non
preualent eis. Alioquin ridiculum est ut dicamus eum qui uinculis
peccatorum suorum ligatus est, et trahit peccata sua sicut funem
15 longum et tamquam iuge lorum uitulae iniquitates suas,⁴ propter
hoc solum quoniam dicitur episcopusᵉ habere huiusmodi potestatem ut soluti super terramᶠ ab eo sint soluti in caelo aut ligati
in terris sint ligati in caelo. Sit⁵ ergo episcopus irreprehensibilis
qui alterum ligat aut soluit, dignus ligare uel soluere in caelo, sit
20 unius uxoris uir, sobrius, castus, ornatus, hospitalis, docibilis,
non uinolentus,ᵍ non percussor, sed modestus, non litigiosus, non
concupitor pecuniarum, bene presidens domui suae, filios habens
subditos cum omni castitate. Si talis fuerit, non iniuste ligabit
super terram et neque sine iudicio soluet. Propterea quaecumque
25 soluerit qui eiusmodiʰ est, soluta erunt et in caelo, et quaecumque
ligauerit super terram ligata eruntⁱ et in caelo. Si enim fuerit quis,
ut ita dicam, Petrus, et non habuerit quae in hoc loco dicuntur
quasi ad Petrum, et putauerit se posse ligare ut sint ligata in caelo,
et soluere ut sint soluta in caelo, ipse se fallit, non intelligens uolun-
30 tatem Scripturae et inflatus incidit in iudicium diaboli.'⁶
Patenter itaque Origenes ostendit, sicut et manifesta ratio habet,

---

ᵃ illud; est *add.* BCD          ᵇ super . . . Matheo: in Matheo super illum
(eumdem C) locum BC          ᶜ docent: quoniam *add.* BC          ᵈ quoniam
BC; quod D          ᵉ episcopus dicitur BC          ᶠ super terram *om.* BCD
ᵍ uiolentus BE *and* ? C          ʰ huiusmodi BCD          ⁱ erunt ligata BCD

---

¹ According to the Victorine *Summa Sententiarum, tract.* VI, *cap.* xi (*PL* 176.
147CD), St. Jerome's authority should not be interpreted so as to preclude the
empowerment by Christ of men to bind and loose. Both God and man bind and
loose, but in different ways. Peter Lombard, *Sententiarum liber* iv, *dist.* xviii, *cap.*
6 (pp. 862–3), agreed with Abelard that priests have the power to declare who is
bound and who loosed.
² Origen, *Commentaria in Matthaeum*, xii. 14, in *Origenes Werke*, x, ed.

they themselves have to judge who are to be bound or absolved by God and to distinguish between the clean and the unclean.[1]

Hence too the observation of Origen on the same passage in Matthew, distinguishing bishops who have merited this grace which has been granted to Peter from the rest in this way:[2] ' "Whatsoever thou shalt bind upon earth". Since', he says, 'those who defend the status of the episcopacy use this text in the manner of Peter, and teach that the keys of the kingdom of heaven have been received from Christ, that those who had been bound by them are bound in heaven and those who had been loosed by them, that is, have received remission, are loosed also in heaven, it should be said that they say well if they have those works on account of which Peter was told "Thou art Peter"[3] and are such that the Church of Christ may be built upon them, if the gates of hell do not prevail against them. Otherwise it is ridiculous that we should say that he who has been bound by the bonds of his sins and trails his sins like a long rope and his iniquities like the reins of a yoked calf[4] has power of this sort just because he is called a bishop, so that those loosed by him upon earth are loosed in heaven or those bound on earth are bound in heaven. Therefore[5] let a bishop who binds or loosens another be blameless and worthy to bind or loose in heaven; let him be the husband of one wife, sober, chaste, of good behaviour, given to hospitality, able to teach; not given to wine, no striker but modest, not quarrelsome, not covetous for sums of money; one that ruleth his own house well, having his children in subjection with all chastity. If he is such a man, he will not bind unjustly upon earth neither will he loose without investigation. Wherefore, whatever he who is like this shall loose shall be loosed also in heaven, and whatever he shall bind upon earth shall be bound also in heaven. For if anyone were, so to say, a Peter, and did not have what in this passage is said to him as it was to Peter, and thought that he could bind so that they are bound in heaven and loose so that they are loosed in heaven, he is mistaken and does not understand the will of Scripture, and being puffed up he falls into the judgement of the devil.'[6]

So Origen clearly shows, just as plain reason also holds, that

---

E. Klostermann, Die griechischen christlichen Schriftsteller der ersten drei Jahrhunderte (Leipzig, 1935), 98[28]–100[26].

[3] Matt. 16: 18.                          [4] Cf. Prov. 5: 22.
[5] Cf. 1 Tim. 3: 2–4.                      [6] Cf. 1 Tim. 3: 6.

quod in his quae diximus Petro concessa esse[a] nequaquam omnibus episcopis a Domino collata sunt,[b] sed his solis qui Petrum non
ex sublimitate cathedrae sed meritorum imitantur dignitate.[1] Non
enim suam uoluntatem sequentes et a uoluntate Dei se auertentes
5 contra diuinae rectitudinem iusticiae[c] quicquam possunt, nec cum
inique aliquid agunt ad iniquitatem Deum inclinare possunt, ut
eum quasi similem sui efficiant. Quales quidem ipse uehementer
arguens et grauiter eis comminans ait,[2] 'Existimasti inique quod ero
tui similis. Arguam te et statuam contra faciem tuam. Intelligite
10 haec qui obliuiscimini Deum', etc. Quis enim magis Deum ob-
liuisci et in reprobum sensum[3] dari dicendus est, quam qui hanc
sibi arrogat potestatem, ut in subiectis pro arbitrio suo ligandis
atque soluendis[d] diuinam sibi subiacere sententiam dicat, ut quod
etiam iniuste presumpserit summam Dei iusticiam peruertere
15 queat, quasi reos uel innocentes facere possit quos uoluerit? Quod
ne umquam presumant, magnus ille doctor aecclesiae Augustinus
et inter ipsos episcopos preclarus occurrit sexto decimo sermone de
uerbis Domini dicens,[4] 'Cepisti habere fratrem tuum tamquam
publicanum, ligas eum in terra, sed ut iuste alliges uide. Nam
20 iniusta uincula disrumpit iusticia.' Beatus quoque Gregorius
patenter asserit et dominicis conuincit exemplis nichil aecclesiasti-
cam potestatem in ligando uel soluendo posse si deuiet ab aequitate iustitiae, et non diuino concordet iudicio. Vnde illud est quod
ait in[e] Euangeliorum omelia uicesima quinta,[5] 'Plerumque contin-
25 git ut locum iudicis teneat, cuius ad locum uita minime concordat,
ac sepe agitur ut uel dampnet inmeritos, uel alios ipse ligatus sol-
uat. Sepe in soluendis uel ligandis[f] subditis suae uoluntatis motus,
non autem causarum merita sequitur. Vnde fit ut ipsa ligandi
et soluendi potestate se priuet qui hanc pro suis uoluntatibus et
30 non pro subditorum moribus exercet. Sepe fit ut erga quemlibet
proximum, odio uel gratia moueatur pastor, iudicare autem digne

---

[a] concessum est ACE; concessa B    [b] collata sunt D; collata esse B;
collatum esse ACE    [c] rectitudinem iusticie BC; iustitie rectitudinem D;
rectitudinis iusticiam AE    [d] ligandum uel absoluendum B; ligandis uel
absoluendis C    [e] in *om.* BCDE    [f] ligandis uel (et D) soluendis CD;
soluendis ac ligandis B

---

[1] Both the *Summa Sententiarum*, VI. xiv (*PL* 176. 152) and Peter Lombard,
*Sententiarum liber* IV, *dist.* xix, *cap.* 1 (pp. 866–9), find that Origen does not
preclude all priests from having the power of binding and loosing, but priests
only use this power rightly and worthily if they are worthy successors of the
Apostles.
[2] Ps. 49: 21–2.                                    [3] Rom. 1: 28.
[4] Augustine, *Sermo* lxxxii, *cap.* iv. 7 (*PL* 38. 509). This passage was familiar
to Abelard's predecessors; see Anciaux, *La théologie du sacrement de pénitence*,
p. 40.

these powers which we say were granted to Peter, were by no means
conferred by the Lord on all bishops, but only on these who imitate
Peter not in the sublimity of his chair but in the dignity of his
merits.[1] For by following their own will and turning away from the
will of God they can do nothing against the rectitude of divine
justice, nor when they do something wickedly can they incline
God to wickedness so as to make him as it were like them. He
himself indeed vehemently accused such and gravely threatened
them, saying:[2] 'Thou thoughtest unjustly that I should be like to
thee: but I will reprove thee, and set before thy face. Understand
these things, you that forget God', etc. For who is to be said to
forget God and to be given over to a base mind[3] more than he
who arrogates to himself the power of saying, in binding and
loosing subjects according to his own judgement, that the divine
decision is subject to him, so that—he has even presumed this
unjustly—he seeks to pervert the supreme justice of God, as if he
could make whom he wanted guilty or innocent? Lest they should
ever presume this, that great doctor of the Church, Augustine,
and one who was also distinguished among bishops themselves,
reacts in the sixteenth sermon on the words of the Lord, by saying:[4] 'You have begun to treat your brother like a publican; you
bind him on earth, but watch that you bind him justly. For justice
breaks unjust bonds.' The blessed Gregory also plainly asserts,
and proves with examples from the Lord, that ecclesiastical power
can do nothing in binding or loosing if it deviates from the fairness
of justice and does not accord with the divine judgement. Hence
what he says in the twenty-fifth homily on the Gospels:[5] 'Frequently it occurs that one whose life does not suit the post at all
holds the post of judge, and it often happens that he either damns
the undeserving or loosens others while being bound himself.
Often in loosing or binding his subjects he follows the promptings
of his own will and not the merits of their cases. Hence it happens
that he deprives himself of the very power of binding and loosing
who exercises this for his own purposes and not for the sake of
the morals of his subjects. It often happens that a pastor is moved
against a neighbour by hatred or by favour, but they cannot judge

[5] Gregory the Great, *XL Homiliarum in Euangelia lib.* ii, *homilia* xxvi. 5 (*PL*
76. 1200A–C). On the citation of this and the following passages by writers before
Abelard see Anciaux, *La théologie du sacrement de pénitence*, pp. 38–41, and
Hödl, *Die Geschichte der scholastischen Literatur und der Theologie der Schlüsselgewalt*, i, BGPTMA, xxxviii. 4 (1960), p. 17.

de subditis nequeunt, qui in subditorum causis sua uel odia uel gratiam secuntur. Vnde per Prophetam,[1] "Mortificabant animas quae non moriuntur, et uiuificabant animas quae non uiuunt." Non morientem quippe mortificat qui iustum dampnat, et non
5 uicturum uiuificare nititur qui reum a supplicio absoluere conatur. Causae ergo pensandae sunt, ac tunc ligandi atque soluendi potestas exercenda est. Videndum quae culpa, aut quae sit penitencia secuta post culpam, ut quos omnipotens[a] per compunctionis gratiam uisitat, illos pastoris sententia absoluat. Tunc enim
10 uera est absolutio presidentis cum interni[b] sequitur arbitrium iudicis. Quod bene quatriduani mortui resuscitatio illa significat, quae uidelicet demonstrat quia prius Dominus mortuum uocauit et uiuificauit dicens, "Lazare, ueni foras",[2] et postmodum is qui uiuus egressus fuerat, a discipulis est solutus.' Item,[3] 'Ecce illum
15 discipuli iam soluunt, quem magister suscitauerat[c] mortuum. Si enim mortuum Lazarum discipuli[d] soluerent, fetorem magis ostenderent quam uirtutem. Ex qua consideratione nobis intuendum est, quod illos debemus per pastoralem auctoritatem soluere, quos auctorem nostrum cognoscimus per resuscitationis[e]
20 gratiam uiuificare. Quae nimirum uiuificatio ante operationem rectitudinis in ipsa iam cognoscitur[f] confessione peccatorum. Vnde et ipsi mortuo nequaquam dicitur "reuiuisce", sed, "ueni foras". Ac si aperte cuilibet mortuo in culpa diceretur, foras iam per confessionem egredere, qui apud te interius per negligentiam lates.
25 Veniat itaque foras, id est, culpam confiteatur peccator. Venientem uero foras soluant[g] discipuli, ut pastores aecclesiae ei penam relaxent[h] qui non erubuit confiteri quod fecit.' Item,[4] 'Sed utrum iuste an iniuste alliget pastor, pastoris tamen sententia gregi timenda est ne is qui subest, et cum iniuste forsitan ligatur, ipsam
30 obligationis sententiam ex alia culpa mereatur.' Item,[5] 'Qui sub manu pastoris est timeat ligari uel iuste uel iniuste, nec pastoris sui iudicium temere reprehendat, ne, etsi iniuste ligatus est, ex ipsa tumidae reprehensionis superbia, culpa, quae non erat, fiat.'
    Ex his Gregorii dictis et diuinae auctoritatis exemplis liquidum

---

[a] omnipotens: deus *add.* BCD      [b] BC *are difficult to read*, B *showing* itim *and* C *perhaps* interni *as in Gregory; om.* D; tantum AE      [c] resuscitauerat BCD      [d] discipuli Lazarum mortuum BC      [e] suscitantem BC; resurreccionis D      [f] cognoscimus A      [g] soluunt BC      [h] amoueant B; debeant C; iniungant E

---

[1] Ezek. 13: 19.                                    [2] John 11: 43.
[3] Gregory the Great, *XL Homiliarum in Euangelia lib.* ii, *homilia* xxvi. 5 (*PL* 76. 1200C–1201A).
[4] Gregory the Great, *XL Homiliarum in Euangelia lib.* ii, *homilia* xxvi. 5 (*PL* 76. 1201B).

their subjects worthily who in their subjects' cases follow their own hatreds or favour. Hence as the Prophet says:[1] "They killed souls which do not die and saved souls alive which do not live." He, indeed, who damns a just man kills a man who is not dying; and he who attempts to absolve a guilty man from punishment tries to restore to life one who is not going live. So cases should be considered, and then the power of binding and loosing should be exercised; it should be seen what fault there is or what repentance has followed after the fault, so that those whom the Almighty visits by the grace of his compunction, those the decision of the pastor may absolve. For then the absolution of him that rules is true, when he follows the judgement of the inward judge. The raising of the man who had been dead for four days shows this well; it demonstrates in fact that the Lord earlier called the dead man and revived him saying: "Lazarus, come forth"[2] and then he who had come forth alive was loosed by the disciples.' Also:[3] 'Behold, the disciples now loose him whom the master had raised from death. For if the disciples were to loose Lazarus when dead, they would disclose a stench rather than virtue. From this consideration we should observe that we ought to loose those through pastoral authority whom we know our Author is reviving through the grace of resurrection. This revival is now discerned indisputably before any right-doing in the confession of sins itself. Whence also this dead man is by no means told: "revive" but: "come forth", as if it were being said openly to any man who died in fault: "come forth now through confession, you who are inwardly hiding in yourself through negligence". And so let the sinner come forth, that is, confess his fault. But let the disciples loose him on coming forth, in order that the pastors of the church may relax the penalty for him who has not been ashamed to confess what he has done.' Also:[4] 'But whether the pastor binds justly or unjustly, none the less the decision of the pastor is to be feared by the flock, lest the subject, even though perhaps unjustly bound, earn that sentence of binding through another fault.' Also:[5] 'He who is under the hand of a pastor, let him fear to be bound either justly or unjustly and not criticize rashly the judgement of his pastor, lest even though he has been unjustly bound, by the very conceit of arrogant criticism what was not a fault becomes one.'

From these sayings of Gregory and the examples of divine

[5] Ibid.

est nichil episcoporum sententiam ualere si ab aequitate discrepat
diuina, iuxta illud propheticum,[1] 'mortificare uel uiuificare uolentes
quos non possunt'. Qui episcoporum quoque sententia ab ipsorum
communione priuantur, cum subiectos iniuste a communione sua
5 priuare presumpserint. Vnde Affricanum concilium ducentesimo
decimo,[a] 'ut non temere quemquam communione priuet episcopus
et[b] quam diu excommunicato suus non communicaret[c] episcopus
eidem episcopo ab aliis non communicetur episcopis, ut magis
episcopus caueat[d] ne dicat in quemquam quod aliis documentis
10 conuincere non potest'.[e2]
    Denique quod dictum est quia 'iniusta uincula disrumpit
iusticia',[3] et[f] 'qui sub manu pastoris est, timeat ligari uel iuste[g] uel
iniuste, nec pastoris iudicium temere reprehendat, ne, etsi iniuste
ligatus est, ex ipsa tumide reprehensionis superbia culpa, que non
15 erat, fiat'[4] et nonnichil affert questionis et uiam, ut arbitror, aperit
solucionis. Quis enim iniuste debeat timere ligari, si hoc iniuste
nullatenus possit fieri, cum 'iniusta uincula disrumpat iusticia'?
Vt ergo utraque salua conseruentur, ita iniuste ligari quis potest
humana sentencia, ut hec tamen iniusta uincula disrumpat diuina
iusticia. Iniuste quidem ligatur cum quislibet excommunicacionem
20 quam non meruit incurrens ab ecclesia religatur ut ei fidelium non
concedatur consorcium. Set hec anathematis uincula Deus disrumpit, quia hanc pastoris sentenciam irritam facit, ut non eum
excludat a gratia quem ille separauit ab ecclesia. Si quis igitur
quod apostolis dictum est, de potestate ligandi et soluendi uel de
25 peccatis remittendis seu retinendis, omnibus eorum uicariis, id
est, episcopis, concedi pariter uelit, ita mihi accipiendum uidetur,

    [a] cc°x AE; cap̄. B; ca°.c.ix C; cum D     [b] et *om.* BCD     [c] communi-
caret DE; communicare A; communicat B; communicauerit C     [d] caueat
episcopus BCD     [e] Explicit A; Explicit 1469 E; B *and* D *also end here. In*
C *the colophon* (Explicit iuxta exemplar) *has been erased and a new hand continues
without interruption from f.* 78[v] *to f.* 79[v]     [f] et: ut *add.* C     [g] uel iuste
*om.* C

    [1] Cf. Ezek. 13: 19.
    [2] This quotation is probably a canon of the second session of the council of
Carthage held in 419. It appears together with the heading ('Ut non temere . . .')
in the collection of Dionysius Exiguus among canons of the African church, can.
133 (*PL* 67. 223B). Crisconius, *Breuiarium Canonicum*, c. 287, refers it to the
council of Carthage, *tit.* 100 (*PL* 88. 936C). Without the heading it appears as
the eighth canon in the Verona MS. of the canons of the council of Hippo held
in 427 (printed in *PL* 56. 878B as a council of Carthage held in 421). However,
A. Boudinhon in J. Hefele–H. Leclercq, *Histoire des conciles*, ii. 2 (Paris, 1908),
app. 5, pp. 1302–8, argued that this particular canon was originally formulated
in the Carthaginian council of 419. It reappears under a new heading in the
collection *Hispana*, xviii. 5, where it is ascribed to the seventh council of Carthage (*PL* 84. 228B). See too J. D. Mansi, *Sacrorum Conciliorum noua et amplissima*

authority, it is clear that the judgement of bishops is worth nothing if it varies from divine fairness, being, according to that prophetic saying,[1] 'willing to kill or to save whom they could not'. When they have presumed to deprive their subjects unjustly from their own communion, they are also deprived by an episcopal decision from communion with them. Whence the 210th canon of the African council: 'Let the bishop not deprive anyone of communion rashly and, as long as his bishop does not communicate with the excommunicate, let not other bishops communicate with the same bishop, so that the bishop should beware more of accusing anyone of what he cannot show by other proofs.'[2]

Finally, what was said—'justice breaks unjust bonds'[3] and 'he who is under the hand of a pastor, let him fear to be bound either justly or unjustly and not criticize rashly the pastor's judgement lest, even though he has been unjustly bound, by this very conceit of arrogant criticism what was not a fault becomes one'[4]— both introduces something of a question and opens, I think, the way to a solution. For who ought to fear being unjustly bound if this cannot be done unjustly at all, since 'justice breaks unjust bonds'? So, in order to keep both statements inviolate, anyone can in this way by a human decision be bound unjustly, with the result none the less that divine justice breaks these unjust bonds. In fact, anyone is bound unjustly when he incurs an excommunication which he has not merited and is separated from the Church, with the result that the fellowship of the faithful is not allowed to him. But God breaks these bonds of the anathema because he makes this decision of the pastor invalid, so that it does not exclude from grace him whom the pastor has separated from the Church. Therefore, if anyone wants what was said to the Apostles concerning the power of binding and loosing or of forgiving or retaining sins to be granted equally to all their vicars, who are the bishops, it seems to me that it should be understood in the following way:

---

*collectio*, t. iv (Florence, 1760), col. 438; also col. 509. The canon is, however, absent from Burchard's *Decretum*, xi, and from Ivo's *Decretum*, *pars* xv and *Panormia*, v. Abelard elsewhere cites the council of Carthage, but his references are to the fifth-century *Statuta ecclesiae antiqua*. Cf. *Epist.* viii, *Theologia 'Scholarium'*, ii. 2, *Theologia christiana*, ii, *Sic et non*, *cap.* 80 and 107 (*PL* 178. 317C, 1043B, 1208D, 1464C, 1501B), and the *Statuta*, c. 99. 5. 1 (*PL* 56. 889A, 881A, 879A–880A, 879A–880B).

[3] Augustine, *Sermo* lxxxii, *cap.* vii. 7 (*PL* 38. 509).

[4] Gregory the Great, *XL Homiliarum in Euangelia lib.* ii, *homilia* xxvi. 5 (*PL* 76. 1201B).

ut hec eorum potestas in excommunicacionis faciende uel re-
laxande arbitrio consistat, ut uidelicet eis liceat quos uoluerint
de subiectis ab ecclesia presenti, ut dictum est, religare uel in
eam recipere. Cum ergo apostolis dicitur,[1] 'quecumque ligaueritis
5 super terram' etc., ut generaliter hoc omnibus episcopis concedi
concedamus, ita intelligendum arbitror, ut quos hic pastores ecclesie quoquomodo, ut dictum est, ligant[a] uel absoluunt, celestis
potestas ita eorum sentenciam iustam uel iniustam confirmat, ut
a subiectis eam per humilitatem conseruari iubeat. Hinc quippe
10 et illud est quod peruersis ait prelatis,[2] 'Que dixerint uobis seruate
et facite.' Et beatus supra[3] Gregorius, quamuis eum qui iniuste
subiectos ligat potestate ligandi et soluendi se priuare dicat, hoc
est, ea se sic indignum facere, precipit tamen sentenciam pastoris,
quamuis iniustam, a subiectis timendam nec esse uiolandam, ut
15 nemo uidelicet quacumque de causa per excommunicacionem
eliminatus ab ecclesia, contra uoluntatem episcopi se in eam
intrudere presumat uel in hoc ei contumaciter resistere audeat, ne
per hoc culpam incurrat quam prius non habebat. Claues itaque
regni celorum apostolis uel Petro traditas potestatem accipimus
20 aperiendi uel claudendi regnum[4] celorum, hoc est, presentem
ecclesiam subiectis, ut diximus, suis tanquam una clauis sit re-
serandi, altera obserandi. Id quoque in remittendis uel retinendis
peccatis intelligi fortassis potest quod in potestate ligandi uel
soluendi omnibus pariter concessum nunc dicimus, ut penam ex-
25 communicacionis pro peccatis inferendam in arbitrio habeant
subiectis imponere uel relaxare. Cum enim Dominus ait, 'quecumque ligaueritis', non quoscumque, ligari uel solui peccata
dixit, ut tale sit peccata solui quantum ea remitti, et eadem ligari
quantum ea retineri uel imponi.
30 Si tamen diligenter huius et illius potestatis donum pensemus,
sicut diuersa in hiis fuerunt tempora, sic et diuersa earum uide-
buntur dona. Ante resurrectionem quippe illa concessa est potestas tam Petro quam ceteris, sicut Matheus scribit.[5] Hec uero in
ipso die resurrectionis, ut Iohannes meminit.[6] Denique et ante re-
35 surrectionem, ut Lucas refert,[7] Dominus 'discipulos uocauit et

[a] ligant: soluunt C

[1] Matt. 18: 18.　　[2] Matt. 23: 3.　　[3] Above, pp. 118–21.
[4] Isa. 22: 22; Rev. 3: 7.　　[5] Matt. 16: 19; 18: 18.
[6] John 20: 23.　　[7] Luke 6: 13.

this power of theirs consists in the decision to determine or relax excommunication, so that it is lawful for them, as was said, to separate from the present Church or to receive back into it those among their subjects whom they would. The Apostles were told:[1] 'Whatsoever you shall bind upon earth' etc., and in order to concede that this was granted generally to all the bishops, I think it must be understood in this way: those whom here the pastors of the church in one manner or another, as has been said, loose or absolve, heavenly power confirms thus their just or unjust decision, and commands subjects to keep it through humility. Hence what he said to perverse prelates:[2] 'What they shall say to you, observe and do.' And the blessed Gregory above,[3] although he says that he who binds his subjects unjustly deprives himself of the power of binding and loosing, that is, makes himself in this way unworthy of it, yet he teaches that the decision of the priest, although unjust, should be feared by subjects and should not be violated. No one in fact, for whatever reason he has been turned out of the Church by excommunication, should presume to force himself into it against the bishop's will or dare in this to resist him stubbornly, lest he thereby incur a fault which he did not have earlier. So, we understand the keys of the kingdom of heaven handed to the Apostles or to Peter as the power of opening or closing the kingdom of heaven,[4] that is, the present Church for their subjects, as we have said. One key is, as it were, for unlocking, the other for bolting. What we now say has been granted equally to all, in the power of binding or loosing, can perhaps also be understood in forgiving or retaining sins; they have it within their judgement to impose upon their subjects or to relax the penalty of excommunication which should be inflicted for sins. For when the Lord said: 'Whatsoever'—not whomsoever—'you shall bind', he said that sins are bound or loosed, so that the loosing of sins is the equivalent of their forgiveness and their binding the same as their being retained or imposed.

But if we carefully consider the gift of this and of that power, just as they took place at different times, so too there will seem to have been different grants of them. In fact, the first power was granted both to Peter and to the others before the resurrection, as Matthew writes;[5] the other one, however, on the very day of the resurrection, as John records.[6] And finally, before the resurrection, as Luke reports,[7] the Lord 'called unto him the disciples and he

elegit duodecim ex ipsis quos et apostolos nominauit', quibus et dicebat,[1] 'uos estis sal terre, uos estis lux mundi.' Quos etiam ad predicacionem mittens[2] et eis potestatem ligandi et soluendi committens, eos iam tunc episcopos sicut et apostolos constitue-

5 rat. Cum ergo post resurrectionem insufflans illis ait,[3] 'Accipite Spiritum sanctum, quorum remiseritis peccata' etc., uidetur hoc donum Spiritus sancti quasi nouum esse et eis specialiter conces-sum fuisse, uel hiis tantum ipsorum uicariis qui gratia ista non fuerint indigni, spirituales pocius quam animales dicendi et in

10 hiis que faciunt discrecionem illam quam supradiximus per Spiri-tum aduerti. Vnde nec Iudas proditor iam defunctus nec Thomas adhuc incredulus[4] huic gratie tunc percipiende digni fuerunt interesse.[5] Siquis tamen secundum suprapositam expositionem omnibus episcopis eque ut apostolis hanc gratiam concessam esse

15 contendat, non inuidemus tante gratie in omnes pariter dilatate, nec contenciose resistimus eis qui se plenitudine potestatis equari uolunt apostolis.[6] Sufficit mihi in omnibus que scribo opinionem meam magis exponere quam diffinicionem ueritatis promittere.[7] Satis hoc tempore manifesta quoque ratio ueritatis in inuidiam

20 uel odium eos etiam qui nomine religionis preminent accendit.

EXPLICIT LIBER PRIMUS

[1] Matt. 5: 13–14.                                    [2] Cf. Luke 9: 2.
[3] John 20: 22–3.                                     [4] Cf. John 20: 24–9.
[5] Abelard also discusses the power of the keys and the role of priests in the reconciliation of the penitent in his eighth Sermon (*In Ramis Palmarum*, PL 178. 440B–441A, 444D). For discussions of Abelard's teaching see Anciaux, *La théologie du sacrement de pénitence*, pp. 286–93, and Hödl, *Die Geschichte der scholastischen Literatur und der Theologie der Schlüsselgewalt*, i, BGPTMA, xxxviii. 4 (1960), pp. 79–86. The compiler of the *Capitula Haeresum, cap.* 12 (PL 182. 1053C–1054A) produced three excerpts not from the *Ethica* but resembling some of the foregoing passages. Cf. also Bernard of Clairvaux, *Epistola* 188 (PL 182. 353C). At the council of Sens Abelard was condemned for teaching *quod potestas ligandi atque soluendi apostolis tantum data sit, non etiam successoribus eorum, Capitulum* 11, ed. J. Leclercq in *Revue bénédictine*, lxxviii (1968), 104. In his *Confessio fidei* (PL 178. 107–8) Abelard conceded that this power was given to all the successors of the Apostles without specifying exactly in what he con-sidered the power to consist. Both Hugh of Saint-Victor in the *De Sacramentis*, ii. 14. 8 (PL 176. 564C–570B) and the author of the *Summa Sententiarum*, VI.

chose twelve of them, whom also he named apostles'. And he said to them:[1] 'You are the salt of the earth, you are the light of the world.' And sending them also to preach[2] and committing to them the power of binding and loosing, he made them bishops then as well as apostles. So when, after the resurrection breathing on them he said:[3] 'Receive ye the Holy Ghost. Whose sins you shall forgive' etc., this gift of the Holy Ghost seems to be, as it were, a new one and to have been granted to them or only to these vicars of them who were not unworthy of that grace; they should be called spiritual rather than animal beings and in what they do that discretion which we have mentioned is perceived through the Spirit. Whence neither Judas the traitor now dead nor Thomas still unbelieving[4] was worthy to be present then to obtain this grace.[5] If, however, anyone according to our exposition contends that this grace has been granted to all bishops just as to the Apostles, we do not envy so great a grace being extended to all equally, nor do we contentiously resist those who want to equal the Apostles in the plenitude of power.[6] It is sufficient for me in everything I write to expound my opinion rather than to put forward a definition of the truth.[7] At this time, moreover, the plain reason of truth inflames to enough envy or hatred even those who are prominent in the name of religion.

THE END OF THE FIRST BOOK

xi (*PL* 176. 147–9), reacted strongly to Abelard and argued that priests can remit sin where true penance is made and according to the merits of the penitent; see on this Anciaux, *La théologie du sacrement de pénitence*, pp. 295–302. Peter Lombard, however, leaned towards Abelard's views in the *Sententiarum liber* III. xviii and xix. 1 (2nd edn., Quaracchi, 1916) pp. 857–69. According to him, God alone remits sin and judges according to truth without following the errors made by priests. Priests declare what they discern and have the power to excommunicate; they have the power of the keys but do not always use it rightly. On the influence of Abelard's teaching in the twelfth century see Anciaux, *La théologie du sacrement de pénitence*, pp. 312 et seq., and Hödl, *Die Geschichte der scholastischen Literatur und der Theologie der Schlüsselgewalt*, pp. 86–115.

[6] Pope Leo the Great's formula, that bishops are called 'in partem . . . sollicitudinis, non in plenitudinem potestatis' (*Epist.* 14, *cap.* 1; *PL* 54. 671) enjoyed great success in subsequent centuries; see J. Rivière, '*In Partem Sollicitudinis.* Évolution d'une formule pontificale', *Revue des sciences religieuses*, v (1925), 210–31. The history of the expression *plenitudo potestatis* is unwritten and it is an open question whether Abelard here alludes to an actual claim by some bishops (cf. Matt. 18: 18) to emulate the papacy in the plenitude of power or critically applies to their activities a phrase associated especially with the heir of St. Peter (cf. Matt. 16: 18–19). On the 'episcopalist thesis' see W. Ullmann, *A History of Political Thought: The Middle Ages* (Penguin Books, 1965), p. 108.

[7] Cf. Abelard, *Theologia 'Scholarium'*, iii (*PL* 178. 1098CD).

INCIPIT SECUNDUS

⟨S⟩uperior *Ethice* nostre libellus cognoscendis uel corrigendis peccatis operam dedit et ipsa peccata distinxit a uiciis que uirtutibus dicuntur contraria. Nunc uero superest ut ordine congruo
5 iuxta illud Psalmiste,¹ 'declina a malo et fac bonum', postquam de malis egimus declinandis ad bona facienda doctrine nostre stilum conuertamus.

Prudencia, id est, boni malique discretio, mater est uirtutum pocius quam uirtus. Ad hanc pertinet pro tempore uel loco et per-
10 sonarum dignitate dispensaciones facere.²

Sicut autem uicia distinximus a peccatis, ita uirtutes illis contrarie uiciis nonnullam differenciam habere uidentur ab hiis quibus beatitudinem promeremur bonis, que in bono consistunt obediencie. Sicut enim uirtutes uiciis contrarie sunt, ita peccatum,
15 quod proprie dicitur Dei contemptus, uidetur aduersum obediencie bonum, id est, uoluntas ad obediendum Deo parata. Que fortassis uoluntas nonnunquam esse poterit, si ad tempus habita nondum ita firma sit ac difficile mobilis, ut uirtus dici possit. Vt enim philosophis placuit, nequaquam uirtus in nobis dicenda est, nisi sit
20 habitus mentis optimus, siue habitus bene constitute mentis. Quid uero habitum uel dispositionem dixerint, Aristoteles in prima specie qualitatis diligenter distinxit, docendo uidelicet eas qualitates que non naturaliter nobis insunt, set per applicacionem nostram ueniunt, habitus uel disposiciones uocari.³ Habitus quidem,
25 si sint difficile mobiles, quales, inquit, sunt sciencie uel uirtutes. Disposiciones uero, si e contra fuerint facile mobiles. Si ergo secundum hoc habitus sit dicenda quelibet uirtus nostra, non absurde uidetur nonnunquam uoluntas ad obediendum parata, cum sit facile mobilis, antequam firmetur nequaquam dicenda
30 uirtus, sicut nec habitus. Quicumque tamen in huius uoluntatis proposito uitam finirent, nequaquam dampnandi sunt estimandi. De qualibus illud est quod in libro Sapiencie legimus,⁴ 'Placens Deo factus dilectus et uiuens inter peccatores translatus est. Raptus est ne malicia mutaret intellectum eius, aut ne fictio
35 deciperet animam illius. Consummatus in brevi, expleuit tempora multa. Placita enim erat Deo anima eius. Propter hoc properauit

¹ Ps. 36: 27.
² Cf. Abelard, *Dialogus* (*PL* 178. 1652A–1653A).
³ *A. M. S. Boetii in Categorias Aristotilis liber* iii (*PL* 64, 240D–241A). Cf. Abelard, *Sic et non*, c. 144 (*PL* 178. 1591AB) and *Dialogus* (1651C–1652A).
⁴ Wisdom 4: 10–11, 13–14.

### THE BEGINNING OF THE SECOND

The preceding little book of our *Ethics* gave attention to the understanding or correction of sins, and it distinguished sins themselves from vices, which are said to be contrary to the virtues. However, it now remains for us in a suitable order—in accordance with the Psalmist:[1] 'Decline from evil and do good'—after dealing with declining from evils to turn the pen with which we teach to doing good.

Prudence, that is, the discernment of good and evil, is the mother of virtues rather than a virtue. To this belongs the making of dispensations on account of time or place or the dignity of persons.[2]

But just as we distinguished vices from sins, so the virtues contrary to those vices seem to be somewhat different from these goods with which we earn beatitude, and which consist in the good of obedience. For just as the virtues are the contrary of the vices, so sin, which is properly said to be contempt of God, seems opposite to the good of obedience, that is, the will which is ready to obey God. Perhaps this will will sometimes be able to exist if, at the time it is possessed, it is not yet so firm and difficult to move that it can be called a virtue. For, as the philosophers have decided, virtue should by no means be said to be in us unless it is a very good habit of mind or a habit of the well-constituted mind. Now what they called habit or disposition Aristotle carefully distinguished in the first species of quality, that is, by teaching that those qualities which are not in us naturally, but come through our application, are called habits or dispositions:[3] habits in fact, if they are difficult to move—such are, he says, the sciences or the virtues—but dispositions if, on the other hand, they should be easy to move. So if, according to this, any virtue of ours is to be called a habit, it does not seem absurd that sometimes the will ready to obey God, when it is easy to move before it is made firm, should not be called virtue at all, just as it should not be called habit. But whoever finish their life with this purpose of will should by no means be thought of as being damned. What we read in the book of Wisdom refers to them:[4] 'He pleased God and was beloved: and living among sinners he was translated. He was taken away lest wickedness should alter his understanding, or deceit beguile his soul. Being made perfect in a short space, he fulfilled a long time. For his soul pleased God. Therefore he hastened to bring

educere illum de medio iniquitatum.' Multi quippe sunt fidelium qui tante constantie non sunt, ut agones martirum sustinere possent, uel non facile in aduersitatibus deficerent. Quorum infirmitati Dominus prouidens non permittit eos temptari supra id quod 5 possunt,[1] nec eos aduersis probat quos pusillanimes uel imbecilles considerat. Qui huius quoque beneficii non immemores et hinc non minimas Deo gratias agentes tanto humiliores existunt quanto se debiliores recognoscunt, nec ab amore Dei possunt esse alieni cuius beneficiis non permanent ingrati, et cui se plus debere faten-10 tur a quo plus in talibus accepisse uidentur.

EXPLICIT IVXTA EXEMPLAR[2]

[1] 1 Cor. 10: 13.
[2] Some idea of the remaining or at least of the projected contents of this second book of the *Ethics* may well be provided in two passages in Abelard's *Expositio* of the Epistle to the Romans. In the first (*Expos*. ii. 4; *PL* 178. 841D–842A) Abelard reserves three questions for lengthier consideration in the *Ethics*. First, since God's gifts are of grace, in what do merits consist? Secondly, do merits consist in will alone or also in deed? Thirdly, does virtue, which is not manifested in action, suffice for beatitude? In the second passage (v. 13; *PL* 178. 950C–951A) Abelard reserves to the *Ethics* a discussion of the duty to love one's neighbour if he is in hell or destined for hell and of the question whether one should will what is not good to be done, e.g. pray for the salvation of all although only a few will achieve salvation.

him out of the midst of iniquities.' Indeed, there are many among the faithful who are not of such steadfastness that they can bear the agonies of the martyrs or who would not easily fail in adversities. The Lord, providing for their weakness, does not permit them to be tempted above that which they are able[1] nor tests with hardships those whom he considers to be faint-hearted or weak. They too, mindful of this favour also and therefore offering God no small thanks, are so much more humble the more they recognize their feebleness; they, who do not remain ungrateful for his favours, cannot be alienated from God's love; in these respects they declare they owe him more from whom they seem to have received more.

THE END ACCORDING TO THE EXEMPLAR[2]

# INDEX OF QUOTATIONS
# AND ALLUSIONS

## THE BIBLE

## OTHER SOURCES

# INDEX OF MANUSCRIPTS

## OTHER SOURCES

# GENERAL INDEX